Praise for *Online, Blended, a Education in Schools*

"Clark and Barbour understand that they have a tiger by the tail. Like any other mega-technology, virtual teaching and learning has enormous potential both for good and for abuse. They have assembled a distinguished cast of scholars to examine the potentials and the perils of K–12 technology-mediated instruction. It is the most thoughtful examination of the issues I have ever read."

—**Gene V. Glass**, *Emeritus Regents' Professor, Arizona State University; Research Professor, University of Colorado, Boulder*

"This volume represents a timely, practical, and scholarly focus on K–12 online, blended, and distance learning edited by leading scholars on the topic. Through case studies of actual teachers in actual schools, primarily in North America but in other countries as well, this book provides compelling insights into the growth and value of new forms of K–12 learning, mediated by information and communication technologies (ICTs). In spite of this growth and value, there is a dearth of literature on these new forms of K–12 learning. As is the case with many educational technology initiatives, our integration of these new forms of learning with ICTs advances at a much faster pace than does our understanding of the effects of that integration. Clark and Barbour's book helps address this problem by drawing on experts and experienced practitioners to highlight effective practices and instructional design and pedagogical approaches while at the same time raising important issues and questions that need to be addressed. The Part One emphasis on research, policy, and management considerations, followed by Part Two's emphasis on actual case studies of implementation, reflect the complementarities and complexities of the phenomenon of this form of K–12 learning. In Part Three, the editors look back at lessons learned and look forward at future directions in order to focus their audience's attention on key issues of policy and practice. A must-read for all those involved with K–12 learning, this book will no doubt become an essential resource."

—**Elizabeth Murphy**, *Internationally recognized researcher on technology-mediated learning; Professor, Faculty of Education, Memorial University of Newfoundland*

"If there is one book you should to read that will bring you into the digital present and future, this is that book. Tom Clark and Michael Barbour take you on a journey with global experts that will change the way you think about education, digital technologies, and the teaching and learning professions."

—**Don Olcott Jr.**, *Professor of Leadership and Open and Distance Learning, Co-Director of the uImagine Digital Learning Laboratory, Charles Sturt University, Australia*

"This book is a must-read for administrators, policy advisors, and school leaders seeking transformation in K–12 learning. Whether innovating on curriculum, assessment, or mobile technology; embracing new digital pedagogies; or preparing students and teachers with the skills and experiences needed in our global society, this book is something [readers] will keep coming back to again and again.

"*Online, Blended, and Distance Education in Schools* brings together leading experts in learning with technology to highlight the depth and breadth of the critical questions and conversations every K–12 leader should be having today.

"With supporting global case studies that highlight innovative practices and up-to-the-minute easy-to-read research, along with the important considerations of scale, sustainability, and equity, this book provides the necessary deep thinking needed to begin and evaluate vision, policies, and strategies required for holistic change and transformation."

—***Aidan McCarthy***, *Global Digital Learning Strategy, Microsoft Corporation*

"This book brings together experts in online and blended teaching, learning, policy, and technology and left me excited, inspired, and yearning for more! Anyone interested in ensuring students are prepared for a world that is not yet invented, needs to read this book!"

—***Michelle Licata***, *Florida Virtual School Teacher of the Year, 2012;*
National Online Teacher of the Year finalist, 2013

ONLINE, BLENDED, AND DISTANCE EDUCATION
IN SCHOOLS

ONLINE
LEARNING &
DISTANCE
EDUCATION
Leadership, Innovation,
Policy, & Practice

Current and forthcoming
titles publishing in our ONLINE LEARNING AND DISTANCE
EDUCATION series edited by Michael Grahame Moore

LEADING THE E-LEARNING TRANSFORMATION OF HIGHER EDUCATION
Meeting the Challenges of Technology and Distance Education
Gary Miller, Meg Benke, Bruce Chaloux, Lawrence
C. Ragan, Raymond Schroeder, Wayne Smutz, and Karen Swan
Available

ASSURING QUALITY IN ONLINE EDUCATION
Practices and Processes at the Teaching, Resource, and Program Levels
Edited by Kay Shattuck
Available

CULTURE AND ONLINE LEARNING
Global Perspectives and Research
Edited by Insugn Jung and Charlotte Nirmalani Gunawardena
Available

WEB 2.0 FOR ACTIVE LEARNERS
by Vanessa Dennen
Publishing Spring 2015

TEACHING SCIENCE ONLINE
Practical Guidance for Effective Instruction and Lab Work
Edited by Dietmar Kennepohl
Publishing Summer 2015

ONLINE, BLENDED, AND DISTANCE EDUCATION IN SCHOOLS

Building Successful Programs

Edited by *Tom Clark and Michael K. Barbour*

Series Foreword by Michael Grahame Moore

Foreword by Cathy Cavanaugh

PUBLISHED IN ASSOCIATION WITH

STERLING, VIRGINIA

COPYRIGHT © 2015 BY
STYLUS PUBLISHING, LLC

Published by Stylus Publishing, LLC
22883 Quicksilver Drive
Sterling, Virginia 20166-2102

Library of Congress Cataloging-in-Publication Data
Online, blended and distance education in schools : building successful
programs / edited by Tom Clark and Michael Barbour. – First Edition.
    pages cm. (Online learning and distance edcuation series)
Includes bibliographical references and index.
ISBN 978-1-62036-163-4 (cloth : alk. paper)
ISBN 978-1-62036-164-1 (pbk. : alk. paper)
ISBN 978-1-62036-165-8 (library networkable e-edition)
ISBN 978-1-62036-166-5 (consumer e-edition)
1. Computer-assisted instruction. 2. Distance education. 3. Internet in
education. 4. Computer-assisted instruction–Case studies. 5. Distance educa-
tion–Case studies. 6. Internet in education–Case studies. I. Clark, Thomas
A., 1952- editor of compilation. II. Barbour, Michael, 1975
LB1028.5.O486 2015
371.33'44678--dc23
2014023197

13-digit ISBN: 978-1-62036-163-4 (cloth)
13-digit ISBN: 978-1-62036-164-1 (paper)
13-digit ISBN: 978-1-62036-165-8 (library networkable e-edition)
13-digit ISBN: 978-1-62036-166-5 (consumer e-edition)

Printed in the United States of America

All first editions printed on acid-free paper
that meets the American National Standards Institute
Z39-48 Standard.

Bulk Purchases

Quantity discounts are available for use in workshops and for
staff development.
Call 1-800-232-0223

First Edition, 2015

CONTENTS

PART THREE: CASE STUDIES ON PRACTICE

PART FOUR: SUMMARY THOUGHTS

Tables

Figures

SERIES FOREWORD
Michael Grahame Moore, Series Editor

In North America, children's elementary and secondary education is usually referred to as "K–12" (i.e., kindergarten through 12th grade). One of the few characteristics of K–12 education that most experts would agree on is that it occurs in a classroom. Indeed, it was unease with that general assumption—that *teaching* should be defined as "the activity which takes place during schooling and within the classroom setting" (ASCD, 1971)—that was the spur to my own quest in the 1970s to define and explain *nonclassroom teaching*, what we came to know as *distance education*: "a family of instructional methods in which the teaching behaviors are executed apart from the learning" (Moore, 1973, p. 4).

In that early research, my focus was almost entirely on higher and continuing adult education, and only some years later did I come to appreciate that such nonclassroom teaching also occurred at the K–12 level, beginning as early as the first decade of the 20th century, most notably in the economies of the United States, Canada, Australia, and New Zealand (Moore, 2002). Of course, it was an underused method in comparison to the traditional classroom, and during those early days when the technology was the postal service, nonclassroom teaching was regarded either as an unsatisfactory substitute for "the real thing"—that is, a teacher at the chalkboard—or, at best, as a type of teacher's aid, serving to complement and support the real thing.

Today's historian of distance education can describe how with each advance in technology educational programs delivered in that kind of supporting role became increasingly appreciated and more generally employed, beginning with an explosion of interest when radio was introduced into the classroom, then television, and in more recent memory "narrow-cast" programs distributed by satellite and cable in such well-known projects as the Star Schools initiative, preceding the unprecedented changes that began with the spread of the Internet in the mid-1990s.

The purpose of this book is to describe and discuss some of this 21st-century experience of distance education in K–12 teaching and learning. While readers may find other themes that excite them, surely one of the most intriguing is the recent and growing shift of perception about distance teaching for schoolchildren from a merely complementary enrichment activity to that of viable alternative pedagogy. If it is not immediately apparent what I am referring to here, perhaps you can take some clue from the currently popular buzzwords "flipped classroom," "blended learning," "virtual classroom," or (dare I?) "homeschooling"!

Whether viewed as merely a complementary pedagogy or a significant alternative to the classroom, distance education is now on the lips of elementary and secondary school teachers and administrators across the globe, just as it has already swept through the worlds of higher and continuing education. However, subject of much talk though it may be, actual understanding of either the basic pedagogical principles or best-quality practice lags far behind the enthusiasm for the technologies that could be the vehicles for such improvements in teaching and learning. In short, there is a huge job to be done in teaching the teachers if today's technologies are to play more than a relatively minor ancillary role as a teacher aid.

Seen in this historical context, it is expedient and timely that Stylus Publishing has chosen in its newest volume in the Online Learning & Distance Education series to put the spotlight on K–12 teaching and learning, and has been able to engage two of North America's leading scholars in this field as its editors. In accepting the challenge of compiling a book that would be informed by research but have, as its central theme, a sharing of experiences by real-world teachers and schools practicing at the cutting edge of contemporary experience, aimed at helping their peers to develop an understanding that reaches beyond merely knowing how to tinker with the technology, Tom Clark and Michael Barbour bring a unique blend of knowledge, deep in experience and wide in its geography. As noted elsewhere, Clark's experiences and studies of K–12 distance education extend back some 30 years, including most of what might be considered the modern age of distance education, while Barbour brings an especially wide knowledge of international K–12 distance education, drawing not only on his career in Canadian schools but also on his comparative education research and scholarship.

Early in the process of conceiving the book, having decided the approach would be to feature the experiences of real teachers in real schools, the editors set out to build on some foundation chapters on such general topics as "quality," "access," and "instructional design" with a series of case studies. In this they decided to complement studies of experiences in schools in North America with a selection from several overseas countries. In going global in this way, as with other books in the series, Stylus is surely in the vanguard of an approach to knowledgemaking that is highly appropriate for the still emerging global society.

Thinking about this, I was reminded, as I read these later chapters, of the preceding book in the series, Jung and Gunawardena's (2014) *Culture and Online Learning: Global Perspectives and Research,* and their proposition that "online learning has the great potential to motivate and engage students in participating in cross-national exchanges of cultures and the creation of new cultures" (p. 8). This is surely an aspiration that deserves every attempt at implementation when we search for how to best apply online technologies in preparing our children in the K–12 schools for employment and citizenship in the 21st-century global economy. Perhaps not everyone will agree, and so let the debate proceed!

To that end, the best contribution this series editor can make at this point is to get out of the way, pausing only to record my thanks to Cathy Cavanaugh, who helped conceive and develop the proposal for this book, and to Tom Clark and Michael Barbour, for their patience and perseverance in what has proven to be a fairly lengthy and challenging process of assembling a wide range of national and international specialists and nurturing them in the preparation of their contributions to this volume.

Michael Grahame Moore
Distinguished Professor of Education Emeritus
The Pennsylvania State University

References

ASCD: Association of Supervision and Curriculum Development. (1971). Criteria for assessing the formal properties of theories of instruction. In R. Hyman (Ed.), *Contemporary thought on teaching* (pp. 123–130). Englewood Cliffs, NJ: Prentice-Hall.

Jung, I., & Gunawardena, L. (2014). *Culture and online learning: Global perspectives and research.* Sterling, VA: Stylus.

Moore M. G. (1973). Towards a theory of independent learning and teaching. *The Journal of Higher Education, 44*(9), 661–679.

Moore, M. G. (2002). The Benton Harbour plan. *American Journal of Distance Education, 16*(4), 201–204.

I was excited to hear that my colleagues Tom Clark and Michael Barbour were developing an edited book that would present global perspectives on online and blended learning in schools. When Tom and Michael asked me to pen this foreword (and a chapter or two), I leapt at the opportunity because this is a topic near to my heart.

A Fulbright Senior Scholarship took me to Nepal, where I saw not only barriers to online and blended learning that far surpassed those in my native United States, but also unexpected opportunities for new applications of e-learning to take root. Inspired by these experiences I took the leap from a tenured faculty position in the United States to an administrative position with the Higher Colleges of Technology in the United Arab Emirates (UAE). In the UAE I have seen just how rapidly online and blended learning can be implemented when there is a national will and vision to do so.

I have known Tom and Michael for many years. Our paths have crossed many times in conferences and projects. Tom coauthored one of the first American textbooks on distance education in 1991 and has remained active in the field ever since, coediting a book on virtual schools in 2005 and evaluating online and blended learning projects. A rising star in the field, Michael began his career as a high school teacher in Canada, where he still resides, while teaching at a university in the United States. His recent works include two coedited books about online and blended learning around the world, and an annual report on K–12 online learning in Canada.

Internationally, an explosion of K–12 online and blended learning activity has occurred in the last few years. In conceiving this book, Tom and Michael asked these questions: What can North American educators learn from international K–12 educators? What can international K–12 educators learn from North America? They then went about finding the people and programs who could help them answer these questions.

The resulting book is a collection of stories about primary and secondary school online and blended learning, based on the sensemaking work of each author. The experts who contributed their stories here have stepped back from the rapids swirling around them to provide their perspectives on specific aspects of e-learning at a single point in time. K–12 e-learning is too broad and complex for any single book to offer a comprehensive view, but a carefully curated and diverse collection of stories like this one does much to advance our understanding. As readers of these stories, we represent unique roles and locations in the global education community. Nonetheless, we share more commonalities than differences, in that we all place our hopes and energies into advancing learning for individual and collective good. Therefore, we can each take lessons from the stories into our settings of practice.

Globally, e-learning for elementary and secondary students has the flexibility to increase access to education and educational quality. It is already being leveraged to alleviate numerous educational problems, including crowded schools, shortages of secondary courses needed by remedial or accelerated students, lack of access to qualified teachers in a local school, and students who need to learn at a pace or in a place different from a school classroom. These are prime opportunities for e-learning, and this book shares examples that begin to close some of these gaps. A fundamental challenge in e-learning is building upon successful practice and research. When one country uses e-learning to increase education access and quality, it provides a model for others that may not be in a position yet to support research and development. Nations with established e-learning systems can learn from other nations that leapfrog the use of e-learning technologies in innovative ways.

Countries and education organizations have opportunities to capitalize on their unique features and assets to become leaders in specific domains of education. For example, in an emerging project in Nepal, students can now engage in project-based learning related to local ecosystems, indigenous cultures and arts, and the political system by contributing data, stories, histories, and media artifacts to an open online repository. The repository also serves as a portal to open education resources, experts, and mentors. This is only one example of what is possible. These kinds of projects require little in the way of technology infrastructure beyond a cellular signal and inexpensive handheld devices that can be charged using solar, wind, or mechanical power. Expanding options for schooling in the developing and developed world is a critical issue. The UNICEF 2011 *State of the World's Children Report* states that 88% of the world's 1.2 billion adolescents live in the developing world, and that nearly half of the children of secondary-school age are unable to attend school at that level. Add to that number the adults who have not completed primary and secondary education, and the result is an audience of billions in need of education in areas where physical schools with classroom teachers cannot quickly accommodate them.

UN secretary general Ban Ki-moon issued a statement last year marking May 17 as World Telecommunications and Information Society Day, and emphasizing the importance of information and communication technology (ICT) as "enablers of modern society." ICTs provide access to cultures, economic opportunity, health care, and education, all of which are especially critical in rural areas, according to the secretary. He specifically mentions transforming lives by connecting village schools to the Internet. As exciting as it is to see the United Nations and many participating countries speaking on behalf of K–12 e-learning and even sponsoring special programs around that day, sustained access to quality educational resources and experiences requires a permanent systemic commitment on the part of collaborating governments and agencies. The United States has taken steps in the right direction with recent initiatives such as the National Broadband Plan for Education, and the European Commission has established a transnational assessment of virtual school and college provision (VISCED).

For best likelihood of success, e-learning programs must be systemic, including teacher education and professional development, ubiquitous mobile learning technology and technical infrastructure, robust digital content, and educational supports. Broad vision and leadership are needed to bring the components of a program together into a system. Education, as a lifelong enterprise, involves families, governments at all levels, K–adult education organizations, education materials publishers, support systems, and infrastructures. Coordinating all of these entities requires vision and leadership that can unite learners, providers, and supporters around the goal of education as a path to social advancement.

This edited volume represents an important step along that path. Each story in this book uses data from research and practice to move us closer to the vision of education for all, everywhere, all the time. I hope you will join me in reading these global perspectives on online and blended learning, in thinking about how we can use e-learning and educational technologies to help transform the world, and in applying the lessons from these stories to enable universal access to quality education. Stories are at the heart of the human experience because they inspire action. There is an abundance of inspiration in these pages.

Cathy Cavanaugh, PhD
Abu Dhabi/Khalifa City Women's College

ACKNOWLEDGMENTS

This book would not have been possible without the contributions of many people. Thanks to Michael Grahame Moore, our series editor, for recognizing the need to include a book on K–12 education in his Online Learning & Distance Education series, and for asking us to act as its editors. Also to Cathy Cavanaugh, the author of our foreword, for her leadership and vision in the field and her ongoing encouragement of our efforts to bring this book to fruition.

We would also like to thank our chapter authors, who include some of the most widely known experts in the fields of educational technology and K–12 online and blended learning, and expert practitioners in the field from around the world: Leanna Archambault, Stephen Baker, Helen Boulton, Ali Carr-Chellman, Cathy Cavanaugh, Rob Darrow, Jhone M. Ebert, Richard E. Ferdig, Joseph R. Freidhoff, David Glick, Stephen Harris, Karen Johnson, Christy G. Keeler, Kathryn Kennedy, Hyeonjin Kim, Kevin Oliver, Allison Powell, Victoria Raish, Jennifer Reaburn, Mickey Revenaugh, Kerry Rice, Raymond M. Rose, Jeonghee Seo, John Smallwood, Alese Smith, Lisa Hasler Waters, Tracy Weeks, and Dazhi Yang.

We would also like thank our acquisitions editor at Stylus, Sarah Burrows, who advocated for our book and helped us at many points along the way, as well as our production editor, Alexandra Hartnett.

PART ONE
Overview

1

ONLINE, BLENDED, AND DISTANCE EDUCATION IN SCHOOLS

An Introduction

Tom Clark and Michael K. Barbour

The last decade has seen dramatic growth in the use of online, blended, and distance learning approaches in elementary and secondary education around the world. Online learning is a type of distance education, the key element of which is "the separation of teacher and learner during . . . a majority of the instructional process" (Verduin & Clark, 1991, p. 11). Watson and Kalmon (2005) defined *online learning* as "education in which instruction and content are delivered primarily over the Internet."

As depicted in Table 1.1, the history of K–12[1] online learning begins with the concepts and systems that made it possible. The independent study high school launched by the University of Nebraska in the 1920s served as a model for distance and online learning programs later on. Enrollments in 1935 were almost all at the University of Nebraska. By 2004–2005, K–12 independent study enrollments peaked at 174,000 nationwide, but about 40% were in online courses (D. Gearhart, personal communication, March 31, 2006).

A wide variety of distance education technologies were used in K–12 education in the United States from the 1930s through the inception of web-based instruction in 1991. Educational radio broadcasts began in 1921 at the Ohio School of the Air (Saettler, 2004). The Wisconsin School of the Air served 330,000 students in classrooms at its peak in 1996 (Bianchi, 2002). Educational television programming began in 1933 at the University of Iowa (Kurtz, 1959), and a network of educational television stations began to appear in the 1950s, after the Federal Communications Commission (1952) reserved TV channels for this purpose. Educational broadcasts from airplane-based transmitters began in 1961 (Jajkowski, 2004), but were supplanted when educational satellite broadcasts began in 1971 (Singh, Morgan & Rosenbaum, 1972). By 1985 the TI-IN network provided high school courses to 150 receive sites in 12 states (Pease & Tinsley, 1986). In the 1980s and 1990s, many states and regions developed broadband networks for educational video programming and other purposes (Hezel Associates, 1998).

TABLE 1.1:

Key dates in the history of K–12 distance and online learning

1921	Educational radio broadcasting begins at Ohio School of the Air
1929	University of Nebraska begins supervised independent study high school
1951	School of the Air launched in Australia
1953	Educational television broadcasting begins at University of Iowa
1961	Purdue University pioneers airplane-based K–12 instruction
1965	Computer-based K–12 learning experiments at Stanford, and a year later at Illinois
1971	Educational broadcasting via geosynchronous satellite begins using NASA's ATS-1
1980s	Audio and computer conferencing technologies used in K–12 instruction
1980	Development of USENET
1982	Development of SMTP e-mail and Internet Protocol Suite
1987	Norwegian distance learning expert Morten Paulsen predicts creation of a "virtual school"
1989	Timothy Berners-Lee demonstrates key functionalities of the World Wide Web
1990s	Many states and regions develop broadband networks for K–12 instruction and other uses
1996	University of Nebraska's CLASS program, Florida Virtual High School, and the VHS consortium begin offering web-based high school courses during the school year
1996	Florida Virtual School launched; many state virtual schools follow
2000	Online charter school provider K12 Inc. founded; Connections Academy launched a year later
2009	State virtual school programs exist in 27 states, report 320,000 course enrollments
	Full-time online schools exist in 24 states, enroll about 175,000 students
2011	More than a million estimated enrollments in K–12 online learning
2013	State virtual school programs exist in 26 states, report 740,000 course enrollments
	Full-time online schools exist in 29 states, enroll 310,000 students
	More than 75% of school districts offer online or blended learning options
2014	State virtual schools served 741,516 course enrollments (one student enrolled in one semester-long course) in 26 states in SY 2013–14.
	Fully online schools served 316,320 students in 30 states in SY 2013–14.

Note. Clark (2012); Watson, Murin, Vashaw, & Gemin (2014)

A series of technological breakthroughs set the stage for the emergence of web-based instruction. Networked computers, the Internet, e-mail, the Web, and broadband were all needed before Morten Paulsen's 1987 vision of a "virtual school" became a reality in the 1990s and 2000s. A virtual school is "an educational organization that offers K–12 courses through Internet- or Web-based methods" (Clark, 2001, p. 1). Laurel Springs School probably offered the first K–12 online program in 1991, using text-based distance education for course delivery in the pre-web era (Laurel Springs School, 2011). University of Nebraska's CLASS program (Smith & Northrup, 1998), Florida Virtual High School (Florida Taxwatch Center, 2007), and the Virtual High School Consortium (Kozma, Zucker, & Espinoza, 1998) all began offering web-based high school courses during the 1996–1997 school year.

The U.S. Department of Education estimated over 1.8 million enrollments in K–12 distance education courses in 2009–2010, many of which were in online courses (Queen & Lewis, 2011). The number of U.S. enrollments, specifically in K–12 online courses, grew to well over a million by 2010–2011 (Watson et al., 2011). From 2009 to 2013, the number of state virtual schools offering state-supported supplemental online learning stagnated, while the number of full-time programs grew, but both types of programs experienced robust enrollment growth. By 2013, 26 of the 50 U.S. states had state virtual schools, a decrease of one state since 2009, while 29 states had fully online multidistrict online schools, an increase of five states during the same four-year period. Course enrollments in state virtual schools grew 119% during this period, while student enrollments in fully online multidistrict programs grew 77%.

District-led programs were also growing rapidly in numbers and enrollments. By 2013, researchers estimated that more than 75% of school districts in the United States offered online or blended learning options (Watson, Murin, Vashaw, Gemin & Rapp, 2013). Other program types saw little growth in 2013-2014. Course enrollments in the 26 state-level virtual schools had leveled off at about 742,000, a 1% increase from the prior year. Full-time online schools served students in one more state than in 2012-2013. Their 316,000 enrollments represented a 2% increase (Watson, Pape, Murin, Vashaw, & Gemin, 2014).

The emergence of K–12 blended learning has brought online learning into the mainstream. Piccianno and Seaman (2009) defined *blended learning* as "part online and part traditional face-to-face instruction" (p. 1). Staker and Horn (2012) defined *blended learning* as "a formal education program in which a student learns at least in part through online delivery of content and instruction with some element of student control over time, place, path, and/or pace, and at least in part at a supervised brick-and-mortar location away from home" (p. 3).

Internationally, there has been a similar explosion of K–12 online and blended learning activity in the last few years. In Canada, the estimated number of online enrollments grew from around 25,000 to 245,000 during the 2000s (Barbour, 2012b). Among 54 countries responding to a 2010 survey, 65% reported that online and blended learning opportunities were available to at least some students (Barbour et al., 2011). In 2011, five years after opening its first online school, China reported about 600,000 enrollments in 200 online schools.

Consideration of the rapidly evolving field led us to ask the following question: What are some key policy and practice needs in the field that might be addressed through advice from experts and program leaders? We believe that the tremendous growth in K–12 online and blended learning programs in recent years is creating new needs for policy development, infrastructure building, teacher/leader training, and program development in areas such as curriculum, instruction, technology, and management.

As blended learning approaches bring online learning into the K–12 mainstream, universities need to prepare K–12 teachers and administrators for the incorporation of online and blended learning into their professional practice. K–12 educators need to learn new ways of teaching and supporting learning. Policymakers need to address related policy and funding issues. This book is designed to meet these needs through chapters contributed by experienced practitioners and experts in the field on key program components and important policy issues.

While North America has taken the lead in development of K–12 online learning and the number of students participating is growing, whether this is having a positive educational impact on student achievement is not yet clear (Barbour, 2012a). The United States has fallen behind many other nations in high school student achievement, based upon recent Program for International Student Assessment (PISA) and Trends in International Mathematics and Science Study (TIMSS) international assessments. This movement is especially alarming because, over the long run, K–12 educational outcomes tend to predict a nation's gross domestic product (Hanushek & Woessmann, 2010). This raises the question: What can North American educators learn from other nations about online, blended, and distance learning? Conversely, as they expand their programs, international educators want to know, *What can we learn from North American programs?* Through the contributed chapters in this book, we seek to provide illustrative program examples from North America and around the world that explore the issues and challenges that programs face, the lessons they have learned, and what they would share with others.

There is also a tremendous need for research in the emerging field of K–12 distance, online, and blended learning. The existing research on K–12 online and distance learning is limited, and the need to study blended learning as well only adds to this challenge. Therefore, we have encouraged chapter authors to reference the related research as feasible in their analyses of key program components, policy issues, and case studies of programs in North America and around the world. The contributed chapters in this book are organized into four parts. We, the coeditors, authored this introductory chapter in Part One, "Overview," and the concluding chapter in Part Four, "Summary Thoughts." Contributor chapters are presented in Part Two, "Research and Policy," and Part Three, "Case Studies on Practice."

Research and Policy

The first three chapters in Part Two address quality online teaching, curriculum, and technology, three key components of a K–12 online and blended learning program. Several of the case study chapters presented in the next section address the fourth key program component: management. The last three chapters in this section address research on K–12 online learning, full-time online charter schools, and equitable access.

In Chapter 2, Kathryn Kennedy and Leanna Archambault focus on ways of identifying, evaluating, and fostering quality K–12 online teaching. These include research-based online pedagogy, frameworks and standards for evaluating online teaching, and ways to foster quality online teaching, including coursework, field experiences, endorsements, certificates, and professional development. They also explore ways to restructure teacher education to prepare teachers for online and blended teaching.

Christy G. Keeler introduces instructional design principles for online teachers and course developers in Chapter 3. She differentiates between traditional and online instructional design issues, and outlines elements necessary when designing online courses at both the macro and micro levels. She argues for a new perspective of instructional design as it relates to online and blended learning.

In Chapter 4, Rob Darrow addresses technology infrastructure, tools, and costs. He explores issues such as connectivity and hardware, learning management systems, and mobile learning devices. He describes tools for communication, social media, and gaming, as well as online content, open education resources, and learning objects. He advocates the use of planning cycles with cost projections, and identifies cost components of online programs that must be considered.

Richard E. Ferdig, Cathy Cavanaugh, and Joseph R. Freidhoff respond in Chapter 5 to this question—What does the research on K–12 online learning tell us?—by encouraging researchers to ask the right questions, answer the critics, and appreciate the complexity. They say researchers should study where online learning works best, and note that some online programs are not high quality. Ferdig, Cavanaugh, and Freidhoff see the distributed nature of online learning as raising new complexities for researchers. They conclude by highlighting effective practice resources.

Victoria Raish and Ali Carr-Chellman provide a case study in Chapter 6 on Pennsylvania cyber charter schools, or charter schools whose coursework is delivered primarily via the Internet. The authors explore the origins and legislative context of cyber charters, evaluations and research on their effectiveness, issues surrounding how they are funded, and the legal and ethical issues they raise. They conclude with recommendations for future research on cyber charters.

In Chapter 7, Raymond M. Rose, Alese Smith, Karen Johnson, and David Glick explore the issues surrounding equitable access in online learning, including equitable access to technology, online courses, and quality instruction. They discuss challenges raised by online learning but also ways that online learning can be used to address equity issues. The chapter concludes with an Access and Equity Checklist for administrators and other stakeholders.

Case Studies on Practice

In Part Three of the book, chapter authors present nine case studies of online and blended programs. Three of the four U.S. case studies illustrate the most common categories of online learning programs in that county—state-led, charter school, and district-led. The fourth documents a program that prepares educators for online teaching, a key component of online learning programs. Case studies of private schools are presented in chapters from Canada and Australia, while barriers to online learning programs in developing nations are explored through a case study on Nepal. The next case study explores the integration of e-learning in selected schools in the United Kingdom, while the final case study describes a national e-learning system for K–12 students in South Korea.

In Chapter 8, Kevin Oliver and Tracy Weeks present a case study of a new state virtual school, the North Carolina Virtual Public School (NCVPS), as informed by program- and project-level evaluation. This chapter addresses program management issues through the lens of evaluation. The authors argue that evaluation can help online learning providers improve their programs and encourage student success. They describe how NCVPS used evaluation findings during its startup period to revise approaches to course design, teaching, policy, and more.

In Chapter 9, Dazhi Yang and Kerry Rice present a case study of Boise State University's state-approved K–12 Online Teaching Endorsement program. Beginning with the research on teaching and standards, and standards development by the state of Idaho, they then describe the program's development and implementation, as well as challenges faced and how they were resolved.

Mickey Revenaugh presents in Chapter 10 a case study of the startup of the Nexus Academy blended charter schools by Connections Academy in two states. She describes how a series of pilots led to development of their own approach to blended learning, which is structured around data-driven personalized learning for every student in a small high school setting. Implementation challenges and lessons learned are described, along with potential applications of such blended models.

In Chapter 11, Jhone M. Ebert and Allison Powell offer a case study on the evolution of a district-led virtual school program in Nevada. District-led programs are the fastest-growing sector of K–12 online learning, and they frequently include blended learning initiatives. The authors describe how online learning and blended learning are being mainstreamed in this large district and share some effective practices.

John Smallwood, Jennifer Reaburn, and Stephen Baker present a study in Chapter 12 of the development of one private online school, Virtual High School (Ontario), from its inception in the mid-1990s to the present day. They document the philosophy, growth, and operations of this school's student-centric, highly challenging, and successful educational model.

In Chapter 13, Cathy Cavanaugh addresses the potential for online and blended learning to meet the needs of all students, based on the case of Nepal, a least-developed country that faces many challenges in its readiness for virtual education. She documents the many barriers faced, but also the success of Open Learning Exchange Nepal, which provides resources, such as an online repository of activities and books, that some public primary schools use. She argues that sustained access to quality educational resources and experiences requires a sustained commitment from governments and agencies.

In Chapter 14, Stephen Harris describes the evolving role of the Sydney Centre for Innovation in Learning, a unit of North Beaches Christian School, in the provision of K–12 online learning. He describes development of the school's model of online and blended learning and the expansion of its educational role in New South Wales. He explains how state-level policy issues have limited growth of online programs in Australia.

Helen Boulton and Lisa Hasler Waters describe in Chapter 15 the use of virtual learning environments (VLEs) to personalize education. The authors see VLEs as the next generation of technology integration. They focus on five schools across the United Kingdom that constitute a diverse cross section of primary and secondary schools, and of virtual and brick-and-mortar schools. They consider how the personalization achieved via VLEs reflects each school's values and mission.

In Chapter 16, Hyeonjin Kim and Jeonghee Seo present the case of Korea's national e-learning system for elementary and secondary students and teachers, the Cyber Home Learning System, which was launched in 2005 with the aim of reducing private tuition expenses and the educational gap between high- and low-income families. The authors review the school's evolution and effectiveness. They conclude with recommendations for improving the system and using it to support the nation's new Smart Education initiative for a 21st-century knowledge society.

The book concludes with a chapter by the coeditors in which we synthesize key findings and lessons learned, and present a global vision for the future of K–12 distance and online learning.

A companion resource for the book is available online. This Classroom Resources Wiki (onlineblendedschooling.wikispaces.com) includes chapter questions, reference links, and related resources.

Note

1. In the United States and Canada, elementary and secondary education is frequently referred to in short as K–12 education (kindergarten through 12th grade). Therefore, learning in schools is often called K–12 learning.

References

Barbour, M. (2012a). The landscape of K–12 online learning. In M. G. Moore (Ed.), *Handbook of distance education* (pp. 574–593). New York: Routledge.

Barbour, M. (2012b). *State of the nation: K–12 online learning in Canada* 5th ed. Victoria, BC: Open School BC / Vienna, VA: International Association for K–12 Online Learning. Retrieved from http://www.openschool.bc.ca/pdfs/iNACOL_CanadaStudy_2012.pdf

Barbour, M., Brown, R., Waters. L. H., Hoey, R., Hunt, J. L., Kennedy, K., . . . Trimm, T. (2011). *Online and blended learning: A survey of policy and practice around the world.* Vienna, VA: International Association for K–12 Online Learning.

Bianchi, W. (2002). The Wisconsin School of the Air: Success story with implications. *Educational Technology & Society, 5*(1), 141–147.

Clark, T. (2001). *Virtual schools: Issues and trends.* Phoenix: WestEd. Retrieved from http://www.wested.org/online_pubs/virtualschools.pdf

Clark, T. (2012, September). History of K–12 online learning. In M. K. Barbour (Ed.), *Virtual school MOOC: Introduction to K–12 online learning research (10 September–07 October 2012).* Retrieved from http://virtualschoolmooc.wikispaces.com

Federal Communications Commission. (1952). *Fourth report and order.* Washington, DC: Author.

Florida Taxwatch Center for Educational Performance and Accountability. (2007). *Final report: A comprehensive assessment of Florida Virtual School.* Tallahassee, FL: Author. Retrieved from www.flvs.net/areas/aboutus/Documents/Research/TaxWatch%20Study.pdf

Hanushek, E. A., & Woessmann, L. (2010). *The high cost of low educational performance.* Paris: Program for International Student Assessment, Organisation for Economic Co-operation and Development.

Hezel Associates. (1998). *Educational telecommunications and distance learning: The state-by-state analysis, 1998–99.* Syracuse, NY: Author.

Jajkowski. S. (2004). *MPATI: The flying classroom.* Retrieved from http://www.chicagotelevision.com/MPATI.htm

Kozma, R. B., Zucker, A., & Espinoza, C. (1998). *An evaluation of the Virtual High School after one year of operation.* Retrieved from http://thevhscollaborative.org/sites/default/files/public/Evaluation%20after%20yr%201.pdf

Kurtz, B. E. (1959). *Pioneering in educational television, 1932–1939.* Iowa City: State University of Iowa.

Laurel Springs School. (2011). *Laurel Springs celebrates 20 years of distance learning.* Retrieved from http://laurelsprings.com/2011/05/20/laurel-springs-20-years

Pease, P. S., & Tinsley, P. J. (1986, October). *Reaching rural schools using an interactive satellite based educational network.* Paper presented at the annual conference of the National Rural and Small Schools Consortium, Bellingham, WA. (ERIC Document Reproduction Service No. ED281681)

Picciano, A. G., & Seaman, J. (2009). *K–12 online learning: A 2008 follow-up of the survey of U.S. school district administrators.* Needham, MA: BABSON Survey Research Group & Sloan Consortium.

Queen, B., & Lewis, L. (2011). *Distance education courses for public elementary and secondary school students: 2009–10* (NCES 2012-009). U.S. Department of Education, National Center for Education Statistics. Retrieved from http://nces.ed.gov/pubs2012/2012008.pdf

Saettler, L. P. (2004). *The evolution of American educational technology.* Charlotte, NC: Information Age Publishing.

Singh, J. P., Morgan, R. P., & Rosenbaum, F. J. (1972). Satellite networks for education. In *Proceedings of the International Telemetering Conference* (pp. 419–439). Woodland Hills, CA: International Foundation for Telemetering.

Smith, K., & Northrup, K. (1998). The CLASS course design model for Web-based instruction. Washington, DC: General Services Administration. (ERIC ED 422877). Retrieved from http://files.eric.ed.gov/fulltext/ED422877.pdf

Staker, H., & Horn, M. B. (2012). *Classifying K–12 blended learning.* San Mateo, CA: Innosight Institute. Retrieved from http://www.innosightinstitute.org

Verduin, J. R., & Clark, T. (1991). *Distance education: The foundations of effective practice.* San Francisco: Jossey-Bass.

Watson, J., & Kalmon, S. (2005). *Keeping pace with K–12 online learning: A review of state-level policy and practice.* Naperville, IL: Learning Point Associates. Retrieved from www.kpk12.com/reports

Watson, J., Murin, A., Vashaw, L., Gemin, B., & Rapp, C. (2011). *Keeping pace with K–12 online learning: An annual review of policy and practice.* Evergreen, CO: Evergreen Education Group. Retrieved from http://kpk12.com/reports

Watson, J., Murin, A., Vashaw, L., Gemin, B., & Rapp, C. (2012). *Keeping pace with K–12 online & blended learning: An annual review of policy and practice.* Evergreen, CO: Evergreen Education Group. Retrieved from http://kpk12.com/reports

Watson, J., Pape, L., Murin, A., Vashaw, L., & Gemin, B. (2014). *Keeping pace with K–12 digital & blended learning: An annual review of policy and practice.* Durango, CO: Evergreen Education Group. Retrieved from http://kpk12.com/reports

PART TWO
Research and Policy

2

IDENTIFYING, EVALUATING, AND FOSTERING QUALITY ONLINE TEACHING

Kathryn Kennedy and Leanna Archambault

K–12 online learning continues to have a lasting impact on the current education landscape in many ways. All 50 states and the District of Columbia have online learning opportunities for K–12 students (Watson, Murin, Vashaw, Gemin, & Rapp, 2011). A handful of states have passed laws requiring that K–12 students take at least one online learning experience prior to graduating high school (Watson et al., 2011). These policy and growth developments in K–12 online learning warrant the need for teachers to be prepared to teach online (Archambault, 2011). But what exactly does quality online teaching entail? In this chapter we focus on identifying, evaluating, and fostering quality teaching in K–12 online learning environments. We divide the chapter into four sections, which include an overview of research on quality online teaching, a collection of research-based frameworks and standards available for evaluating online teaching and course design, a summary of how the field is fostering quality online teaching, and an exploration of where the field might go in terms of restructuring teacher education to prepare teachers for K–12 online and blended teaching.

What Do We Know? Research on Quality Online Teaching

Teacher quality is typically guided by education policy in accordance with standards from accrediting bodies, such as the National Council for Accreditation of Teacher Education (NCATE) and the Teacher Education Accreditation Council (TEAC). In addition, standards from professional organizations, including the American Association of Colleges for Teacher Education (AACTE), the National Education Association (NEA), and the Association of Teacher Educators (ATE), guide teacher education programs in their design of programs that have the potential to graduate quality teachers. Specifically for online teaching, standards designed to help ensure quality have been established by professional organizations, such as the International Association for K–12 Online Learning (iNACOL), the Southern Regional Education Board (SREB), and the National Education Association (NEA). A cross-reference of how these standards align is available in existing literature (see Kennedy, 2010, and Kennedy & Archambault, 2012b). Together with these standards, the Quality Matters (2011) standards as well as a white paper produced by SRI International for the Virtual High School Global Consortium are key resources in defining quality online courses (Yamashiro & Zucker, 1999).

In addition to existing standards and reports, studies have been conducted that report on qualities of effective online teachers. DiPietro, Ferdig, Black, and Preston (2008) found that quality online teachers need to provide extra support and understand course pacing. They also need to be willing to explore new technologies, have exemplary organizational skills, and use technology effectively. They have to possess strategies in addressing inappropriate behavior in the online environment, have an appreciation for and an abundance of knowledge of their subject area, and be willing to constantly monitor and ensure their students' safety in the online classroom. Online teachers should be able to motivate students, establish deadlines for assignments, offer supplemental work for students who need help, monitor student progress, and maintain flexibility with time. They should have an understanding of how learning occurs, be available to their students, be willing to self-evaluate by using data-driven strategies, assess students in meaningful ways, and acknowledge and use students' interests in their course(s). Most importantly, they need to form meaningful and supportive relationships with students, build and facilitate community to enhance the learning environment, provide timely feedback, and address technology access issues for students (DiPietro et al., 2008).

Kearsley and Blomeyer (2004) shared their ideas for effective online teaching, including providing prompt feedback, preparing engaging learning activities, motivating students, allowing for student-to-student interaction, and promoting critical and reflective thinking from students. Fuller, Norby, Pearce, and Strand (2000) found that an online instructor should appreciate the need for one-on-one interaction with their students, allow for flexibility, and provide a significant amount of feedback. Various combinations of these qualities are sought by those looking for educators to teach in online or blended environments. In addition to these qualities and skills, teachers also must be prepared in online pedagogy (Lowes, 2007), online course design (Dabner, Davis, & Zaka, 2012), and online course facilitation within the course online and at the students' traditional school, if applicable (Davis & Niederhauser, 2007; Harms, Niederhauser, Davis, Roblyer, & Gilbert, 2006).

Brennan (2003) found that in order to help ensure effective student learning outcomes, online pedagogy needs to address a variety of factors. Among these are the level to which a learner-centered environment is created, whether approaches are used that enable learners to build new knowledge and skills based upon the ones they have already acquired, the quality of the design of online materials and the engagement with those materials, the use of teaching and learning methodologies that develop cognitive skills, the level of interactivity among all participants, and whether a consistent level of appropriate feedback exists, as well as the opportunity for self-testing, review, and reflection. While there is no way to ensure the right combination of these factors to produce quality online instruction, the interaction among them is what currently constitutes effective online pedagogy (Brennan, 2003).

Evaluating Quality in Online Teaching and Learning: Standards for Online Teaching

Standards that are often used in the evaluation of online teachers include the National Education Association's (NEA; 2006) *Guide to Teaching Online Courses,* the International Association for K–12 Online Learning's (iNACOL; 2011b) *National Standards for Quality Online Teaching,* and the Southern Regional Education Board (SREB; 2006) *Standards for Quality Online Teaching.* A cross-reference of these standards is available (Kennedy & Archambault, 2012a) that categorizes the standards using the following classifications: qualifications, professional development, and credentials; curriculum, instruction, and student achievement; online pedagogy; ethics of online teaching; communication/interaction; assessment and evaluation; feedback; accommodation and diversity awareness; management; technological knowledge; and design. For instance, the classification of "online pedagogy" within the cross section highlights two organizations' standards, including iNACOL and SREB. The first seven are from iNACOL:

- Standard A Summary: Knows the primary concepts and structures of effective online instruction and is able to create learning experiences to enable student success.
- A1: Knows and understands the current best practices and strategies for online teaching and learning and their implementation in online education.
- A2: Knows and understands the role of online learning in preparing students for the global community they live in, both now and in the future.
- A3: Knows and understands the instructional delivery continuum (e.g., fully online to blended to face-to-face). . . .
- Standard C Summary: Plans, designs, and incorporates strategies to encourage active learning, application, interaction, participation, and collaboration in the online environment.
- C1: Knows and understands the techniques and applications of online instructional strategies, based on current research and practice (e.g., discussion, student-directed learning, collaborative learning, lecture, project-based learning, forum, small group work). . . .
- C6: Knows and understands differentiated instruction based on students' learning styles. (iNACOL, 2011b, pp. 4, 6)

The last three are from SREB, whose third standard was adopted by iNACOL as Standard C, with revised indicators.

- Standard 3 Summary: Plans, designs, and incorporates strategies to encourage active learning, interaction, participation, and collaboration in the online environment.
- 3.1: Demonstrates effective strategies and techniques that actively engage students in the learning process (e.g., team problem-solving, in-class writing, analysis, synthesis and evaluation instead of passive lectures). . . .
- 3.5: Leads online instruction groups that are goal-oriented, focused, project-based and inquiry-oriented. (SREB, 2006, p. 4)

In addition to this cross-reference, a research-based analysis of the standards for online teaching is available as well (Ferdig, Cavanaugh, DiPietro, Black, & Dawson, 2009). In this analysis, it was found that (a) the varying roles of educators in K–12 online learning environments needed to be included in standards and best practices within the field, (b) data collection at K–12 online learning programs must improve in order to provide a better foundation for making recommendations to the field in terms of best practices and standards, and (c) teacher education programs need to provide guidance to new and existing teachers regarding online pedagogy.

In addition to standards that evaluate online teaching, there are also standards that guide design of online courses. iNACOL (2011a) has developed such a set of standards. Note that the iNACOL standards in their current form have yet to be tested and validated. Two additional frameworks that are also used include the SRI evaluations of the Virtual High School (VHS) and Quality Matters standards. Together, these sets of online teaching and course standards contain the current understanding of factors composing effective online teaching.

iNACOL is most explicit about teachers and their roles, while the VHS and Quality Matters reports concentrate more on describing the instructional functions. Within the iNACOL (2011a) *National Standards for Quality Online Courses*, key elements illustrate teachers' roles in online learning environments, including being able to perform the following functions:

- Providing "multiple learning resources and materials to increase student success" (p. 8).
- Differentiating learning to meet "students' needs and incorporate varied ways to learn and master the curriculum" (p. 10).
- Organizing "units and lessons that fall into a logical sequence . . . provid[ing] multiple learning opportunities for students to master the content" (p. 10).
- Planning "activities that engage students in active learning" (p. 10).
- Providing "multiple learning paths, based on student needs that engage students in a variety of ways" (p. 11).
- Providing "opportunities for students to engage in higher-order thinking, critical reasoning activities, and thinking in increasingly complex ways" (p. 11).
- Accommodating student needs by "adapt[ing] learning activities" (p. 11).
- Structuring the course to allow for "opportunities for appropriate instructor-student interaction, including opportunities for timely and frequent feedback about student progress" (p. 12).
- Designing the course to allow for "explicit communication/activities (both before and during the first week of the course) that confirms whether students are engaged and are progressing through the course" (p. 12).
- Providing "opportunities for appropriate instructor-student and student-student interaction to foster mastery and application of the material" (p. 12).
- Enabling students "access to resources that enrich the course content" (p. 12).
- Structuring the course to permit the addition of "content, activities, and assessments to extend learning opportunities" (p. 14).

- Designing the course with "rich media . . . in multiple formats for ease of use and access in order to address diverse student needs" (p. 14).
- Applying knowledge learned through professional development of "the behavioral, social, and . . . emotional aspects of the learning environment" (p. 14).

These quality course standards outline some of the key pedagogical factors involved in quality online teaching. In the next section we delve into ways in which quality online teaching is being fostered and cultivated.

Fostering Quality Online Teaching

The field is fostering quality online teaching in many ways, including preservice and in-service field experiences for teachers in colleges of education; state-endorsed online teaching endorsements or university-endorsed certificates; and professional development opportunities provided by universities, nonprofit organizations, professional organizations, virtual schools, or other K–12 online learning programs. Our primary focus here is on the role of university teacher education programs in fostering quality.

Preservice and In-Service Training in Teacher Education Programs

In 2007 Iowa State University began TEGIVS (Teacher Education Goes Into Virtual Schooling) a Fund for the Improvement of Postsecondary Education (FIPSE) project that helped introduce preservice teachers to K–12 online teaching and learning through a partnership with Iowa Learning Online (Davis et al., 2007). The University of Florida, University of Central Florida, and University of South Florida followed suit in 2009 with the help of Florida Virtual School (Kennedy, 2010). Through various online teaching endorsements and online teaching certificates, a number of universities around the country—including, but not limited to, Wayne State University, Arizona State University, Georgia Southern University, Utah State University, Boise State University, University of California, and South Dakota State University—have begun training their in-service and preservice teachers in online pedagogy and course design. Many of these programs also provide a field experience element so that the prospective online teachers can work alongside an online teacher mentor. Barbour (2012) highlights specifics related to these programs. While this list of universities continues to grow, a 2011 survey of teacher education programs reported only 1.3% of them offer field experiences in K–12 online learning programs, such as virtual schools (Kennedy & Archambault, 2012b).

Because of this, many virtual schools have developed various forms of teacher mentoring opportunities and professional development for those new to online teaching (Davis & Rose, 2007; Kennedy & Archambault, 2012b; Wortmann et al., 2008). Wortmann et al.'s (2008) report titled *Online Teacher Support Programs: Mentoring and Coaching Models* provides a detailed look at how mentoring occurs in various virtual school models. Kennedy and Archambault (2012b) brought together researchers and practitioners from the field on the topic of teacher mentoring in virtual schools. In addition, Boise State University created a series of reports regarding professional development for K–12 online teachers (Rice & Dawley, 2007, 2008, 2009; Rice, Dawley, Gasell, & Florez,

2008). Guidelines have been developed for professional development of online teachers (Southern Regional Education Board, 2009).

Future Directions for Teacher Education Programs

With the rise in K–12 online and blended learning environments, teachers need to be prepared accordingly. In-service teachers will need to have professional development for online teaching, especially if they teach in school districts that are adopting online learning. District-led programs represent one of the fastest-growing sectors of K–12 online and blended learning (Watson et al., 2011). Teacher education programs can be a source of this in-service professional development. As the need for K–12 online teachers increases, new teachers may be recruited directly from their teacher education programs. Because of this, teacher preparation programs will need to examine what it means to prepare teachers for 21st-century teaching and learning environments, providing them the necessary skills and dispositions to be quality online instructors. For example, teacher education programs should consider a greater degree of meaningful technology integration and the modeling of evidence-based quality online and blended teaching in both preservice and in-service teacher education programs. More research studies on standards for online teaching and effective online and blended teaching practices are needed to support this effort.

References

Archambault, L. M. (2011). The practitioner's perspective on teacher education: Preparing for the K–12 online classroom. *Journal of Technology and Teacher Education, 19*(1), 73–91.

Barbour, M. (2012). Virtually unprepared: Examining the preparation of K–12 online teachers. In K. Kennedy & L. Archambault (Eds.), *Mentoring and virtual schools: Supporting teachers in K–12 online education*. Vienna, VA: International Association for K–12 Online Learning.

Brennan, R. (2003). *One size doesn't fit all: Pedagogy in the online environment*. Kensington Park, Australia: National Centre for Vocation Education Research, Australian National Training Authority.

Dabner, N., Davis, N., & Zaka, P. (2012). Authentic project-based design of professional development for teachers studying online and blended teaching. *Contemporary Issues in Technology and Teacher Education, 12*(1). Retrieved from http://www.citejournal.org/vol12/iss1/currentpractice/article2.cfm

Davis, N. E., & Niederhauser, D. S. (2007). New roles and responsibilities for distance education in K–12 education. *Learning and Leading, 34*(7), 10–15.

Davis, N. E., Roblyer, M. D., Charania, A., Ferdig, R., Harms, C., Compton, L. K. L., & Cho, M. O. (2007). Illustrating the "virtual" in virtual schooling: Challenges and strategies for creating real tools to prepare virtual teachers. *Internet and Higher Education, 10*(1), 27–39.

Davis, N. E., & Rose, R. (2007). *Professional development for virtual schooling and online learning*. Vienna, VA: International Association for K–12 Online Learning. Retrieved from http://www.nacol.org/docs/NACOL_PDforVSandOlnLrng.pdf

DiPietro, M., Ferdig, R. E., Black, E. W., & Preston, M. (2008). Best practices in teaching K–12 online: Lessons learned from Michigan Virtual School teachers. *Journal of Interactive Online Learning, 7*(1), 10–35.

Ferdig, R. E., Cavanaugh, C., DiPietro, M., Black, E. W., & Dawson, K. (2009). Virtual schooling standards and best practices for teacher education. *Journal of Technology and Teacher Education, 17*(4), 479–503.

Fuller, D., Norby, R., Pearce, K., & Strand, S. (2000). Internet teaching by style: Profiling the on-line professor. *Educational Technology & Society, 3*(2). Retrieved from http://ifets.ieee.org/periodical/vol_2_2000/pearce.html

Harms, C. M., Niederhauser, D. S., Davis, N. E., Roblyer, M. D., & Gilbert, S. B. (2006). Educating educators for virtual schooling: Communicating roles and responsibilities. *Electronic Journal of Communication, 16*(1–2). Retrieved from http://www.cios.org/EJCPUBLIC/016/1/01611.HTML

International Association for K–12 Online Learning (iNACOL). (2011a). *National standards for quality online courses.* Vienna, VA: Author. Retrieved from http://www.inacol.org/resources/publications/national-quality-standards

International Association for K–12 Online Learning (iNACOL). (2011b). *National standards for quality online teaching.* Vienna, VA: Author. Retrieved from http://www.inacol.org/resources/publications/national-quality-standards

Kearsley, G., & Blomeyer, R. (2004). Preparing teachers to teach online. *Educational Technology, 44*(1), 49–52.

Kennedy, K. (2010). Cross-reference of online teaching standards and the development of quality teachers for 21st-century learning environments. *Distance Learning: A Magazine for Leaders, 7*(2), 21–28.

Kennedy, K., & Archambault, L. (2012a). Design and development of field experiences in K–12 online learning environments. *Journal of Applied Instructional Design, 2*(1), 35–49. Retrieved from http://www.jaidpub.org/wp-content/uploads/2012/08/KennedyArchambault-3.pdf

Kennedy, K., & Archambault, L. (Eds.). (2012b). *Mentoring and virtual schools: Supporting teachers in K–12 online education.* Vienna, VA: International Association for K–12 Online Learning.

Lowes, S. (2007). Professional development for online teachers. In C. Cavanaugh & R. Blomeyer (Eds.), *What works in K–12 online learning* (pp. 161–178). Eugene, OR: International Society for Technology in Education.

National Education Association. (2006). *Guide to teaching online courses.* Washington, DC: Author. Retrieved from http://www.nea.org/home/30103.htm

Quality Matters. (2011). *Quality Matters rubric standards 2011–2013 edition with assigned point values.* Baltimore: Author. Retrieved from http://www.qmprogram.org

Rice, K., & Dawley, L. (2007). *Going virtual! The status of professional development for K–12 online teachers: Results from phase one of the Going Virtual! study series.* Vienna, VA, and Boise, ID: North American Council for Online Learning and Boise State University. Retrieved from http://edtech.boisestate.edu/goingvirtual/goingvirtual.htm

Rice, K., & Dawley, L. (2008). Professional development for K–12 online teachers: Where do we go from here? *Technology and Teacher Education Annual, 19*(1), 667–673.

Rice, K., & Dawley, L. (2009). The status of professional development for K–12 online teachers: Insights and implications. *Journal of Technology & Teacher Education, 17*(4), 523–545.

Rice, K., Dawley, L., Gasell, C., & Florez, C. (2008). *Going virtual! Unique needs and challenges of K–12 online teachers.* Boise, ID, and Vienna, VA: Boise State University and the International Association for K–12 Online Learning. Retrieved from http://www.distance-educator.com/Article16104.phtml

Southern Regional Education Board. (2006). *Standards for quality online teaching.* Atlanta: Author. Retrieved from http://publications.sreb.org/2006/06T02_Standards_Online_Teaching.pdf

Southern Regional Education Board. (2009). *Guidelines for professional development of online teachers*. Atlanta: Author. Retrieved from http://www.sreb.org/page/1295/publications.html

Watson, J., Murin, A., Vashaw, L., Gemin, B., & Rapp, C. (2011). *Keeping pace with K–12 online learning: An annual review of policy and practice*. Evergreen, CO: Evergreen Education Group.

Wortmann, K., Cavanaugh, C., Kennedy, K., Beldarrain, Y., Letourneau, T., & Zygouris-Coe, V. (2008). *Online teacher support programs: Mentoring and coaching models*. Vienna, VA: International Association for K–12 Online Learning.

Yamashiro, K., & Zucker, A. (1999). *An expert panel review of the quality of Virtual High School courses: Final report*. Menlo Park, CA: SRI International.

3

INSTRUCTIONAL DESIGN
Teaching With Intention

Christy G. Keeler

Curriculum (n.): What to Teach. Instruction (v.): How to Teach.

Students enrolled in Algebra I can be quite certain they will learn the same concepts as students anywhere in the world who take Algebra I. Some will enjoy the experience while others will hate it. In all cases, teachers teach the content—or curricula—of Algebra I. The difference is *how* they teach. That "how" is instructional design.

Quality design is of great importance in online contexts because single lessons are delivered multiple times (Dick & Carey, 1996). A teacher at a brick-and-mortar high school might teach the same lesson five times in one day (making minor adjustments between each class period), but will not teach that lesson again for another year. On the other hand, an online course offers a lesson that is exactly the same each time students visit it. Traditional classroom teachers can make minor adjustments to lessons based on numerous factors like whether the heater went out or there was a school assembly. Online courses cannot take individual and unique events into account because there is no consistent circumstance in which students complete their lessons. For this reason, online lessons need to have a consistent layout so that students can quickly pick up where they left off, and so that lessons engage students so that they can stay actively involved with the content.

While minor changes are possible in online courses, time and financial constraints as well as the complication of having several students engaged in different parts of courses simultaneously make this a daunting task. Instead, full courses tend to remain intact except when undergoing major revisions (usually on a six-year cycle). Except supplemental instruction (e.g., individual tutoring) and administrative assistance (e.g., technology support), online course designers must plan for every possible reaction and response that might occur during student enrollment; they must create the "finished product" before school begins (Smith & Ragan, 2005, p. 4).

What Is Online Instructional Design?

Gagné, Briggs, and Wager (1992) describe *instruction* as a "deliberately arranged set of external events designed to support internal learning processes" (p. 11). They further state that "*events of instruction* . . . considered, chosen, and represented in the

21

communications and other stimulation offered to the learner . . . will lead to rapid, obstacle-free learning" (p. 11). Simply stated, the goal of instructional design is to create a desirable state in which students can learn (Gagné et al., 1992). The instructional designer, then, is to use precision, care, and expertise along with theoretical, practical, and research-based methods to systemically identify means of preparing an effective, efficient, and appropriate course of action that will ease the process of learning. They create environments conducive to learning by specifying *how* learning should happen. Smith and Ragan (2005) add, "[Instructional designers] try to design solutions that are not only functional but also attractive or appealing to the end-user" (p. 4). This latter point is particularly true when working with adolescents. The art of instructional design is finding the best match among content objectives, teaching strategies, and intended student populations.

How Are Online Courses Developed?

K–12 virtual schools offer online courses to students but do not always create their own courses. Instead, many purchase rights to use courses designed by content providers. For example, K12 Inc. develops courses ranging from kindergarten science to AP macroeconomics. An online school such as Nevada Virtual Academy, a public school in Nevada, uses K12 Inc. courses with its own Nevada-certified teachers to "teach" those courses by monitoring students as they progress through predeveloped courses. The teachers' administrative responsibilities include activities such as keeping students on task, assisting with accessing materials, and coordinating schedules with students and their site facilitators. Instructionally, they monitor students' academic progress (e.g., grading assessments)— intervening as needed to provide individual assistance such as tutoring, introducing alternative learning resources, and facilitating group learning sessions. Their job is distinctly different from that of the course designer. The designer prepares all instructional units in advance and has no control over course implementation. Content providers provide the courses; virtual schools, sometimes also the content providers, teach those courses. Examples of content providers include Connections Academy, K12 Inc., Florida Virtual School, and APEX.

Each virtual school must begin by deciding how it will procure its courses—buying or leasing them from outside providers or developing its own. This choice alone can define a school. Because of the quality, cost, and availability of courses through content providers, most contemporary K–12 online schools rely on leasing or purchasing content instead of creating their own.

Design Models

When many people think of online course design, they envision a professor sitting at a computer deciding how to organize his or her own course. The professor chooses resources to make available to students, uploads lectures (often videos of the professor delivering a lecture in front of a camera or slideshows with voice-overs), and writes multiple-choice and essay questions. Online course design allows professors to develop courses in real time as semesters progress and also allows quick course modification. This is not the model common to K–12 online course designers.

The three basic K–12 course design models are teacher-as-designer, design team, and template design. All approaches usually rely on preexisting course design structures based on course management system limitations and traditional educational styles and theories. As such, courses tend to be separated into units and further into lessons, with formative evaluation occurring within lessons and summative evaluation occurring at the end of units and courses. Within these limitations and traditions, designers generally have license to create any events that they feel contribute to student learning that are manageable within an online environment.

In the first model, the designer and teacher are the same person. A single individual determines course content, organizes it into units, prepares lessons and assessments, and teaches the course. While there are many benefits to being both the designer and teacher, there are also costs. Some of these include the length of the design and development process, which alone can take a single designer 500 hours (T. Layton, personal communication, October 30, 2002) also, the model limits available resources. Collective teams know of and have access to a wider knowledge base than any single designer.

In the second model, teacher-as-designer model, the design team model, takes advantage of a wide range of specialists working collectively. Ideally, teams consist of a curriculum (or content) specialist, instructional designer, visual designer, web programmer, and teacher. The content specialist provides a standards-based list of curricular goals and objectives for the full course; creates a scope and sequence indicating natural delineations and connections between and within curricular topics; and provides the instructional designer with research-based, content-specific writing, resources, and guidance. The instructional designer, who also serves as the project manager, uses the curricular scope and sequence in conjunction with educational theory, research, and contemporary practice to select and organize learning modules, events of instruction, educational resources, and assessment. This designer is also responsible for ensuring that the course meets a variety of standards and laws.

Based on content, course organization, instructional goals, and needed resources, a visual designer works with the instructional designer to conceive a visual "feel" for the course and works with the web programmer to translate those visual elements into functional, aesthetically appealing, and age-appropriate online pages. The visual designer's job is to create visual branding for the course at both the macro and micro levels while focusing on content themes and visual consistency. The goal is to create a user-friendly, content-specific experience while ensuring seamless attention to mastering course objectives. The designer, based on the instructional plan, will also create page layouts and lesson-specific visual elements (e.g., the appearance of avatars, games, or models). The web designer then merges the instructional and visual design plans in a way that allows students to transparently progress within the online environment. Finally, the teacher serves as a quality control agent with a focus on course delivery. The teacher envisions teaching and learning within the environment while identifying issues that might prove unwieldy or difficult for students or teachers. The teacher looks for inconsistencies in content and design and judges the ease of progressing through course content based on the intended age of students (see Figure 3.1).

Figure 3.1: Design team roles

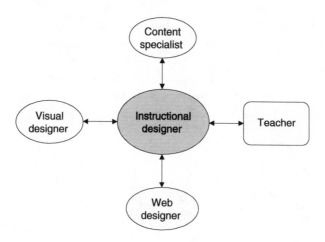

Given the special skills and knowledge of individuals within a design team, it is difficult to imagine a single individual creating a higher-quality course. Additionally, the design team model enhances the overall course creativity and makes learning more attractive to K–12 students than is possible with other models.

A third model is the sole use of templates. While the previous team approach allows for much greater creativity and variety in instructional methodologies, the template design model still allows substantive flexibility within individual events of instruction while forcing consistency within and across courses. When designing using the template method, course designers receive a general shell in which they fill in curriculum and instruction. When contracted to develop a course, an instructional designer or design team may receive template requirements such as those appearing in Figure 3.2. However, a design team may go beyond sole use of templates in its design approach.

In Figure 3.2, each lesson includes five sections: "You will learn," "You should know . . . ," "Lesson," "Assigned activities," and "Test yourself."

See Figure 3.3 for an example of how Connections Academy implements this design method.

Courses offered through Connections Academy share this template for all lessons within all its courses. While the number of screens/pages varies by lesson, all lessons progress through "Getting Started," "Instruction," "Activity," and "Review."

Many online schools now rely on third-party content providers using design team or template models. Courses, particularly those with nontemplate designs, are extremely time intensive and costly to produce. Online schools can review courses from a variety of content providers, choose a provider they feel offers the highest-quality courses at the most reasonable prices, and then focus on working with students. This economic model is beneficial for all parties. Content providers can afford the expense of building high-quality courses, sometimes as much as $1 million per course. Economies of scale—due to the possibility of leasing courses to a wide market of virtual schools—provide financial resources needed to access expert design teams. Regardless, there are relatively few major

Figure 3.2: Template screen shots

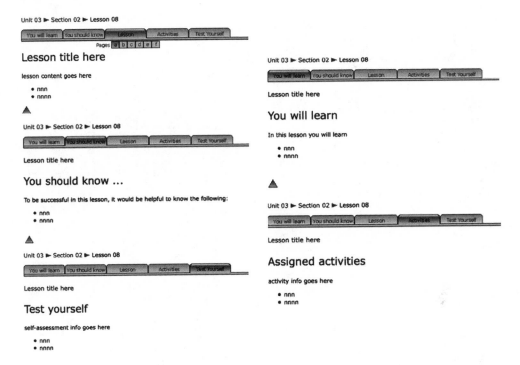

content providers. Some educators worry that privatization of content may lead to a small number of corporate entities controlling knowledge and its delivery methods in K–12 environments (Bracey, 2004). To counter this criticism, content providers often rely on predeveloped, third-party resources. One example is use of third-party videos by Discovery Streaming, BrainPop, or Khan Academy. By partnering with other educational companies, content providers take advantage of exceptional, reliable, and accessible resources while not being the only providers of actual content.

Instructional Design Elements

Because every design element within each course has a single goal—student attainment of content objectives—course designers must focus on this goal in every decision they make regarding course structure. They ask questions such as

- Where might it be best to introduce course goals so as to inform learners of broad concepts while not detracting from student focus on mastering individual objectives?
- How might the course structure assist learners in making connections between individual objectives and course goals?

The instructional designer forms a plan based on these and many other questions. Creating the plan begins with developing a broad structure identifying where each

Figure 3.3: Connections science lesson (eighth-grade) screen shot

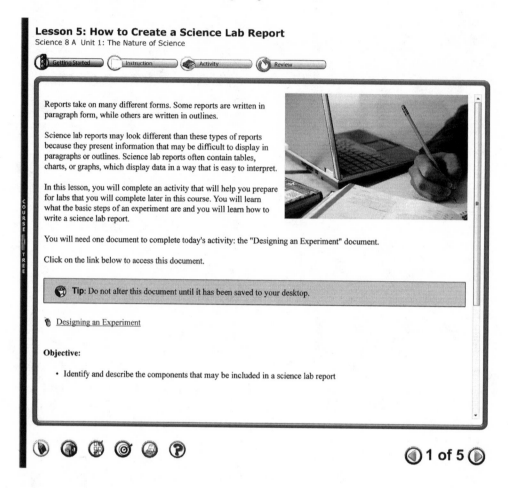

instructional element would most likely appear in a course, and continues on to decisions about instructional problems, learner characteristics, task analysis, instructional objectives, content sequencing, instructional strategies, and evaluation instruments (Morrison, Ross, & Kemp, 2007).

A Design Schema

Courses, structures intended to teach sets of self-contained, predetermined content goals, exist at two levels—macro and micro—both of which are an "arrangement of resources and procedures used to promote learning" (Gagné et al., 1992, p. 20). The macro level is the overall course design and serves as a shell in which all learning can occur. It considers topics such as course curriculum, unit sequencing, style consistency, and course management. The micro level delves into individual "events of instruction" (Gagné et al., 1992) spanning multiple mini-units, lessons, or modules, each with the goal of guiding students toward mastering singular curricular objectives. Think of macro-level design as what traditional teachers do before the first day of school (e.g., long-term unit planning, making classroom bulletin boards, arranging seating), and micro-level planning as weekly lesson planning (i.e., "What will I do Wednesday after the vocabulary quiz?").

Combining the macro and micro levels leads to a three-tiered schema—course, lesson, and assessment (wherein assessments appear both within and outside of lessons)—common in all K–12 online courses. Moving from conceptual theory to designing actual courses requires breaking the macro and micro levels into manageable, research-supported subparts. Figure 3.4 outlines the broad schema and element subsets used when instructional designers begin developing online courses.

Macro-Level Design

The macro level, which subsumes the "course level" (see Figure 3.4), is where designers make decisions about course organization and policies that overlay the entire course. In terms of content, they determine the standards basis for the course. Based on that decision, they prepare the course scope and sequence.

Designers also consider a variety of principles encompassing visual and website design factors at this level. They determine how lessons will "look" by defining step-by-step lesson subparts (e.g., objectives, activities), choosing color and other visual palettes and themes, deciding on technical (e.g., video formats) and nontechnical (e.g., textbooks, lab kits) resources, and choosing programming methods (e.g., use of Flash). Finally, at the course level, designers add the equivalent of a syllabus that overviews course rules, identifies means of teacher communication, states whether the course is linear or nonlinear, and details available course options. The macro level is where designers explain evaluation procedures; outline support resources; provide a navigable structure, grade book, and scheduling tool; and list required materials and expectations. At this level, students do not learn; they simply gain an overview of what they will learn.

Micro-Level Design

The macro level provides a "shell" for the course. Within that shell are replicable mini-shells in the form of broad units separated into lessons. Just as in traditional classrooms, certain elements are consistent in each lesson. A teacher in a traditional classroom may always start class with an advance organizer, provide a brief content presentation, have students engage in an activity, and evaluate how well students mastered the day's objectives. This lesson design model is nearly universal because educational theory, research, and practice dictate the pattern. While some design differences may exist between lessons, most follow this standard outline. For the purpose of consistency—a design principle itself—instructional designers working on K–12 online courses, even when using nontemplate designs, develop a standard iterative shell for all lessons within any given course. Despite these micro-level similarities, there can be great variety in both instruction and assessment.

Lesson-Level Design

Lessons are the cornerstone of learning. There students master content objectives needed to meet course goals and designers ask questions such as, "What media might be best for introducing the concept of plate tectonics?" Determining the combination of methods

Figure 3.4: Instructional design schema

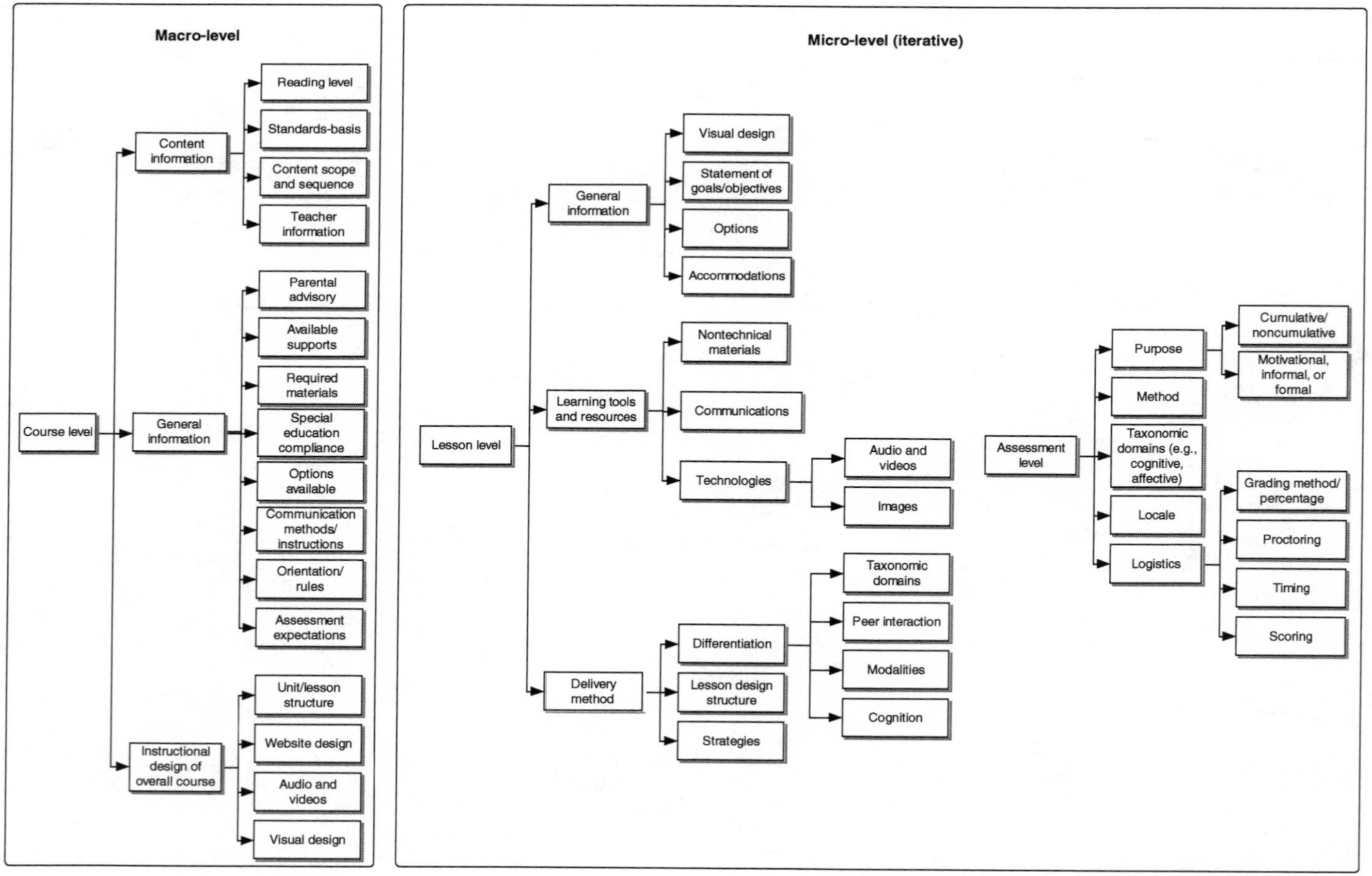

Macro-level

Course level
- Content information
  - Reading level
  - Standards-basis
  - Content scope and sequence
  - Teacher information
- General information
  - Parental advisory
  - Available supports
  - Required materials
  - Special education compliance
  - Options available
  - Communication methods/ instructions
  - Orientation/ rules
  - Assessment expectations
- Instructional design of overall course
  - Unit/lesson structure
  - Website design
  - Audio and videos
  - Visual design

Micro-level (iterative)

Lesson level
- General information
  - Visual design
  - Statement of goals/objectives
  - Options
  - Accommodations
- Learning tools and resources
  - Nontechnical materials
  - Communications
  - Technologies
    - Audio and videos
    - Images
- Delivery method
  - Differentiation
  - Lesson design structure
  - Strategies
    - Taxonomic domains
    - Peer interaction
    - Modalities
    - Cognition

Assessment level
- Purpose
  - Cumulative/ noncumulative
  - Motivational, informal, or formal
- Method
- Taxonomic domains (e.g., cognitive, affective)
- Locale
- Logistics
  - Grading method/ percentage
  - Proctoring
  - Timing
  - Scoring

leading to the greatest levels of student learning is the primary concern of instructional designers at this stage.

Designers are aware that some instructional activities are better for use with specific content and individuals. Foreign-language lessons require two-way communication, language arts require reading and writing, math challenges students with problems to analyze and solve, and science stretches students to engage in laboratory experiments. Despite these common content-specific methods, all courses benefit when incorporating a wide array of instructional events. Lectures may work well for auditory learners, whereas demonstrations may be better for visual learners. Similarly, students who excel artistically may perform better on visual, physical, or other performance-based assessments than students who prefer highly interrelational activities such as communications or critiquing. Audiobooks may be better suited to use with students who exhibit reading disabilities, audio cues may work best in foreign-language classes, and project-based learning and portfolios may be wise to use in business classes.

Student preferences, student abilities, and content interact to affect student success with instructional activities and assessment types. To ensure that lessons address all these factors, instructional designers must engage in "a systemic and reflective process of translating principles of learning and instruction into plans for instructional materials, activities, information resources, and evaluation" (Smith & Ragan, 2005, p. 4), and they must deliver these resources in age-appropriate and engaging ways for 21st-century K–12 learners (Ohanian, 2004).

A few areas that designers must consider include communications and instructional strategies as well as assessment design and special-needs accommodations—each of which correspond to elements at the micro level of the design schema in Figure 3.4.

Communication strategies. A strength of online education is its ability to leverage multiple forms of media—text, audio, visual stills and streams, and more—for the purposes of learning. Each of these is a form of communication from the course to the student. Despite this strength, a key to successful course completion is not one-way static communication but the interaction that occurs within teacher-student and student-student communication (Plough & Barbour, 2012).

The Distance Learning Resource Network (2000) identifies communication as one of the major challenges facing online education. It asks, "How do educators create a sense of community online?" and answers by offering several suggestions:

- Provide activities that clearly value differences and voices of all.
- Share photos when appropriate.
- Create student/teacher introductions and web pages.
- Use bulletin boards, chats, and e-mail.
- Provide opportunities for interaction so that participants can make a personal connection.
- Create offline occasions for the learning community to interact.

Increased communication is particularly important in K–12 contexts, where social development is an essential part of the growth experience. In a traditional school, students regularly interact with one another in both academic and nonacademic (e.g., lunch, recess, sports, and club) roles. It is especially important to include real-time and audiovisual interactions in younger grades, where reading and writing are just in their developmental stages and students cannot easily communicate with the written word.

According to Keeler (2003), online schools are taking advantage of communications-related research. University-level courses generally limit communications to threaded discussion and e-mail requirements. K–12 online schools, however, have added to these methods by moving toward synchronous and video options. In fact, many schools (e.g., Florida Virtual School, Connections Academy) even require regular telephone or video-conferencing contacts between teachers and students. Many also offer (and some require) weekly real-time lessons using synchronous audio, video, and collaborative whiteboard technologies. Furthering communication with the intent of increasing socialization and academic motivation, many K–12 online schools routinely offer online clubs, physi-cal field trips, and real-time tutoring. In most cases, instructional designers who create courses for mass use are not privy to the social contexts in which their students will learn. Designing communication requirements into courses increases the likelihood of commu-nication occurring regardless of school expectations. Designers are also generally limited to asynchronous formats for this same reason.

Instructional strategies. While higher education online courses often depend on the "read-the-textbook, answer-the-questions" format, K–12 content providers are far beyond reliance on this single strategy. Simply lecturing and testing may be acceptable in higher education, but full-lesson lecture is seldom the best instructional methodol-ogy for K–12 learners. It fails to motivate children and adolescents to actively engage in their learning. Lecture, in online contexts, appears in two formats: (a) audio or video of a content lecture (i.e., a "talking head"), or (b) large blocks of text (i.e., the equivalent of reading a textbook). Another common strategy is use of workbook-style pages (Ohanian, 2004). Content delivered via these methods is necessary but should not serve as the sole instructional strategy.

In a cross-school analysis of lesson strategy types (Keeler, 2003), high school online courses relied on lecture in over half of the lessons (see Figure 3.5). But these lessons did not rely only on lecturing; instead, they integrated multiple methods. For instance, a science lesson on temperature conversions may begin with a reading-based content introduction (a "lecture" by the study's standards), follow with a virtual simulation of the conversion process, and conclude with drill-and-practice. A social studies lesson about slavery, on the other hand, may have students view a video and then role-play being slaves and plantation owners during a live lesson. Both of these examples exemplify qual-ity design structures for adolescent learners, whereas dependence solely on lecturing is unlikely to fully engage them.

Assessment design. Assessment can be informal or formal, and its purpose can be preassessment, self-assessment, formative or summative evaluation, or motivational. Assessments can be graded or not graded, provide immediate feedback or require teacher review, require proctoring, or be optional. In online contexts, informal and motivational assessments generally appear as self- or computer-graded questions embedded within lessons. Formative evaluation tends to occur at the ends of lessons, and formal, summa-tive assessment generally occurs either outside lessons (at the course level in the form of semester-long projects or exams) or as single lessons devoted only to taking a test or

Figure 3.5: Instructional strategies

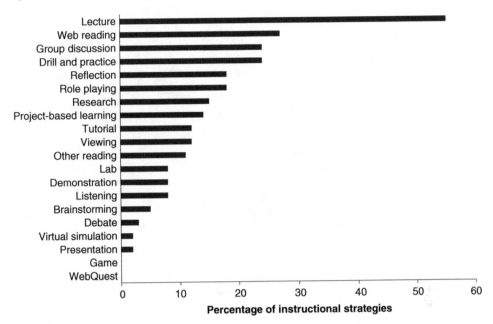

completing an activity. Whereas informal evaluation tends to appear as multiple-choice questions, formal, graded assessment takes many forms and in many cases includes multiple formats in a single assessment. A math lesson on volume may require students to solve equations in multiple-choice format *and* respond to several short-answer prompts (e.g., "How would you determine the area of a multistory building?"). Students receive immediate feedback on the multiple-choice questions but must await teacher grading for feedback on their written (or spoken) responses.

Assessment is not always quite so simple. Students in an art class may need to demonstrate a skill (e.g., drawing in two-point perspective), or students taking a foreign language may need to respond verbally to audio prompts. Translating traditional assessment methods is relatively simple when working within a cognitive taxonomy, but more complex when evaluating within the affective and psychomotor domains. Instructional designers have innovatively incorporated many alternative assessment techniques addressing these other domains. An art course may provide instructions for making clay using common household items, deliver a video demonstration on sculpture creation, direct students to create their own sculptures, and have students take a picture of their product to e-mail to the teacher. A music course may require students to participate in real-time video lessons during which they play an instrument. A language arts course may require that students create and submit an audio file of an interpretive reading of a self-written poem. Figure 3.6 identifies assessment types identified in Keeler's (2003) study of high school online courses.

K–12 designers must employ new assessment types that allow collaboration, reflection, and interactivity (Swan, 2003). Researchers should continue to guide the

Figure 3.6: Assessment types

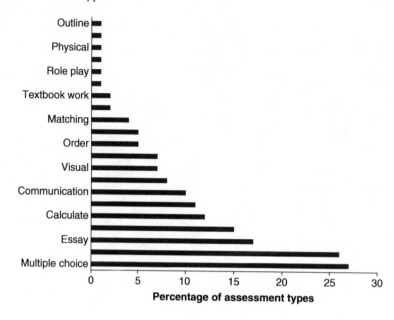

development of next-generation tests, especially as complex scoring rules linked with online computer-assisted assessment make it possible to evaluate more complex types of learning while instructional designers continue to experiment with innovative techniques.

Special-needs accommodations. Despite guidelines for accommodating individuals with special needs, many online courses still present barriers (Burgstahler, 2004; Edmonds, 2004). In part, this is because many designers believe erroneously that assistive technologies alone can remove all access barriers. Burgstahler (2004) cautions that access alone is not enough to provide adequate accommodations, given that poorly designed courses "erect new barriers to equal participation." He identifies two basic approaches to designing for accessibility: (a) avoiding certain data or methods, and (b) offering alternative methods, features, or formats. Keeler, Richter, Horney, Anderson, and Ditson (2007) support his notion by recommending that designers include variety and options in their courses.

Keeler and Horney (2007) list five categories of elements requiring designer attention: accessibility, website design, technologies used, support systems, and instructional methodologies. The accessibility category focuses on content access for all learners. Literature and guidelines are replete with recommendations on this topic and broadly break recommendations into visual, hearing, and other physical accommodations (e.g., Architectural and Transportation Barriers Compliance Board, 2001; Bohman, 2004; Burgstahler, 2004; Rowland, 2004; World Wide Web Consortium, 1999, 2004). Keeler and Horney (2007) confirm that online course designers are including many recommended accessibility options for individuals with hearing impairments, but many courses in their sample imposed barriers for students with visual impairments.

An example of problematic elements originates in the rule that when images appear on screen, they must include textual equivalents, which could be as simple as adding descriptive text to a graphic or as complex as describing a painting or figure in detail. More complex graphics may be impossible to fully describe because the visual stimuli induce indescribable emotional responses (e.g., Edvard Munch's *The Scream*). Most accessibility considerations focus on assisting students with physical disabilities. Little research addresses the needs of students with cognitive disabilities, and no research directly addresses possible means of assisting students with emotional handicaps. Designers must ensure functional and consistent educational experiences for all potential enrollees, including assurance that assistive technologies (including use with third-party resources) will work as needed for all lessons and lesson subparts.

A common design error regardless of student ability is repetition of a single strategy. For example, students with attention-deficit disorders or reading disabilities may struggle with large blocks of text. They may be able to digest material when employing the strategy sparingly and when supplemented with alternative approaches such as audio and video. There will be cases, nonetheless, when variety is still not enough. Accommodating students with special needs is a legal and ethical action for students with direct needs, but it is educationally beneficial for *all* learners.

Conclusion

In *The Mismeasure of Man*, Stephen Gould (1981) warns researchers that their biases affect the questions they ask and, ultimately, their results. Questions posed by researchers who are advocates of online education must recognize that their questions and methods of answering them are inherently biased. K–12 online education is at a point when questioning the basic understanding of instructional design is important. Researchers need to look objectively to determine what is occurring, why it is occurring, and whether it is in the best interest of learning.

While educators are often open to new technologies, they often cannot envision how those technologies might be effective (Cuban, 1986, 2002). Russo (2001) reminds us that we must not think of the future solely in terms of what is available and what we know today; designers must seek innovations beyond what is currently known. Dede (1996), Fitzgerald and Lester (1997), and Jones (1997) identify avatars and electronic mentors as possible future instructional tools.

Moving toward innovation, instructional designers are beginning to pursue techniques for including, promoting, and measuring more complex learning, critical thinking, and cognitive engagement within online environments (Shaffer, Squire, Halverson, & Gee, 2005). Some even recommend using alternative assessment formats such as collaborative assessment, game-based assessment, project-based learning, and electronic portfolios (Twigg, 2000). There is also research focusing on using emerging technologies for assessment purposes (Baker, Dickieson, Wulfeck, & O'Neil, 2008), and several researchers (Gee, 2007; Gee & Levine, 2009; Shaffer et al., 2005; Squire, 2005) theorize about using massively multiplayer online role-playing games (MMORPGs) and multiuser virtual environments (MUVEs) to deliver and assess content knowledge. Chris Dede and colleagues at Harvard (Clarke, 2009; Dieterle & Clarke, 2009; Ketelhut,

Dede, Clarke, Nelson, & Bowman, 2008; Metcalf, Clarke, & Dede, 2009) are experimenting with the use of immersive and gaming technologies to assess advanced cognition of specific content. Their work extends general educational immersive resources by focusing on specific content and specific assessment objectives. Perhaps future students will complete biology dissections using virtual models and haptic gloves.

Within the current K–12 online course design structure, much room exists for growth and variation. Instructional designers must rise to the challenge of being imaginative, creative, and ingenious while questioning the overall structure and beliefs of online instructional design. Is the macro/micro separation valid within the new context? Are categories or elements redundant or missing from the current functional schema? These are questions for the current and next generation of K–12 instructional designers.

References

Architectural and Transportation Barriers Compliance Board. (2001). *Web-based intranet and Internet information and applications.* Retrieved from http://www.access-board.gov/sec508/guide/1194.22.htm

Baker, E., Dickieson, J., Wulfeck, W., & O'Neil, H. (Eds.). (2008). *Assessment of problem solving using simulations.* New York: Lawrence Erlbaum Associates.

Bohman, P. (2004). *Cognitive disabilities part 1: We still know too little, and we do even less.* Logan, UT: Web Accessibility in Mind. Retrieved from http://www.webaim.org/techniques/articles/cognitive_too_little

Bracey, G. W. (2004). *Knowledge universe and virtual schools: Educational breakthrough or digital raid on the public treasury?* Tempe: Arizona State University.

Burgstahler, S. (2004). *Real connections: Making distance learning accessible to everyone.* Seattle: University of Washington. Retrieved from http://www.washington.edu/doit/Brochures/Technology/distance.learn.html

Clarke, J. (2009, April 13–16). *Studying the potential of virtual performance assessments for measuring student achievement in science.* Paper presented at the American Educational Research Association, San Diego, CA.

Cuban, L. (1986). *Teachers and machines: The classroom use of technology since 1920.* New York: Teachers College Press.

Cuban, L. (2002). *Oversold and underused.* Cambridge, MA: Harvard University Press.

Dede, C. (1996). The evolution of distance education: Emerging technologies and distributed learning. *American Journal of Distance Education, 10*(2), 4–36.

Dick, W., & Carey, L. (1996). *The systematic design of instruction* (4th ed.). New York: HarperCollins.

Dieterle, E., & Clarke, J. (2009). Multi-user virtual environments for teaching and learning. In M. Pagani (Ed.), *Encyclopedia of multimedia technology and network* (2nd ed., pp. 1033–1041). Hershey, PA: Idea Group.

Distance Learning Resource Network. (2000). *Challenges and solutions for online instructors.* Retrieved from http://www.dlrn.org/library/dl/challenges.html

Edmonds, C. (2004). Providing access to students with disabilities in online distance education: Legal and technical concerns for higher education. *American Journal of Distance Education, 18*(1), 51–62.

Fitzgerald, P., & Lester, J. (1997). Knowledge-based learning environments: A vision for the twenty-first century. In P. Martorella (Ed.), *Interactive technologies and the social studies* (pp. 111–127). Albany: State University of New York Press.

Gagné, R., Briggs, L., & Wager, W. (1992). *Principles of instructional design* (4th ed.). San Diego: Harcourt Brace Jovanovich.

Gee, J. P. (2007). Reflections on assessment from a sociocultural-situated perspective. *Yearbook (National Society for the Study of Education), part 1,* 362–375.

Gee, J. P., & Levine, M. H. (2009). Welcome to our virtual worlds. *Educational Leadership, 66*(6), 48–52.

Gould, S. J. (1981). *The mismeasure of man.* New York: W. W. Norton.

Jones, G. R. (1997). *Cyberschools: An education renaissance* (2nd ed.). Englewood, CA: Jones Digital Century.

Keeler, C. (2003). *Developing and using an instrument to describe instructional design elements of high school online courses.* (Unpublished doctoral dissertation.) University of Oregon, Eugene.

Keeler, C., & Horney, M. (2007). Online course designs: Are special needs being met? *American Journal of Distance Education, 21*(2), 65–75.

Keeler, C. G., Richter, J., Horney, M., Anderson, L., & Ditson, M. (2007). Exceptional learners: Differentiated instruction online. In C. Cavanaugh & R. Blomeyer (Eds.), *What works in K–12 online learning* (pp. 125–142). Eugene, OR: International Society for Technology in Education.

Ketelhut, D. J., Dede, C., Clarke, J., Nelson, B., & Bowman, C. (2008). Studying situated learning in a multi-user environment. In E. Baker, J. Dickieson, W. Wulfeck, & H. O'Neil (Eds.), *Assessment of problem solving using simulations* (pp. 37–58). Mahwah, NJ: Lawrence Erlbaum Associates.

Layton, T. (2002). Personal communication, October 30.

Metcalf, S. J., Clarke, J., & Dede, C. (2009, April 24–26). *Virtual worlds for education: River City and EcoMUVE.* Paper presented at the Media in Transition International Conference, MIT, Cambridge, MA.

Morrison, G., Ross, S., & Kemp, J. (2007). *Designing effective instruction.* New York: John Wiley & Sons.

Ohanian, S. (2004). *The K12 virtual primary school history curriculum: A participant's-eye view.* Tempe: Arizona State University.

Plough, C., & Barbour, M. (2012). Odyssey of the mind: Social networking in cyberschool. *International Review of Research in Open and Distance Learning, 13*(3). Retrieved from http://www.irrodl.org/index.php/irrodl/article/view/1154/2148

Rowland, C. (2004). *Cognitive disabilities part 2: Conceptualizing design considerations.* Logan, UT: Web Accessibility in Mind. Retrieved from http://www.webaim.org/techniques/articles/conceptualize

Russo, A. (2001). E-learning everywhere. *School Administrator,* 10. Retrieved from http://www.aasa.org/publications/sa/2001_10/russo.htm

Shaffer, D. W., Squire, K. D., Halverson, R., & Gee, J. P. (2005). Video games and the future of learning. *Phi Delta Kappan, 87*(2), 104–111.

Smith, P. L., & Ragan, T. J. (2005). *Instructional design* (3rd ed.). Hoboken, NJ: John Wiley & Sons.

Squire, K. (2005, April 12). *Game, play, and culture: When video games enter the classroom.* Paper presented at the American Educational Researcher Association Annual Meeting, Montreal.

Swan, K. (2003). Learning effectiveness: What the research tells us. In J. Bourne & J. C. Moore (Eds.), *Elements of quality online education, practice and direction* (pp. 13–45). Needham, MA: Sloan Center for Online Education.

Twigg, C. A. (2000). *Innovations in online learning: Moving beyond no significant difference.* Retrieved from http://www.center.rpi.edu/Monographs/Innovations.html

World Wide Web Consortium. (1999). *Web content accessibility guidelines 1.0: W3C recommendation 5-May-1999.* London: Author. Retrieved from http://www.w3.org/TR/WCAG10

World Wide Web Consortium. (2004). *Web content accessibility guidelines (WCAG) 2.0: W3C working draft 19 November 2004.* London: Author. Retrieved from http://www.w3.org/TR/2004/WD-WCAG20-20041119/

4

TECHNOLOGY INFRASTRUCTURE AND TOOLS

Rob Darrow

In 2000, e-mail was the main technology used for communication, and the World Wide Web was a bunch of static web pages—no Facebook, no Twitter, no blogs, no wikis. The iPod was not yet invented. Most people accessed the Internet via a dial-up connection. Conversations were just beginning to happen in school districts across the nation about online learning.

The superintendent of one K–12 school district in California declared, "One of the things we are doing to prepare for the future are 'Virtual Classrooms' . . . where students can take courses on the Web" (Darrow, 2002, p. 18). The district's director of technology then set out to hire someone to take on the task of creating these virtual classrooms; thus, I came to serve as the founding principal of the district's online school.

Imagine if you were the person hired to create a K–12 online learning program today. Where would you start? Technology infrastructure and technology tools are key components of the planning and implementation of any blended or online learning program and must be addressed early on in the planning process.

Technology Infrastructure

The technology infrastructure needed to implement an effective online and blended learning program has evolved over time with the invention of new technologies, technology applications, and storage options. This section focuses on connectivity and hardware, selecting a learning management system, and mobile learning. Each one of these areas needs to be part of the three-year plan for an online or blended learning program and the costs should be projected out as well.

Learning Management Systems

The terms *online platform*, *learning platform*, *course management system*, *learning management system*, and *virtual learning environment* are all used to describe a system that houses online courses. The technical terms most used in K–12 online learning are *course management system* (CMS) and *learning management system* (LMS). Both platforms hold content, provide tools for online learning, and support a closed environment for individual teachers to offer online learning to students.

The main difference between a CMS and an LMS is that the CMS focuses on courses, course development, and data and reports related to courses, while an LMS focuses on an entire school, district, or entity; course content; and data and reports related to the entire organization. In most cases, schools or districts will choose an LMS. However, many content providers now include an LMS as part of their overall product, thus reducing the need to purchase an LMS. Ultimately, organizations need an LMS to track and report performance improvements. The basic functions that exist in all such systems include enrolling learners, communicating with students, assessing performances, and storing and activating learning materials (Theis, 2005).

Most schools or school districts choose to use an LMS to organize coursework. However, an online course could also be put together using various Web 2.0 features, online tools, and Google apps. An LMS also allows a school or district to develop and maintain its own online content and courses, in addition to any proprietary course content. Effective teachers will want to supplement any purchased online content with their own teaching strategies and other content and tools that are developed daily across the Web.

In selecting an LMS, the following criteria should be considered (Ellis, 2009):

- Administration tools
- Analytics and reporting
- Content access
- Content development
- Content integration
- Skills management
- Assessment capabilities
- Configurability
- Security
- Cost

In addition, prior to making a final LMS selection, talk to people at other institutions that have already adopted the potential LMS. Key questions to ask include the following:

- What lessons did you learn during the LMS implementation process?
- Were there any unanticipated challenges or issues?
- What worked well? What would you do differently?
- How did you provide training and technical support for your staff and teachers?
- How is the LMS provider's customer service?

Karrer (2010) wrote a valuable series of blog posts that address the various aspects of LMS selection, including forming the selection team, writing the request for proposal, and conducting the process as a whole. As Requests for Proposals (RFPs) are commonly posted online, those interested in writing RFPs for an LMS for their school can view hundreds of rubrics and criteria by conducting a simple Google search, such as "school district RFP [request for proposals] LMS."

Figure 4.1: Percentage of LMS usage in higher education across four countries: United States, Canada, United Kingdom, and Australia

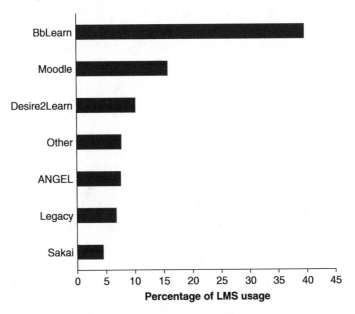

The use of open-source LMSs is growing in the United States and internationally among higher education institutions, which can be seen as a leading indicator for technology adoption in K–12. Kroner (2013) and his colleagues identified the primary LMS of higher education institutions in the United States, Canada, the United Kingdom, and Australia (see Figure 4.4). Blackboard was the most common LMS, followed by Moodle. They documented steady growth of open-source LMSs such as Moodle, Canvas, and Saki over time. In the United Kingdom, Blackboard retained a majority of the market, while in the United States its share had fallen below 50%, but it remained the most common LMS. In Canada and Australia, Moodle had become the most common LMS.

Connectivity and Hardware

The meaning of the term *hardware* has become blurred with that of other technology terms, such as *software, online, cloud-based,* and *web-based.* Traditionally, *hardware* referred to the physical location of computer programs such as a server or computer. Most everything that runs on the Internet is based on a physical computer or server somewhere in the world. In this section, *hardware* refers to the various technology systems that are used to operate an online program.

Many components are involved in connectivity, including the device used to connect, how the device connects to the Internet (wireless or hardwired), the Internet provider, the connection to the Internet, the connection to the LMS, and the server upon which the LMS operates. If any of these components are not working correctly, then the result is either a slower connection speed or limited or no access. Connectivity problems are becoming less frequent as bandwidth becomes more plentiful and less expensive.

The following are responses to typical organizational questions and can guide any program in establishing the most cost-effective and technically effective connectivity and technology infrastructure needed for a successful online program:

Where and how will students access the LMS and the Internet to complete online courses?

Some programs provide web-enabled devices such as notebook computers or tablets that are loaned to students while other programs expect students to provide their own device.

Many programs develop a computer lab where students may complete their online work, but a lab requires some type of adult supervision to operate properly. Other programs have computers set aside in a school or public library for use by online students. If students are expected to access online courses "anywhere, anytime," then recommended devices for this purpose should be communicated to students and parents.

Will the LMS and course content reside on a local managed server or on an online provider's server?

Human or financial costs are associated with each option. Technical and human resources must be available locally if the LMS is to be hosted on a local server. The key advantage of paying an online provider to host an LMS, either on its own server or one it rents, is that the company then has the responsibility to make sure the LMS is always working and will fix any problems that may develop.

Which systems (e.g., LMS, student information system, attendance) will produce the types of reports needed for the program?

Performance measures and data need to be gathered to measure the success of the program. The measures and data needed in each system should be identified prior to program implementation. The various systems may include a

- Learning management system, or LMS (course content, grade book, online discussion board, etc.).
- Student information system, or SIS (information about students, phone numbers, grades, transcripts).
- Testing management system (benchmark testing, end of course testing, organized student by student).
- Attendance system (reports that generate funding for the school).

In an ideal world, all technology systems would seamlessly integrate with one another. In the real world, very few technology systems seamlessly integrate with one another, which is one reason that many commercial online course providers have developed their own LMS within which all needed technology tools and reports can be integrated seamlessly.

More often than not, online and blended learning administrators, teachers, and staff need to access a variety of systems in order to gather the needed data and to provide students with an overall effective online program. One issue is how student attendance will be gathered from online students and how that is recorded in the established attendance system, which is usually separate from the LMS. Another example is that few LMSs have the capability of providing online collaboration between teachers and students, so in most cases the LMS and online collaboration tools will be separate systems. Parents and students need to understand up front the use of a variety of systems and the reasoning for doing so.

Mobile Learning Technologies

The U.S. Department of Education (2012) sponsored a series of online events during Connected Educators Month, including a presentation that featured a panel of six young people from sixth to twelfth grade talking about their personal use of technology, particularly in learning. The moderator asked questions such as, "How do you use the Internet in school?" and "What is your favorite technology to use for an assignment?" Clearly, the moderator expected answers related to the World Wide Web and computers. But the young people talked about apps and their cell phones and their tablets instead.

The first cell or mobile phone not connected to a house or vehicle was patented in the early 1970s (Cooper et al., 1973). By 2014, there were about 6.9 billion mobile phone subscriptions (active SIM cards) worldwide, and an estimated 2.3 billion mobile broadband subscriptions (International Telecommunications Union, 2014). As mobile network technology options have expanded, so have the types of mobile devices, such as smartphones, e-book readers, tablets, and mini-tablets. No doubt that the convergence of cheaper and faster mobile technologies—networks, devices, and bandwidth—will produce other devices in the future.

Research in the area of mobile learning (m–learning) highlights the teaching and instruction perspective as well as the end user (student) perspective. Keegan (2002) wrote that "mobile learning is a harbinger of the future of learning" (p. 9). Mobile devices, when used intentionally for instruction, can increase the occurrence of formal and informal learning by students. The applications of mobile learning vary widely, from K–12 to higher education and corporate learning settings, from formal and informal learning to classroom learning and distance learning.

Park (2011) suggests a framework (see Figure 4.2) of how learning will shift from e-learning to ubiquitous learning (u-learning), noting that "as mobile devices are becoming increasingly ubiquitous, many . . . practitioners have integrated them into their teaching and learning environments" (p. 1). The technologies used are dynamic and flexible, and learning is the focus rather than technology.

Attewell, Savill-Smith, Douch, and Parker (2010) documented the uses of mobile devices by students in the United Kingdom of 30 MoleNet (Mobile Learning Network) projects conducted by postsecondary institutions, including some through consortia involving schools. About 87% of the students were age 14 through 19, so the findings appear applicable to K–12 learners. The team's research identified a number of ways in which mobile devices (e.g., phones, notebooks, PDAs) were being utilized effectively to support teaching and learning, including individual study, group work, data collection, Internet access and remote learning, recording of activities/reflections/diaries, formative

Figure 4.2: Comparisons and flow of e-learning, m-learning, and u-learning

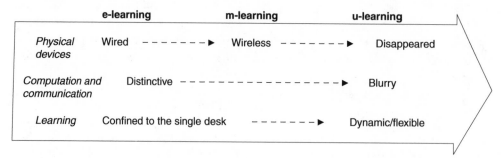

assessment, student-to-teacher and peer-to-peer communication, observation of teachers and students, and student surveys.

When surveyed, representatives of the 30 projects involved in this research identified the benefits of mobile learning with which they most strongly agreed. These benefits included the following:

- Enables differentiated instruction
- Supports different ways of learning
- Provides access for more learners
- Allows learning to take place in different places and in different times
- Increases interest, engagement, and motivation of learners
- Enables learners to collect evidence of their skills in different ways

Note that the Apple iPad was not released to the public until 2010; therefore, this new tablet technology was not included in the research. About 195 million tablets were sold to end users worldwide in 2013, with Android (61.9%) and Apple (36.0%) dominating the market (Gartner, 2014).

In the United States, a number of school districts have implemented one-to-one initiatives using iPads or other tablets. One example is the Corcoran Unified School District in Central California (2011), where every sixth- to 12th-grade student now has a district-purchased iPad that is used daily in teaching and learning.

Bring Your Own Device (BYOD) initiatives are also providing new opportunities for blended and online learning in other nations. A roundtable process involving schools from across Australia revealed a variety of BYOD deployment models, ranging from the school mandating the device to bring and then managing it to having students bring any device and their own network connection, with the school providing other educational services (Sweeney, 2012).

Reports about student use of mobile devices and tools illustrate teen preferences for use of texting and wall posting over the use of e-mail. A recent Pew Internet study (Madden, Lenhart, Duggan, Cortesi, & Gasser, 2013) indicated that in 2012, over 78% of young people (age 12–17) owned a cell phone. Another Pew study found growing use by teens of mobile devices to access the Internet. As Figure 4.3 shows, while almost nine in

Figure 4.3: Percentage of teens using the Internet in last 30 days by device

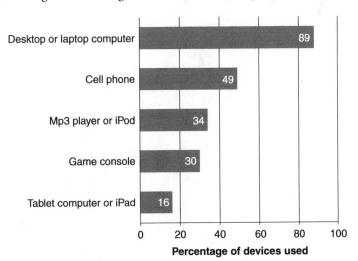

10 teens reported using a computer in the last 30 days to access the Internet, nearly half reported using a cell phone to go online (Lenhart, 2012).

In order to implement mobile learning one-to-one or BYOD initiatives in online and blended learning, a variety of factors must be considered. Project managers made a number of recommendations for those planning for mobile teaching and learning:

- Start with the pedagogy, not the device. Ensure that the planned use of the technologies is appropriate and supportive for the specific learning context.
- Consider how the functions of the technologies can be used to improve the learning experience and to overcome previous barriers to learning.
- The functionality required should be the primary influence when deciding which technologies to purchase. This will depend greatly on the learning context—the subject area, learning locations, learner level, current issues identified, and so on.
- Try a number of devices before making large purchases to check how they match up against requirements and their compatibility with existing infrastructure.
- Test devices before use in sessions designed to gain confidence and eradicate problems. (Attewell et al., 2010, p. 108)

The challenge for educators is determining which mobile devices and applications (apps) work for different functions in an online or blended learning environment. To find out, they need to ask questions such as

- Is there a mobile device that should be promoted for learning, or is this decision best left in the hand of the learners?
- Should our institution create an app that allows mobile device users to access the CMS or use their device in specific learning contexts?

- Is it necessary to provide content to students both via the Web and via a mobile device or app?
- If mobile devices are used to promote learning, should the educational focus be on the devices, the apps, or both?

Educators should be engaged in a process of continuous evaluation of devices, tools, apps, and software that may better facilitate learning. For example, can a cell phone more effectively check grades online? Can a tablet work better for synchronous online chats? What apps best work for the course content being delivered? The use of mobile learning tools is an emerging technology that all educators are just beginning to understand and apply to teaching and learning.

Perhaps the best method to evaluate the success of mobile devices, apps, or software is to observe what students are using, ask students for their input, and embrace whatever devices students are using to provide multiple access points for learning. If education is to become more student-centric with more student control over learning, then mobile devices and apps will need to be embedded in the classroom—whether face-to-face, blended, or online.

Technology Tools

A number of online technology tools now exist that can enhance the online and blended learning experience, including tools for communication and productivity, gaming, open educational resources, and learning objects.

Communication/Productivity Tools and Social Media

Communication is the key to a successful online or blended learning course, just like it is in a face-to-face classroom. Many elements go into curriculum delivery, including pedagogy, content, multiple ways to access content, and design. In the design of effective online and blended learning courses, the mode of ongoing communication will ensure a higher online completion rate. The Community of Inquiry model (Swan et al., 2008) set forth a framework for online courses and course design that includes social presence, cognitive presence, and teaching presence. Social presence is the degree to which participants feel connected within the online environment. Communication is one of the strategies that cause students to feel connected and to increase social presence.

Effective communication in online courses (and face-to-face courses) is a result of using synchronous and asynchronous tools. Table 4.1 identifies a number of types of synchronous and asynchronous tools that online and blended teachers can use to increase the social presence in their courses.

Meeting the needs of all online learners is often easier to accomplish than in a face-to-face classroom. Communication online can be written, audio, or visual. A number of free and paid ($$) online tools are available (see Table 4.2). Using a variety of communication modes and mediums for instructional delivery helps ensure student engagement and success. According to Roblyer and Wiencke (2004), "Increased interaction in distance courses is associated with higher achievement and student satisfaction."

TABLE 4.1:
Synchronous and asynchronous communication tools

Synchronous	*Asynchronous*	
• Face-to-face meeting • Google Docs/Google Hangouts • Phone call • Chat rooms • Instant messaging • Texting • Online collaboration/ videoconferencing • Quizzes	• Blogs • Bulletin boards/ announcements • Calendar events • E-mail • Discussion boards • Facebook and similar tools • Grade book	• Photo sharing • Podcasts • Surveys and polls • Twitter • Video • Wikis • Tests and quizzes

Various Web 2.0 and social media tools can assist teachers in creating content and teaching online; students can use them to complete assignments to demonstrate their knowledge. Just as with the selection of content and an LMS, teachers and administrators should intentionally select tools based on lesson objectives. Two of the earliest Web 2.0 tools that teachers used were blogs and wikis. Teachers have employed blogs to communicate with students and parents, to communicate their ideas to others, and to chronicle their classroom experiences.

Weblogs, or blogs, are web pages often likened to online personal journals. Winer (2003) defines a *blog* as "a hierarchy of text, images, media objects and data, arranged chronologically." Richardson (2006) identified four things that blogging allows students to do: (a) reflect on what they are writing and thinking as they write and think it, (b) carry on writing about a topic over a sustained period of time, (c) engage readers and audience in a sustained conversation that leads to further thinking and writing, and (d) synthesize disparate learning experiences and understand their collective relationship and relevance.

Various studies have indicated that blogs can increase student engagement for writing, can provide a communication vehicle for teachers, and can provide a way for educators to share their opinions. Subject-specific teachers have found that blogs provide communication with students and also allow students to reflect on their learning. For example, an 11th-grade precalculus teacher found that blogging "increased collaborative learning and nurtured a community of learners, created a student-centered learning environment, provided a place for reflection, and provided enrichment to the class" (MacBride & Lachman, 2008, p. 179).

The *wiki* is a Web 2.0 tool that provides collaborative features and active learning opportunities in a web-based environment (Hazari, North, & Moreland, 2009). A major appeal of wikis is that collaborative content can be created, changed, and tracked easily. Users are able to quickly start expanding any page or site for discussion, posting assignments, and various collaborative projects. With a wiki, teachers and students can easily put information on the Web for use by other teachers and students and for each other's use.

TABLE 4.2:
Examples of visual, audio, and writing tools used in online and blended learning

Visual Tools	Audio Tools	Writing Tools	
Photo/image/slide sharing	**Online collaboration/ screen sharing/ videoconferencing**	**Creation tools**	**Social bookmarking**
Flickr	Adobe Connect ($$)	Camtasia ($$)	Delicious
Google Picasa	Blackboard Collaborate ($$)	Glogster	Diigo
PhotoBucket	Google Hangout	Google Docs	
Pinterest	Join.me	Jing	**Storage/sharing**
Slideshare	WebEx ($$)	Museum Box	Dropbox
		Myebook	Google Docs
Video creation/ sharing		Prezi	Evernote
Animoto	**Audio creation/ sharing**	Storyjumper	
Blabberize	Podcasting	Storybird	**Brainstorming tools**
Kerpoof	Pandora	Screencast	Bubbl.us
TeacherTube	VoiceThread	ToonDooSpaces	Popplet
TedEd		Wallwisher	
Vimeo		Weebly	**Wikis**
Voki		Zoho	Pbworks
YouTube			WetPaint Central
		Social networking	Wikispaces
		Edmodo	
		Facebook	**Blogs**
		Google Plus	Blogger
		Schoology	Tumblr
		Twitter	Wordpress

Note. $$ = tool that must be purchased.

Students and teachers can use tools such as blogs and wikis for productivity purposes as well as for communication. A number of online technology tools are designed specifically for productivity uses. For example, teachers can guide students as they create video, audio, and writing content and combine it in multimedia presentations they share with others.

Gaming

A *game* can be defined as "a form of play which has rules and a goal" (Koster, 2012, para. 2). "Gamification" is increasingly seen in business, where companies have built gaming-type challenges or badges into their corporate websites (Singer, 2012). The consulting firm Deloitte (2012) reported in its top tech trends report that games "are becoming embedded in day-to-day business processes, driving adoption, performance, and engagement" (para. 12). A Pew Internet study found that "game elements and competition are interspersed throughout the platforms that have made social networks like

Facebook and Twitter popular" (Anderson & Rainie, 2012, p. 2). Gamification has made its way into educational sites, such as the Khan Academy, where students are rewarded with badges for certain levels of achievement. Paid games available through Xbox or Wii provide other opportunities to incorporate gaming into education.

Outstanding educators have always incorporated a variety of games into the learning process—whether simple games like flash cards or more complex games such as simulations. Early educational computer games, such as *Where in the World Is Carmen Sandiego?* and *The Oregon Trail,* found their way into many classrooms. Once the Internet became prevalent, many of these games were replicated online, and new online games were developed. Educators may incorporate games into the curriculum as a way of reinforcing basic and critical thinking skills, extend learning through homework or remediation, or as the curriculum itself, such as through simulations. For instance, in 2009, Florida Virtual School and 360Ed, Inc., formed a partnership to develop *Conspiracy Code,* one of the first online games specifically designed for an online learning program; the entire American history course curriculum was written into the game (Florida Virtual School and 360Ed, Inc., 2009).

Games can engage students and improve learning results. Boise State University has created an online, quest-based 3D Game Lab where educators can receive professional development and create standards-based curricular activities. Students were more likely to choose, complete, and highly rate 3D Game Lab quests that had attractive design elements, like tutorial videos, badges, and novel digital text tools (GoGo Labs, 2012). The Education Development Center studied the *Mission U.S.* role-playing online video game, finding that over 1,000 students who played the game scored significantly higher on a test of historical knowledge than comparison students who did regular textbook study (Corporation for Public Broadcasting, 2012). The game players were better able to see multiple points of view and explain the causes of the Revolutionary War.

Online Educational Resources and Learning Objects

In 2002, 22 experts from around the world issued a declaration supporting the development of open educational resources (OERs) available to everyone and advocated for "technology-enabled, open provision of educational resources for consultation, use and adaptation by a community of users for non-commercial purposes" (UNESCO, 2002). OERs are typically made freely available over the Web or the Internet and include full online courses, course materials, modules, textbooks, videos, documents, simulations, audio files, and any material that is used to support learning.

The amount of OERs continues to grow every year as more and more educators and programs put their content on the Web to be freely shared with others. An additional term—*learning objects*—is often used in relation to OERs. Learning objects refer to the idea that digital materials can be designed and produced in such a manner as to be reused easily in a variety of pedagogical situations (Wiley, 2006). However, the "only difference between an online learning object and an open educational resource is the declaration that it is open" (Mendonca, McAndrew, & Santos, 2011, p. 2).

Many OERs are already being used in traditional classrooms. The rich primary source collections of the U.S. Library of Congress or the British Library are just two examples. Learning object and OER repositories both house digital objects that can be used in online or blended learning courses. Some of the early repositories developed include Curriki (www.curriki.org) at the K–12 level. In addition, various open textbook initiatives have been established, such as CK-12 (www.ck12.org) and Flatworld Knowledge (www.flatworldknowledge.com).

Regardless of the type of OER, learning object, or repository, the question becomes: How can they be used in an online or blended learning course? At each stage of development, there are opportunities to use OERs within the course content. Some OERs may suffice for an entire online course while others may provide the videos needed for instruction, such as the Khan Academy videos in math (www.khanacademy.org) or Smart History for the teaching of art (http://smarthistory.khanacademy.org). Ultimately, the course developer or teacher decides how to best incorporate the endless amount of OERs that currently exist.

Many OERs are not visible through a Google search. However, there are specialized searches just for OERs (UNESCO, 2011), including OER Commons (www.ercommons.org), open courseware consortium (www.ocwconsortium.org/courses/search), and the Creative Commons Search (http://search.creativecommons.org).

The OER Commons (n.d.) website states, "We believe a culture of sharing resources and practices will help facilitate change and innovation in education." The creator of the open-source LMS Moodle, Martin Dougiamas, perhaps best summarizes the beliefs of many involved in the open education movement in an article he posted online titled "Social Constructionism as a Referent." He wrote that these five points characterize social constructionism and form some of the background for the development of Moodle:

1. All of us are potential teachers as well as learners—in a true collaborative environment we are both. . . .
2. We learn particularly well from the act of creating or expressing something for others to see. . . .
3. We learn a lot by just observing the activity of our peers. . . .
4. By understanding the contexts of others, we can teach in a more transformational way (constructivism). . . .
5. A learning environment needs to be flexible and adaptable, so that it can quickly respond to the needs of the participants within it. (Dougiamas, 2006, para. 3)

Conclusion

Technology is one of the key components of an online or blended learning program. Program developers must make decisions early on about technology infrastructure, such as how students will access the LMS and Internet, where the LMS and content will reside, and how the various information systems will generate needed performance data. Putting an LMS in place is a major undertaking, and one of the build-or-buy decisions that must be made. Use of open-source LMSs is increasing, which increases local needs for customization and technical support.

Mobile learning technologies bring a new dimension to learning, and new challenges for programs and educators. Many K–12 students already use mobile technologies for texting and the Internet. A wide range of Web 2.0 communication and productivity tools now exist online that can be integrated into online and blended learning, including blogs, wikis, and social media, and a variety of visual, audio, and writing tools that can be used to create, share, and collaborate. Gaming is also being integrated into online and blended learning. Well-designed games can attract and engage students and may improve their achievement and depth of learning.

OERs and learning objects can be integrated as well. OERs naturally support a social constructivist approach to teaching and learning. Ultimately, the course developer or teacher must decide how to best incorporate the many technology tools available. Online and blended programs and educators should keep the focus on how specific functionalities of these tools can improve student learning experiences and outcomes.

References

Anderson, J. Q., & Rainie, L. (2012). *The future of gamification.* Washington, DC: Pew Internet and American Life Project. Retrieved from http://www.pewinternet.org/Reports/2012/Future-of-Gamification.aspx

Attewell, K. J., Savill-Smith, C., Douch, R., & Parker, G. (2010). *Modernising education and training.* MoleNet Initiative. London: LSN.

Cooper, M., Dronsuth, R. W., Mikulski, A. J., Lynk, C. N., Mikulski, J. J., Mitchell, . . . Sangster, J. H. (1973). *U.S. Patent No. 3,906,166.* Washington, DC: U.S. Patent and Trademark Office.

Corcoran Unified School District. (2011). *One2one: How we did it.* Corcoran, CA: Author. Retrieved from http://one2one.corcoranunified.com/how-we-did-it

Corporation for Public Broadcasting. (2012). *Results of a comparison group study of American History and Civics Initiative's Mission U.S.* Washington, DC: Author. Retrieved from http://www.cpb.org/features/missionus

Darrow, R. (2002, November). *Clovis Unified CAL online report to governing board.* Clovis, CA: Clovis Unified School District. Retrieved from http://onlineschool.cusd.com/calonline/programinfo/reports/2002FinalBoardReport.pdf

DeLoitte. (2012). *Tech trends 2012.* London: Deloitte Development LLC. Retrieved from http://www.deloitte.com/view/en_US/us/Services/consulting/technology-consulting/technology-2012/index.htm

Dougiamas, M. (2006). *Social constructionism as a referent.* Moodle. Retrieved from http://docs.moodle.org/en/Pedagogy

Ellis, R. K. (2009). *A field guide to learning management systems.* Alexandria, VA: American Society for Training and Development. Retrieved from http://www.astd.org/~/media/Files/Publications/LMS_fieldguide_20091

Florida Virtual School and 360Ed Inc. (2009). *FLVS and 360 Ed launch Conspiracy Code.* Orlando: Author. Retrieved from http://www.360ed.com/media/downloads/360Ed%20Conspiracy%20Code%20Press%20Release.pdf

Gartner. (2014). *Gartner says worldwide tablet sales grew 68 percent in 2013.* Press release. Retrieved from http://www.gartner.com/newsroom/id/2674215

GoGo Labs. (2012). *Attractive quest design.* Boise, ID: Author. Retrieved from http://gogolabs.net/wp-content/uploads/2013/01/AttractiveQuestDesign1.pdf

Hazari, S., North, A., & Moreland, D. (2009). Investigating pedagogical implications of Wiki technology. *Journal of Information Systems Education, 20*(2), 187–198.

International Telecommunications Union. (2014). *The world in 2014: ICT facts and figures.* Retrieved from http://www.itu.int/en/ITU-D/Statistics/Documents/facts/ICTFactsFigures2014-e.pdf

Karrer, T. (2010, October). LMS satisfaction features and barriers. *e-Learning Technology*. Retrieved from http://elearningtech.blogspot.com/2007/09/lms-satisfaction-features-and-barriers.html

Keegan, D. (2002). *The future of learning: From eLearning to mLearning, ZIFF papiere 119*. (ERIC Document Reproduction Service No. ED 472435)

Koster, R. (2012, March 13). *"X" isn't a game!* Raph Koster's Website. Retrieved from http://www.raphkoster.com/2012/03/13/x-isnt-a-game/

Kroner, G. (2013, October 15). *Data-driven campus LMS strategy*. Retrieved from http://edutechnica.com/2013/10/15/data-driven-campus-lms-strategy

Lenhart, A. (2012). *Teens, smartphones and texting*. Washington, DC: Pew Internet and American Life Project. Retrieved from http://www.pewinternet.org/Reports/2012/Teens-and-smartphones.aspx

MacBride, R., & Lachman, A. L. (2008). Capitalizing on emerging technologies: A case study of classroom blogging. *School Science and Mathematics, 108*(5), 173–183.

Madden, M., Lenhart, A., Duggan, M., Cortesi, S., & Gasser, U. (2013). *Teens and technology 2013*. Washington, DC: Pew Internet and American Life Project. Retrieved from http://www.pewinternet.org/Reports/2013/Teens-and-Tech.aspx

Mendonca, M. M., McAndrew, P., & Santos, A. (2011). Freeing up access to learning. In A. Baldazzi, L. Ricci, & V. V. Baros (Eds.), *E-Learning quality assurance* (pp. 121–138). Rome: Gangemi Editore S.P.A. Retrieved from http://oro.open.ac.uk/31481

OER Commons. (n.d.). *OER community*. Retrieved from http://www.oercommons.org/community

Park, Y. (2011, February). A pedagogical framework for mobile learning. *International Review of Research in Open and Distance Learning, 12*(2), 78–102.

Richardson, W. (2006). *Blogs, wikis, podcasts, and other powerful web tools for classrooms*. Thousand Oaks, CA: Corwin Press.

Roblyer, M. D., & Wiencke, W. R. (2004). Exploring the interaction equation: Validating a rubric to assess and encourage interaction in distance courses. *Journal of Asynchronous Learning Networks, 8*(4). Retrieved from http://www.sloan-c.org/publications/jaln/v8n4/v8n4_roblyer.asp

Singer, N. (2012, February 4). You've won a badge. *Business Day*. Retrieved from http://www.nytimes.com/2012/02/05/business/employers-and-brands-use-gaming-to-gauge-engagement.html?_r=0

Swan, K. P., Richardson, J. C., Ice, P., Garrison, D. R., Cleveland-Innes, M., & Arbaugh, J. B. (2008). Validating a measurement tool of presence in online communities of inquiry. *eMentor, 2*(24). Retrieved from http://www.e-mentor.edu.pl/artykul/index/numer/24/id/543

Sweeney, J. (2012). *Nine conversations for successful BYOD decision making*. Hazelbrook NSW, Australia: Intelligent Business Research Services. Sponsored by Dell. Retrieved from http://i.dell.com/sites/doccontent/business/solutions/brochures/en/Documents/2012-nine-conversations-byod-education_au.pdf

Theis, G. J. (2005). *Perceived learning and performance needs of organizations seeking a learning management system* (Unpublished doctoral dissertation). University of Minnesota. Retrieved from ProQuest Digital Dissertations. (AAT 3167659)

UNESCO. (2002). *UNESCO promotes new initiative for free educational resources on the Internet*. New York: Author. Retrieved from http://www.unesco.org/education/news_en/080702_free_edu_ress.shtml

U.S. Department of Education. (2012, August 29). *Connected education: Students speak*. Washington, DC: Author. Retrieved from http://connectededucators.org/cem

Wiley, D. (2006). *The current state of open educational resources.* Paris: Organisation for Economic Co-operation and Development.

Winer, D. (2003, May 23). What makes a weblog a weblog? *Weblogs at Harvard Law.* Retrieved from http://blogs.law.harvard.edu/whatmakesaweblogaweblog.html

5

RESEARCH INTO K–12 ONLINE AND BLENDED LEARNING

Richard E. Ferdig, Cathy Cavanaugh, and Joseph R. Freidhoff

To truly understand K–12 online and blended learning research, you have to dig deeper into the components that make up K–12 online and blended learning. In other words, there are so many variations in design, instruction, facilitation, purpose, and content, no single study will answer everything we need to know about K–12 online learning. It is more important to explore the components and the research surrounding them.

In addition to digging deeper, any K–12 online and blended learning educator should consider at least five key areas: (a) asking the right question, (b) answering the critics, (c) appreciating the complexity, (d) understanding resources, and (e) exploring current research.

Asking the Right Question

As researchers, we are constantly asked: Does K–12 blended and online learning work (Ferdig, 2011)? Sometimes hidden and sometimes present in that question is the added query: Does K–12 blended and online learning work better than face-to-face education? Teachers, parents, researchers, policymakers, and the media seem to consistently seek one study that will definitely answer whether K–12 online and blended learning is better than everything that has come before it. But people who are interested in the research often ask the wrong question. They inquire only as to which one (i.e., blended/online or face-to-face) works better.

The better question is, Under what conditions can K–12 online and blended learning work? We do not have a huge research database on K–12 online and blended learning. As we begin to build one, we shouldn't spend time focusing our research energy on comparison studies. Rather, we need to understand when and where and why certain initiatives worked or failed to work.

Asking this question instead led us to a research summary (Ferdig, 2011) that says,

- High-quality programs have high-quality teaching and course worth.
- Successful online and blended students are self-directed and -motivated.

- Most colleges of education are not preparing teachers to teach in virtual schools or programs. This is problematic because teaching online and in blended settings requires a different skill set from instructors who teach in face-to-face programs.
- Online and blended education can work to increase graduation rates for students who have been expelled or have dropped out. However, this is only true for programs that build on remedial and advanced support; those that mirror traditional face-to-face programs that the students dropped out of will fail.
- Successful online programs train their teachers, but they also train their students. We mistakenly believe that because students have iPads, Mp3 players, cell phones, Facebook, and Twitter, they know how to learn online. That just isn't true. Students need to learn how to learn online.
- High-quality programs push the boundaries with technology while using data to help explore which initiatives are working and which are not.

Answering the Critics

Another important aspect of understanding research is to know that K–12 online and blended education has undergone extreme scrutiny for a number of possible reasons. For instance, many assume that online courses will replace teachers with computers. In other cases, schools are faced with limited budgets and have to make choices between programs. Regardless of the reason, we can gather two things from these continual critiques.

First, current and emergent researchers in this area need to understand that due to the scrutiny, many online and blended programs have not necessarily opened their doors to detailed examination by outsiders, which is one reason the research database is so limited. This situation has improved over time, but given the critiques, researchers need to understand that research requires a long-term and mutually beneficial relationship with schools. Researchers need to find a way to collaborate with the schools so that the outcomes improve the research field while also improving teaching and learning in those contexts.

Second, there are illegitimate and legitimate critiques of K–12 online and blended learning. In illegitimate critiques, the critic has no deep knowledge of K–12 online learning. For instance, research tells us that high-quality online and blended education is a multifaceted process that involves such things as high-quality and interactive content, teachers with strong and specific pedagogical skills, training for parents and students, and strong mentoring and scaffolding opportunities. Some illegitimate critics do not understand online and blended education; they don't recognize these factors. They see online and blended education as replacing all teachers with machines, or they picture a student sitting alone watching videos for eight hours a day. As a matter of fact, one of the most raised concerns, particularly related to online education, is that online students get no social interaction. Many of these critics do not realize that online students often spend more time interacting with their peers and teachers than face-to-face students do. They don't understand that online classes often require students to leave the computer to exercise (i.e., physical education class), to go visit a pond (i.e., science experiment), or to go to a museum (i.e., history or social studies).

Research on K–12 online and blended learning requires a deep understanding of the complexity of the environment. Researchers also need to understand that their research may come under attack from those who simply do not understand the same complexity.

However, some critics understand online and blended education and seem to have two legitimate critiques. First, not all online and blended education is of high quality. A lot of programs present technology-based education as simply a recording of lectures or online PowerPoint slides. They do not understand that high-quality online and blended education is a process that takes time, energy, research, and data. Quality organizations like the Florida Virtual School or Michigan Virtual School, for instance, are so successful because they put effort into the varied needs of their teachers, mentors, and students. Critics often see programs that are not done well, and most of them are failing because the program coordinators do not understand or are not given the resources to conduct high-quality online and blended instruction.

A second legitimate critique comes from the research. For the last 100 years of educational technology research (from educational radio to the TV, and from the personal computer to the iPad), people have tried to compare and find out which is better. Some people try to claim that online and blended education always works and always works better than face-to-face education for all students. Salomon and Gardner (1986) demonstrated that almost any question about technology that compares such scenarios will end with no significant difference. Students are able to learn as well in online classrooms as in conventional classrooms (Swan, 2003). Some research studies provide evidence that K–12 online and blended learning works better; in other cases the data suggest face-to-face education works better.

For example, a meta-analysis by Cavanaugh, Gillan, Kromrey, Hess, and Blomeyer (2004) found no significant difference between K–12 student learning outcomes in face-to-face and distance education, while a subsequent meta-analysis by Means, Toyama, Murphy, Bakia, and Jones (2009) found that K–12 online learning students performed modestly better than face-to-face students, and that students in courses that blended elements of online and face-to-face learning had higher performance gains relative to face-to-face students than those in fully online courses.

If you have enough studies, you will find research supporting both sides of the story. Critics are concerned—and rightly so—with claims that online education works all the time for all learners under all conditions. They read the U.S. Department of Education report and assume it means that online education just gets better all the time. This isn't the case.

No study can conclude definitively that online and blended education is always better than brick-and-mortar or vice versa. The research shows that K–12 online and blended education is as good as—and sometimes is better and sometimes worse than—face-to-face education. Researchers in K–12 online learning realize this, and we're beginning to ask a much more important question: Under what conditions do these programs succeed or fail?

For parents, this literally means ignoring the question of which one is better and addressing the question of what their student is hoping to achieve in online or blended settings. Is the child motivated and self-directed? Does the course you're reviewing come from an online school or program that trains its teachers and students, relies on cutting-edge tools and current pedagogy, and provides opportunities for advanced or remedial scaffolding for its students?

Teachers of online and blended education require a different set of skills. Some skills overlap with face-to-face education, but simply putting content online—whether you call it online education or flipping the classroom—won't succeed or fail just because it's online. Teachers need to learn to teach and interact in online and blended environments.

For schools interested in such an approach, online education is an important tool by which students not only have access to content but also content delivered in a medium that is similar to their own digital world. Perhaps more importantly, in addition to the content, they are receiving 21st-century digital skills that will be critical in their personal and professional lives (Ferdig, 2010).

Appreciating the Complexity

Researchers need to understand that doing work in K–12 online and blended settings is a complex venture. In traditional schooling, we often see a research connection among the teacher, the content, and the student (see Figure 5.1). This approach is obviously simplified, yet most of the research addresses student issues (e.g., performance, preparedness, and learning styles), teacher issues (e.g., preparation, performance, and professional development), or content (e.g., quality of content). In online and blended learning, the connection becomes much more complex (see Figure 5.2).

While still obviously simplified, you have a student who is learning content from a teacher. That student may or may not be at the same school as the teacher. Therefore, you probably also have a face-to-face mentor. The student also has the support of parents and others (e.g., siblings or other students who may have taken that class). Parental and other support also happens in face-to-face environments, but emerging research from Erik Black (2009) has demonstrated that the online content and the lack of a physical presence promote parent or caregiver participation in online environments. You still have the content, but this time the content is delivered through various technologies and

Figure 5.1: Relationship among teacher, student, and content

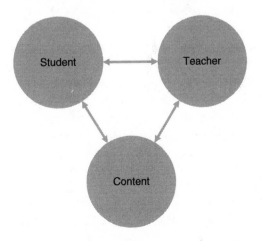

Figure 5.2: Relationships among multiple factors in online and blended settings

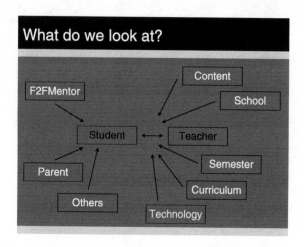

could come through various providers. Some virtual schools have more than 10 different providers of Algebra I. Finally, you have students taking the course who come from a variety of schools. The courses they are taking might be offered at various timelines and with varied synchronous or asynchronous requirements.

This is not to suggest that traditional schooling or research into traditional schooling is simple. Looking at the added complexities in Figure 5.2 provides good evidence as to why it is so important to dig deeper into the various components in order to understand research findings in online learning. It also helps researchers understand why it is so difficult to do the "gold standard research" (randomized controlled trials) that some have called for.

Understanding Resources

All researchers interested in online and blended learning need to ask the right questions, be able to address critics and critiques, build mutually beneficial relationships with online and blended schools, and understand the complexity of the tasks they are undertaking. Research is sparse in this field, and we need more of it. That does not mean, however, that we are without research. Before engaging in a deeper discussion of existing research, one should understand where to find it. Technology changes quickly, and staying aware of emerging research that will impact our field is important. In addition to the typical journals and web searches, three locations contain updated research databases or other information that impacts our work.

The first is the International Association for K–12 Online Learning (iNACOL) website, located at www.inacol.org. Its website, and particularly its resources section, contains articles, books, and reports on information relevant to parents, teachers, educators, policymakers, and researchers in our field.

The second is a research clearinghouse cohosted by iNACOL and Michigan Virtual University (see http://k12onlineresearch.org). An original database hosted by the

Bell South Foundation and the AT&T Foundation supported the Virtual School Clearinghouse (see www.vsclearinghouse.com). This new clearinghouse, supported by a Next Generation Learning Challenge grant, hosts articles and publications that directly relate to K–12 online and blended learning.

Finally, researchers in the field should be aware of the *Keeping Pace* reports created and distributed each year by John Watson and his colleagues at Evergreen Education Group (see http://kpk12.com). These reports provide research and practitioner-based snapshots of online and blended learning in the United States. Understandably these reports are U.S.-centric in nature; however, the information provided can also give international researchers insight into movements in our field.

Exploring Current Research

What does the research say about online and blended learning? As we've said, the research tells us that teaching and learning in these situations is as good as, sometimes better than, and sometimes worse than teaching and learning in face-to-face environments. Under what conditions does K–12 online and blended learning work? K–12 online and blended programs work when

- Educators are innovative with technology but still focus on the importance of pedagogy.
- Schools use data collection and data analytics to share data with all parties involved in the process.
- Organizations spend time providing continuing, personalized professional development for teachers, students, and mentors.
- Schools use mentors to support the learning processes of students and teachers.
- Administrators institute review procedures so that overall policies as well as course content and technology implementations are consistently examined for effectiveness.
- Schools support internal and external research and researchers to be able to examine what works and how to change practices that are no longer effective to the organization, the teachers, and the students.
- Programs, administrators, and teachers recognize the required flexibility of online and blended programs.
- Everyone involved realizes the important but changing role of the teacher.
- Those wishing to implement blended and online solutions understand the culture of the environment, school, parents, and students of the proposed program.
- Implementers recognize the importance of iterative design; it involves multiple stakeholders and is a recursive process.
- Educators understand that blended and online learning is not a panacea for all the problems that exist in education; it comes with its own set of advantages and disadvantages.
- Administrators understand that there are multiple models and that not every model is right for every situation (DiPietro, Ferdig, Black, & Preston, 2008; Ferdig & Cavanaugh, 2011; Ferdig, Cavanaugh, & Freidhoff, 2012).

Future Research

The research that does exist in this arena is promising. It suggests that there are both high-quality and low-quality programs. High-quality programs value pedagogy and the personnel involved in these decisions; low-quality programs attempt to purchase a solution without any real willingness to engage those in the existing culture. Future research needs to find a way to dig deeper into the area. Instead of asking if it works, we need to understand when and how it works—or fails to work. As new technologies evolve, this research will help remind us that no single technology will cure what ails education; however, certain technology can drive specific fixes. In return, this research will also help drive the creation and implementation of new technologies for teaching and learning in K–12 settings.

References

Black, E. W. (2009). *An evaluation of familial involvements' influence on student achievement in K–12 virtual schooling* (Unpublished doctoral dissertation). University of Florida. Retrieved from ProQuest Dissertations and Theses. (Accession Order No. AAT 3367406)

Cavanaugh, C. S., Gillan, K. J., Kromrey, J., Hess, M., & Blomeyer, R. (2004). *The effects of distance education on K–12 student outcomes: A meta-analysis.* Retrieved from http://files.eric. ed.gov/fulltext/ED489533.pdf

DiPietro, M., Ferdig, R. E., Black, E. W., & Preston, M. (2008). Best practices in teaching K–12 online: Lessons learned from Michigan Virtual School teachers. *Journal of Interactive Online Learning, 7*(1), 10–35.

Ferdig, R. E. (2010, August). *Continuous quality improvement through professional development for online K–12 instructors.* A keynote presentation at Michigan Virtual University's fifth annual Collaboration of the Minds conference, East Lansing.

Ferdig, R. E., & Cavanaugh, C. (Eds.). (2011). *Lessons learned from virtual schools: Experiences and recommendations from the field.* Vienna, VA: International Association for K–12 Online Learning.

Ferdig, R. E. (2011). Does online learning work? In J. Watson, A. Murin, L. Vashaw, B. Gemin & C. Rapp, *Keeping pace with K–12 online learning* (pp. 40-42). Evergreen Education Group, Evergreen, CO.

Ferdig, R. E., Cavanaugh, C., & Freidhoff, J. (2012). *Lessons learned from blended programs: Experiences and recommendations from the field.* Vienna, VA: International Association for K–12 Online Learning.

Means, B., Toyama, Y., Murphy, R., Bakia, M., & Jones, K. (2009). *Evaluation of evidence-based practices in online learning: A meta-analysis and review of online learning studies.* Washington, DC: U.S. Department of Education. Retrieved from http://www.ed.gov/rschstat/eval/tech/ evidence-based-practices/finalreport.pdf

Salomon, G., & Gardner, H. (1986). The computer as educator: Lessons from television research. *Educational Researcher, 15*(1), 13–19.

Swan, K. (2003). Learning effectiveness: What the research tells us. In J. Bourne & J. C. Moore (Eds.), *Elements of quality online education: Practice and direction* (pp. 13–45). Needham, MA: Sloan Center for Online Education.

6

CYBER CHARTER SCHOOLS

An Alternative to Traditional Brick-and-Mortar Schooling?

Victoria Raish and Ali Carr-Chellman

"Cyber charter schools are quietly gaining momentum across the country and have begun to challenge traditional definitions of public schooling by delivering instruction from beyond the classroom walls" (Huerta, Gonzales, & d'Entremont, 2006, para. 1). E-learning, or virtual learning, is a rapidly growing field within the public education sector. The federal government believes that cyber charter schools can be a valid alternative to public schools under the provisions of No Child Left Behind. If a high-needs school fails to make Adequate Yearly Progress in student achievement for two or more years, its students may have the option to transfer to a cyber charter school that is not in danger of failing (Hassel & Terrell, 2004). Cyber charter schools are part of a relatively recent educational choice movement that has the potential to dramatically alter the public education landscape.

There are many variations on K–12 online learning, but this chapter predominantly focuses on *cyber charter schools*, which are defined as charter schools in which coursework is delivered primarily via the Internet. Using the state of Pennsylvania as a focus point, we consider the formation of cyber charter schools under a unique legislative context. We then explore how these schools are funded and how this impacts decisions in public education. Then we share some of the reasons that students enroll in cyber charter schools rather than traditional public schools, which include educational choice, special needs, problems in school, and homeschooling experience. We next provide an update on research about the effectiveness of cyber charter schools. Some of the evaluations of their academic programs are explored, with a focus on student achievement levels when compared with traditional public schools. We look at the relationship between local districts and small cyber charters started with a specific local need or educational goal in mind.

Funding formulas are a major point of tension between traditional and cyber charter schools. We attempt to follow the money and examine whether the way in which cyber charter schools are funded in Pennsylvania serves the public good. Another important funding issue that we explore is the for-profit nature of cyber charter educational management companies and their strategic alliances. These alliances are considered one of the more troubling features of this new and promising form of public education. We delve into some of the new legal and ethical issues they raise, such as their alignment with each state's rules for traditional public and charter schools and the extent to which cyber charters are able to serve the public interests and the best interests of the students they enroll. We conclude with a look at some of the different avenues for future research on cyber charter schools and questions for future researchers to consider.

What Are Cyber Charter Schools, and Where Did They Come From?

You may have heard many related terms for online learning: *virtual learning, distance education, e-learning, cyber learning*, and more. To be specific here, both charters and cyber charters are charter schools. A *charter school* is defined here as an "independent public school created through formal agreements with a state or local sponsoring agency, designed and operated by parents, community members, or entrepreneurs, and allowed to operate free from some of the regulations that traditional public schools face" (Huerta & Gonzales, 2004, p. 2). A cyber charter school typically falls under the same state regulations as a brick-and-mortar charter school. In most places, charter schools must be "chartered" or given their charge by the state or district in which they geographically operate.

A cyber charter school differs from a brick-and-mortar charter in several respects. As noted previously, cyber charter schools are charter schools in which coursework is delivered primarily via the Internet. There is no physical location where students attend school, and students from any part of the state or other designated service area can typically enroll. The teacher is at a remote location, and parents are typically expected to take a more active role in their child's schooling. As is explained further in the section on legislation, early Pennsylvania cyber charters were approved by local school boards and often served students in limited geographic areas. Over time, large cyber charter schools emerged that enrolled students statewide.

According to Bogden (2003), very few people who are sufficiently familiar with charter schools truly understand the differences between brick-and-mortar and cyber charters. An essential difference is the delivery method of instruction. However, that would oversimplify the differences in the very essences of these two kinds of schools. While both offer parents some form of choice and options in their children's educational experiences, they tend to have dramatically different structures and societal implications. Typically, the students' teacher is far away, and the cyber charter school depends on the parents for student guidance and supervision. This is particularly true in the younger grades (Thomas, 2002). Bogden (2003) saw major differences in the types of students the two kinds of schools serve, noting that many cyber charter students were formerly homeschooled, and that cyber charters provide a free home-based education while relieving parents of instructional duties.

One of the primary reasons that cyber charters effectively change the rules that govern charter schools is that they can draw from a large geographic area that represents more than one public school's district. This leads to one of the basic funding issues that we consider later; with the lack of geographic boundaries, no uniform allotment per cyber charter exists within Pennsylvania. Each traditional public school has a different per-pupil allocation. This situation incentivizes cyber charters to enroll students from districts with a high per-pupil allocation.

Another challenge that arises with the lack of geographic boundaries is proctoring for exams and assessing students. All public school students must take state assessments in a proctored setting. There are proctoring centers where cyber charter students can go to take a state assessment or final exam, but what if students are from a remote area or do not have transportation? Must the cyber charters transport those students to a center? The auditor general in Arizona recommended "supervising, or proctoring, final exams to ensure academic integrity. It also recommended requiring students to pass those exams to get course credit" (Ryman & Kossan, 2011). Four years later, it appears that four of the state's biggest online schools still do not require proctoring for final exams. Other Arizona cyber charters do require students to come in for these exams, but many complain that the cost is prohibitive. Teachers also need to be concerned about summative assessments and how to best determine if the students truly understand the material presented.

In Pennsylvania, cyber charters and traditional charters both must include in their charter requests the number of years the issuing charter will be valid, the mission and curriculum of the school, the anticipated number of students to be served, and how they will measure student learning (Ahn, 2011). Cyber charters must meet additional criteria centered on the online method of delivery, as stated on the Pennsylvania Department of Education (PDE) website. Since the computer is the medium through which content is primarily received, cyber charters need to provide

> information on the school year calendar, including school day, an explanation of the amount of online time required, the manner in which teachers will deliver instruction, the technology which will be provided by the cyber charter school to the student, what technical support will be available to students and parents, and the methods used to ensure the authenticity of student work and adequate proctoring of examinations. (Pennsylvania Department of Education, 2012, Section 1747-A)

Some of these things are tricky to specify. For example, trying to equate face-to-face time with cyber charter "seat time" is nearly impossible. The more ephemeral aspects of the learning process, some of which are exceedingly difficult to measure, come into play as the learner engages in the cyber charter learning experience. In the end, cyber charter students must demonstrate the same competencies, but efforts to monitor these kinds of seat-time criteria do not ensure student success.

We believe that these differences require a new set of policies and regulations to ensure student success and proper oversight of the cyber charters. We assert that these differences may look superficial but are only the telltale signs of a much deeper iceberg— one that creates significant issues for broader social discourse on the purpose and meaning of education in our society.

What Legislation Exists to Help Cyber Charters Get Started? And Where Are We Now?

As is typical in other states, Pennsylvania did not specifically address cyber charters in its original charter school laws, many of which were written before virtual schools became prominent. Today, cyber charters must be approved by the PDE (Pennsylvania Department of Education, 2012), but this was not always so. When early cyber charters first applied for accredited school status, a local school board could approve the measure. The first Pennsylvania cyber charter, SusQ-Cyber, remained a local school. It was approved by five districts in the county it served (Huerta et al., 2006). The next cyber charter formed in Pennsylvania broke the geographical barrier and attracted students from across the state. After this, there were significant challenges to a single school district approving a school that could draw from a much larger population pool. Legislation emerged as part of Pennsylvania Public School Code Act 88 that gave more well-defined guidelines for the cyber charters as well as the home districts of the students.

Additional legislation for starting a cyber charter school comes from the Charter School Law, specifically sections 1719-A, 1743-A(c) and (d), 1747-A, and 1748-A. These sections required the cyber charter schools to provide information about the governance structure of the school, education goals, financial plan, planned curriculum, privacy of student information, and other details (Pennsylvania Department of Education, 2012). The Pennsylvania System of Cyber Charter Review (PASCCR) is what the charter school has to submit to the state annually (Watson, Murin, Vashaw, Gemin, & Rapp, 2012).

What Is the Appeal of Cyber Charter Schools?

The number of cyber charter schools is exploding across the country. A total of 26 states offered cyber charter school options in 2009 compared with just 13 in 2003 (Brady, Umpstead, & Eckes 2010). In the 2010–2011 school year, an estimated 275,000 K–12 students were enrolled in fully online schools (Watson et al., 2012). For the 2012–2013 school year, two states permitted online schools that had not previously done so. The majority of students in these schools were in cyber charter schools. In Pennsylvania, approximately 32,322 students were enrolled (Watson et al., 2012).

Cyber charters are enjoying unprecedented growth for many reasons. One of the compelling advantages that a cyber charter school offers is significant flexibility over traditional public schools. For many parents, particularly those who might otherwise homeschool or tutor their children, this flexibility goes beyond mere convenience; it is essential. Such high levels of flexibility and autonomy naturally need to be countered with cautious accountability. Other reasons that families may choose the cyber charter route include having children with special needs, feeling that the school isn't serving their children well, and frustration with the system of public schooling. Some parents want to avoid types of socialization that they believe are inherent in traditional schooling, or they have concerns about curricula such as sex education. Parents may seek, based on their religious views, to avoid what they see as the teaching of secular humanism and evolution in public schools, or to focus only on perspectives that support their worldview (Carr-Chellman & Sockman, 2009). Cyber charter schools do not provide this curriculum. If the parents wish to teach this viewpoint, they must do it with supplemental curricula.

While the majority of students who enroll in a cyber charter school these days come from a traditional brick-and-mortar school, many still had been homeschooled prior. Many homeschooling parents are social and religious conservatives (Carr-Chellman & Marsh, 2009). Cambre (2009) addressed the issue of cyber charter schools and the endorsement of religion. Since cyber charter schools rely on parents to take a primary role in the child's education, parents may be heavily involved in curricular decisions even though the school receives public funding. A state needs to carefully define what counts as attendance in a cyber charter school to ensure that the state is not publicly funding religion when a parent teaches religious subjects. However, the policing of parents' inclusion of religious teaching within the cyber charter school day is nearly impossible.

A potential downside of parent choice for cyber charters is that many parents view this as a temporary schooling option. Miron and Urschel (2012) suggested that 31% of parents intend to enroll their child for less than a year; K12 Inc. statistics confirmed that 67% of the students had been in the school for less than two years. No reason was given for this choice, but it can certainly affect student performance if they do not have consistency in their instruction.

In general, cyber charter schools serve less of the special-needs population than traditional public and charter schools. They invest less in special education and serve fewer students with moderate or severe special needs (Miron and Urschel, 2012). "K12 [Inc.] enrolls an increasing number of students with disabilities, but it spends less than half as much per pupil as charter schools on special education instruction and a third of what districts spend on special education instruction" (p. iv). Smaller cyber charter schools may also not have the resources to devote to a wide range of special education programs. However, as we detail later in this chapter, at least one small cyber charter has this student population as its focal point.

Parents and students who choose cyber charters may be unsatisfied with public schools in general. They may feel unhappy with the school's safety or with their academic program selection. Parents can feel frustrated by the lack of accountability, success, and innovation in their school district. They may also see the need for a different schedule than their school district offers. They naturally seek an alternative for their children, and a cyber charter school may be their choice. Cyber charter school parents interviewed in a study by Carr-Chellman and Marsh (2009) thought that public school teachers did not want to spend the time necessary with each student. Cyber charter school parents believe that programs are more individualized and that they will have the ability to constantly monitor student progress (Kim, Kim, & Karimi, 2012). Parents of students in rural or urban schools may lack either school alternatives or the financial means to choose which school their child can attend. With the advent of cyber charters, these parents could finally feel as though they have some say in the school their children attend (Hassel & Terrell, 2004). Parents of students in remote or isolated areas may feel that their local school cannot offer the variety of courses needed to help their children live up to their full potential. They can feel connected in spite of the geographical barriers if they believe that their child can get a more balanced education through a cyber charter (Marsh, Carr-Chellman, & Sockman, 2009).

Homeschooling parents have chosen not to have their children socialized in a traditional school setting for a variety of reasons. In addition to opportunities to learn, students may be exposed to cultural values and mores different from those at home. Students may see drug use, sexual relations, and gang activities. They may be bullied at school and internalize these experiences. Some parents in the mostly conservative homeschool movement took a moderate gamble in joining the technology bandwagon. They had three general reasons for doing so. According to Marsh et al. (2009), these parents saw that cyber charters offered customized curriculum and a lack of financial risk, and believed that making this choice can help "change the world" (p. 35).

Once students are enrolled in a cyber charter school, they may discover that it is not what they expected. The level of interaction, socialization, physical exercise, and many other variables may catch some students off guard. For example, many students report that they do not participate in any discussion forums, and if they do, the discussions are asynchronous and do not replicate face-to-face contact (Kim, Kim, & Karimi, 2012).

The personalized advertisements one encounters when browsing the Internet demonstrate the trend toward increasing personalization through technology. Parents may feel that they can personalize everything else for their children, so why not public schooling? This might naturally attract a parent whose child may have special needs that the parent feels are not being met by their home district. Zogby (2002) propounded the belief that "cybers have the power to combine customized curriculum of charter schools with easy access and flexibility of the Internet—making these schools uniquely adaptable to the students' individual needs" (p. 273). Students on both ends of the academic spectrum can be attracted to a cyber charter. It can simultaneously allow a student who is behind to catch up without worrying about other students and allow a student who is gifted to work ahead without engaging in rote learning (Greenway & Vanourek, 2006).

Current Research Into the Effectiveness of Cyber Charters

The overarching goal of any public school should be the successful education of its students. While a cyber charter school can cause states to reevaluate the definition of a *successful education*, every school still strives to reach certain standards. There are conflicting reports of cyber charters that do no worse than traditional public schools on assessment reports and others that do significantly worse. In one sense, any type of school can excel or fail depending on the many factors that make a successful school. On the other hand, the differences in how cyber charter school students engage in the learning process warrant research into how those students are learning.

A National Education Policy Center study found that children enrolled in one of the cyber charter schools operated by K12 Inc. were falling behind in both attendance and test scores. Math scores for these students were 14% to 36% lower and reading scores 2% to 11% lower than those of their counterparts in other schools (Chadband, 2012). The four-year graduation rate of 49.1% in schools operated by K12 Inc. was much lower than the public school average of 79.4% (Miron & Urschel, 2012). Considering that many jobs and financial achievement require at least a high school diploma, it should be a priority for schools to have as many graduates as possible (Alliance for Excellent Education, 2006).

A finding in Colorado shows that students who switch from a traditional brick-and-mortar school to a cyber charter school fare significantly worse on their state reading exams after two years in the cyber charter school (Hubbard & Mitchell, 2011). A study of full-time virtual high schools in Arizona showed that three schools scored above the statewide average while three others scored lower. They all had significantly lower graduation rates than the statewide average (Ryman & Kossan, 2011).

In a study of Pennsylvania charter school performance from 2007 through 2010 (Center for Research on Education Outcomes, 2011), each cyber student's state achievement test results was compared with those of students enrolled in the cyber student's local traditional public school who had similar demographics and prior test scores. On average, the cyber students had significantly smaller gains than their traditional public school peers in reading (–13%) and math (–24%). All eight cyber charter schools had significantly worse average learning gains in reading and math when compared to their traditional public school counterparts. While these results are worrisome, school achievement should not be decided by only one measure of achievement. These studies did not examine the learning differences of the different populations, and the Pennsylvania study did not always account for significant differences between the brick-and-mortar populations and cyber charter populations on a wider number of variables. Proponents of cyber charters believe that many students come to their schools as a last resort and thus would be significantly further behind in their schooling or are present because of special scheduling needs and may be advanced among their peers (Hubbard & Mitchell, 2011). Limited research exists on the effectiveness of cyber charters, and more factors need to be examined in determining if these schools are truly succeeding and in what ways.

Relationships Between Cyber Charters and School Districts

Not all cyber charter schools have a negative relationship with school districts. The three cyber charter schools examined by Ahn (2011) set out to serve unique student populations that were not being reached by traditional brick-and-mortar schools, or for whom some districts could not provide services. Therefore, the cyber charters and districts were not in conflict over these students. The development of new cyber charters is continuing in Pennsylvania, where four more were approved to open for the 2012–2013 school year. These schools all have different mission statements and plan on serving different student populations. At least two of them are being backed by nonprofit organizations. One of them plans to have brick-and-mortar buildings within a 45-minute drive of any student enrolled (Chute, 2012a). Two of the schools have specified in their mission statements the cultures they are intending to serve. One of the goals of Esperanza Cyber Charter School is to celebrate the Hispanic culture. No two cyber charters are the same, and cyber charters *can* respond to local needs.

Another example is the Education Plus Academy Cyber Charter School (EPACS), whose mission is to be "an alternative learning charter cyber-school that provides accessible, quality, evidence-based educational services for children aged 5–21 (grades K–12) and their families, and specializes in services for students who are academically behind and/or have learning disabilities/differences" (Education Plus Academy Charter School, 2012). The EPACS curriculum is tailored to students with disabilities through specialized programs, expert special education staff, and leadership activities for the student body.

Many school districts are starting their own full-time online learning programs, at least partially in response to the popularity of the cyber charter schools and the consequent budget dips. This development can be seen as a positive, because it may be encouraging traditional public schools to reinvent themselves and make them more responsive to students' needs. Pittsburgh Public Schools is advertising that cyber charter students who would return to the district's own online school would be eligible for Pittsburgh

Promise, a scholarship program for any student who graduates from a Pittsburgh public high school and attends certain colleges (Chute, 2012b). This school district is not the only one seeking to entice students to return to their home districts.

Following the Money

When students transfer from a home district school to a cyber charter, state funding follows them. The home district school may lose a few students, but often not enough to furlough teachers or combine classes. Some Pennsylvania school districts are using public relations efforts or incentives to try to lure students back to their home district. For example, the Mid-Penn school district has put up billboards near a major cyber charter school office to entice students to return to their district. One school district, Solanco in Pennsylvania, has even offered students a $1,000 incentive if they return to that school district (Hall, 2011). This idea is certainly novel, but it brings up another ethical issue entirely: Can a public school district use its funds to advertise and incentivize?

The financial implications of cyber charter funding are perhaps the most critical issue of concern for school districts. It needs to be made clear how states fund cyber charters, what they do with the money, and what happens when previously homeschooled students enroll in cyber charter schools.

Different states have different ways of funding cyber charter schools. The major issues for consideration when forming a cyber charter law are adjusting the funding of the cyber charter to reflect what it costs to run the school, clarifying how these schools will be held responsible for the most important part of any school (i.e., how students are learning), and what government entity is responsible for monitoring the cyber charter schools (Brady et al., 2010; Huerta et al., 2006). The fine line is ensuring that cyber charters are for the public good and effectively facilitate learning, while also allowing them to innovate and devise new ways of educating.

In Pennsylvania, cyber charter schools receive the per-pupil state allocation that would have been provided to the student's home school district. This does not represent what it costs to educate the student at the cyber charter school; rather it represents what it is *estimated* to cost in the home district to educate the child. A major point of contention is that when a student who was homeschooled and thus not using tax dollars signs up for a cyber charter, the resulting costs are entirely new to the state and the home school district. Many home districts feel threatened by this because they have never taught these students before and are now being forced to pay for their education at a cyber charter school (Carr-Chellman & Marsh, 2009). The loss of revenues and added costs can cause great consternation for traditional school districts, raising grave concerns for their longer-term financial planning. Naturally, the question then arises: What is the cyber charter's operator doing with that money?

With the advent of cyber charters, the money still followed the students, as it had in the case of brick-and-mortar charter schools, but based on the student's district of residence, the program provider selected by a cyber charter might receive $6,000 in per-pupil allocations for one student and $12,000 for another (Carr-Chellman & Marsh, 2009). Legislative efforts to change this approach have failed.

Cyber charter operators clearly have different funding needs than a traditional school would. They do not have to pay for facilities for the students, transportation, meals, and utilities. K12 Inc.–operated schools spend more money on instructional materials and administration than their brick-and-mortar charter school counterparts, but the salaries and benefits for faculty and staff are much lower (Miron & Urschel, 2012). Schools run by K12 Inc. necessarily have to spend more on computers and developing effective learning management systems, but how much is not clear. Miron and Urschel strongly recommend more transparency in reporting finances. Another recommendation of theirs is to make funding contingent upon students completing courses, creating an incentive for K12 Inc. to become more focused on achieving student success rather than on padding the pockets of its investors. However, such a plan might lead to unintended consequences, such as cyber charters making courses less rigorous to increase pass rates. Cyber charters also have no limits on spending for advertising or lobbying.

Legality and Ethics of Cyber Charter Schools

In this section, we scrutinize the for-profit nature of many cyber charter school operators. Concerns have been raised that, rather than using money to improve student learning, they recruit students who would not be a good fit in a cyber charter simply to boost enrollments and revenue.

The board of the largest cyber charter provider, K12 Inc., is made up of a variety of professionals from different backgrounds, who are all very accomplished and many of whom have a prominent role in the charter school movement. The manner in which K12 Inc. operates makes it difficult to know precisely how profitable the company is, but profits appear to be quite substantial. Because it costs less to operate a cyber charter school than a traditional brick-and-mortar school, it is reasonable to assume that K12 Inc. reaps large profits from the cyber charters that it operates (Bracey, 2004). The largest online school that K12 Inc. operates was expected to bring in $72 million in 2011, which is 10% of its overall revenue (Saul, 2011).

In a lawsuit filed in 2012 on behalf of investors, K12 Inc. was accused of "high-pressure sales strategies aimed strictly at enrolling students, irrespective of the students' suitability for online education; administrative pressure to pass enrolled students, regardless of academic performance; and overall failure of K12 students to maintain grade-level performance in math and reading" (Birch, 2012; Faruqi & Faruqi LLP, 2012, para. 3). Lawsuits such as this one encourage critical thinking with regard to the future of cyber charter schools.

Conclusion

Public schools were established in our society for the public good, but we, as a society, may no longer agree on what those goals may be. Until recently, the general public would not have included "making money" as one of the laudable goals for the system of public education. We may agree that we would like schools to prepare their *learners* to become moneymakers, but the system itself has always been considered more comparable to public roads and libraries. This outlook may be changing as we see for-profit companies focusing their attention on cyber charter global markets. Further research needs to follow this area closely.

Technology has the potential to significantly improve learning for students and reach those who live in relative geographic isolation. Online learning has the potential to "expand educational access, providing high-quality learning opportunities, improving student outcomes and skills, allowing for educational choice, and achieving administrative efficiency" (Barbour & Reeves, 2009, p. 1). While hopeful in theory, evidence does not support that this theory is lived out in practical applications, at least in terms of full-time online cyber charter schools.

We believe that evaluative measures for cyber charters need to be reexamined and altered from those used to assess brick-and-mortar schools. A thorough analysis of student performance with more than one marker is needed to get a clear idea of how these virtual schools are serving their students. We need to ask the following questions: Why is the school here? How does the school operate? Who does it invite into its membership? How is that membership determined? How are funds allocated—how much to student support, to curricular materials, to advertising or lobbying? Who provides oversight for a statewide cyber charter? What does the cyber charter offer to the local community that houses it? These questions must be answered to help us understand the whole cyber charter picture from a systemic perspective.

Cyber charter schools need to make it clear, to both parents and students, that enrolling will involve a great deal of independent learning and parental involvement to ensure that students are attending to and completing their work. A cyber charter school is not for everyone. Cyber charter schools should make enrollment recommendations based on whether a student's match to cyber learning suggests that the student is likely to succeed in the school.

Funding and budget reports also need to be made transparent so that the community and legislative bodies can see what the schools are spending money on and how much money they need for each student. It is unfair to assume that they need as much as a brick-and-mortar school would, but discrepancies in funding should not be based on the allotment of individual districts. A statewide formula might be devised to establish base-level funding and ensure that each student has the resources needed to succeed in any setting. Companies and schools that are interested in education should also be fully vested in the public good. Being more concerned with profit margins than school outcome is not a good indicator of true investment in the public good.

Online learning has the potential to serve a student base that brick-and-mortar schools are not reaching, but more research needs to be done before we strategically expand cyber charter schools. Case studies should be completed of cyber charter schools that are succeeding. We do believe that small cyber charters that meet a local need or educational goal can have a positive relationship with school districts. We need to determine what curriculum, administrative leadership, professional development, and student resources help to make cyber charter schools the best they can be, while keeping in mind that no one-size-fits-all formula exists for a great school.

Of ongoing concern is how cyber charter students are faring in inquiry-based fields such as science, technology, engineering, and math. There is not much empirical evidence to evaluate the best ways to teach science- and mathematics-based fields online. How much collaboration, interactive content, and teacher-mediated learning is necessary to effectively teach difficult concepts? Are cyber charters willing and able to provide this level of essential support? These are critical questions that need further investigation if full-time online learning is going to help our nation remain a player in an increasingly globalized world.

References

Ahn, J. (2011). Policy, technology, and practice in cyber charter schools: Framing the issues. *Teachers College Record, 113*(1), 1–26. Retrieved from http://ahnjune.com/wp-content/uploads/2011/11/Final-Policy-Technology-and-Practice-in-Cyber-Charter-Schools-Framing-the-Issues.pdf

Alliance for Excellent Education. (2006). *Understanding high school graduation rates in Pennsylvania.* Washington, DC: Author. Retrieved from http://www.all4ed.org/files/Pennsylvania_wc.pdf

Barbour, M. K., & Reeves, T. C. (2009). The reality of virtual schools: A review of the literature. *Computers and Education, 52*(2), 402–416.

Birch, B. A. (2012). K12 Inc. under investigation for potential securities fraud. *Education News.* Retrieved from http://www.educationnews.org/online-schools/k12-inc-under-investigation-for-possible-securities-fraud/

Bogden, J. (2003, Autumn). A new breed in the education corral. *State Education Standard,* 33–37.

Bracey, G. (2004, April). *Knowledge universe and virtual schools: Digital breakthrough or raid on the public treasury?* Phoenix: Education Policy Research Unit. Retrieved from http://epsl.asu.edu/epru/documents/EPSL-0404-118-EPRU.pdf

Brady, K., Umpstead, R., & Eckes, S. (2010). Unchartered territory: The current legal landscape of public cyber charter schools. *Brigham Young University Education and Law Journal, 2,* 191. Retrieved from EBSCO Host (AN=53889277).

Cambre, B. M. (2009). Tearing down the walls: Cyber charter schools and the endorsement of religion. *TechTrends, 53*(4), 61–64.

Carr-Chellman, A. A., & Marsh, R. M. (2009). Pennsylvania cyber charter school funding: Follow the money. *TechTrends, 53*(4), 49–55.

Carr-Chellman, A. A., & Sockman, B. (2009). Selecting Silicon: Why parents choose online charter schools. *TechTrends, 53*(4), 32–36.

Center for Research on Education Outcomes. (2011, April). *Charter school performance in Pennsylvania.* Stanford, CA: CREDO Project, Stanford University. Retrieved from http://www.thefinancialinvestigator.com/wp-content/uploads/2012/02/PA-State-Report_20110404_FINAL.pdf

Chadband, E. (2012, July 25). Virtual schools not passing the test. *NEA Today.* Retrieved from http://neatoday.org/2012/07/25/virtual-schools-not-passing-the-test/

Chute, E. (2012a, June 28). City schools take on cyber rivals with Pittsburgh online academy 6-12. *Pittsburgh Post-Gazette.* Retrieved from http://www.post-gazette.com/stories/local/neighborhoods-city/city-schools-take-on-cyber-rivals-642213/?print=1

Chute, E. (2012b, July 9). State approves 4 new cyber charter schools. *Pittsburgh Post-Gazette.* Retrieved from http://www.post-gazette.com/stories/news/education/state-approves-4-new-cyber-charter-schools-643994

Education Plus Academy Charter School. (2012). *About us.* Wayne, PA: Author. Retrieved from http://edpluscharter.org/

Faruqi & Faruqi LLP. (2012, January 30). *Faruqi & Faruqi, LLP, files securities class action suit against K12 Inc. and certain of its executives.* New York: Author. Retrieved from http://www.faruqilaw.com/cases/summary/id/491

Greenway, R., & Vanourek, G. (2006). The virtual revolution: Understanding online schools. *Education Next, 6*(2), 34–41. Retrieved from http://media.hoover.org/documents/ednext20062_34.pdf

Hall, S. (2011, December 18). With cyber charter competition, school districts start to advertise. *The times-tribune.com.* Retrieved from http://thetimes-tribune.com/news/with-cyber-charter-competition-school-districts-start-to-advertise-1.1246396

Hassel, B. C., & Terrell, M. G. (2004). *How can virtual schools be a vibrant part of meeting the choice provisions of the No Child Left Behind act?* Paper presented at the No Child Left Behind Leadership Summit, July 12–13, Orlando. Retrieved from http://nmoled.org/Hassel-Terrell-VirtualSchools.pdf

Hubbard, B., & Mitchell, N. (2011). Online K–12 schools failing students but keeping tax dollars. *I-News Network.* Retrieved from http://www.inewsnetwork.org/special-reports/online-K-12-schools/2

Huerta, L., & Gonzales, M. (2004). *Cyber and homeschool charter schools: How states are defining new forms of public schooling.* Phoenix: Education Policy Research Unit. Retrieved from http://epsl.asu.edu/epru/articles/EPRU-0401-49-OWI.htm

Huerta, L. A., Gonzalez, M. F., & d'Entremont, D. (2006). Cyber charter schools: Can accountability keep pace with innovation? *Phi Delta Kappan, 88*(1), 23–30. Retrieved from http://web.ebscohost.com. (AN=22295157)

Kim, P., Kim, F., & Karimi, A. (2012). Public online charter school students: Choices, perceptions, and traits. *American Educational Research Association, 49*(3), 521–545.

Marsh, R. M., Carr-Chellman, A. A., & Sockman, B. R. (2009). Selecting silicon: Why parents choose cyber charter schools. *Tech Trends, 53*(4), 32–36.

Miron, G., & Urschel, J. L. (2012). *Understanding and improving full-time virtual schools: A study of student characteristics, school finance, and school performance in schools operated by K12 Inc.* Boulder, CO: National Education Policy Center. Retrieved from http://nepc.colorado.edu/publication/understanding-improving-virtual

Pennsylvania Department of Education. (2012). *Charter school authorizer toolkit.* Harrisburg, PA: Author. Retrieved from http://www.portal.state.pa.us/portal/server.pt/community/charter_school_authorizer_toolkit/18759

Ryman, N., & Kossan, P. (2011). The race to online: Arizona experiments with virtual K12 schools. Will they work for your child? *AZCentral.com.* Retrieved from http://www.azcentral.com/news/education/online-school

Saul, S. (2011, December 12). Profits and questions at online charter schools. *New York Times.* Retrieved from http://www.nytimes.com/2011/12/13/education/online-schools-score-better-on-wall-street-than-in-classrooms.html?pagewanted=all

Thomas, W. (2002). *Virtual learning and charter schools: Issues and potential impact.* Retrieved from http://info.sreb.org/programs/EdTech/pubs/PDF/Virtual_Learn_Charter_School.pdf

Watson, J., Murin, A., Vashaw, L., Gemin, B., & Rapp, C. (2012). *Keeping pace with K–12 online and blended learning.* Evergreen, CO: Evergreen Education Group. Retrieved from http://kpk12.com/cms/wp-content/uploads/KeepingPace2012.pdf

Zogby, C. (2002, October 8). *Possible anticompetitive efforts to restrict competition on the Internet.* Testimony of Secretary of Education Charles B. Zogby: Federal Trade Commission workshop. Retrieved from http://www.ftc.gov/opp/ecommerce/anticompetitive/021008antitrans.pdf

7

ENSURING EQUITABLE ACCESS IN ONLINE AND BLENDED LEARNING

Raymond M. Rose, Alese Smith, Karen Johnson, and David Glick

Challenging issues of providing equitable access to quality education for all students are nothing new in education. Every aspiring teacher in the United States learns about *Brown v. Board of Education* (1954) as a cornerstone of our current public education system and its attempts to address racial disparities. Our understanding of educational equity now extends well beyond race to include issues of socioeconomic status (SES), ethnicity, special needs, gender, and geographic location. Although many American educators have been dedicated to teaching without marginalizing any child, major disparities in educational opportunity persist. Few educators today would question the goal of providing equitable access to educational opportunities across racial groups, although rich discussions and disagreements certainly exist regarding the best methods for doing so. Online learning brings dramatic new solutions to this challenge of equitable opportunity. As so eloquently stated in the *National Broadband Plan* (Federal Communications Commission, 2010), "We believe that where you start doesn't determine where you finish, that demography isn't destiny, that privilege isn't a necessary prologue to success" (p. 10).

Online and blended learning can challenge traditional policy and practice, disrupting status-quo educational systems that are based on an outdated industrial model. It can provide courses suited for the pace and flexibility of 21st-century learning and help prepare students for the university and workplace. School leaders are beginning to recognize the potential of online courses for providing access to advanced courses, low-incidence courses, courses for credit recovery, and courses designed for students with special circumstances. They are also recognizing the advantages of blended learning, such as expanding learning time (Cavanaugh, 2009).

About 28 states now have state virtual schools that offer courses that would otherwise be unavailable. District-led online learning programs have emerged as the fastest-growing type of online learning program. These programs frequently incorporate blended learning (Watson, Murin, Vashaw, Gemin, & Rapp, 2012). As online and blended learning programs proliferate, challenges to ensuring equitable access to courses continue to grow.

In this chapter, we argue that online and blended education and virtual schools can be a critical tool in our search for equitable education across all aspects of our public education system, and caution that without proper planning, virtual schools could perpetuate or even exacerbate disparities in our system. We present three major themes: equitable access to technology, equitable access to online courses, and equitable access to quality instruction. Our focus is on U.S. K–12 education; those interested in international equitable-access issues should consult Cavanaugh's foreword and Chapter 13 in this volume.

Equitable Access to Technology

Equitable access to technology, including access to the Internet through reliable, high-speed connections and to sufficiently fast and enabled computers at the student level, is an essential component of providing equitable access to online information, including online courses. The challenge of equitable access to technology has changed as our definitions of *technology* have evolved. "Universal service" was a key component of the Communications Act of 1934 promulgated by the Federal Communications Commission (FCC, 1934) that focused on equitable telephone service. In the 1980s, when computers began to be more than just a novelty in classrooms, educators talked about tech equity and the "information haves and have-nots." At that time, the most advanced schools were using Apple IIe or Commodore PET computers with 5½-inch floppy discs and 64 KB of RAM. The National Telecommunications and Information Administration (NTIA, 1994) published *Falling Through the Net*, the first major survey analyzing information haves and have-nots. By 1998 the term *digital divide* was a commonplace reference to the gap between people with access to computers and people without it (Hoffman, Novak, & Schlosser, 2000).

Since then, that definition has evolved further, first to include the division between schools that had Internet access and those that did not. By 2008, 98% of schools had Internet access (U.S. Department of Education, National Center for Education Statistics, 2010). More recently, the digital divide has come to describe the disparity between schools that have high-speed Internet access and truly sufficient computing capacity and those that do not. Computing capacity means everything from the capacity of broadband coming into the school to the number of computers of sufficient speed and capacity available for student use. For online courses in particular, access to technology must also include sufficiently flexible firewalls and filtering systems that do not prohibit students from accessing critical interactive tools and multimedia. Without attention to the fundamental access issues, the potential exists for online courses to become just another way to separate haves and have-nots, rather than a tool to help address disparities in educational opportunity.

For the purposes of virtual schooling, we focus specifically on students' ability to access and use technology with sufficient frequency and bandwidth to take advantage of all that online courses have to offer. The National Center for Education Statistics reports that since 1999 there have been virtually no differences in school access to the Internet by school characteristics (U.S. Department of Education, National Center for Education Statistics, 2006), and that by 2005 94% of all public school instructional rooms had access to the Internet (U.S. Department of Education, National Center for Education Statistics, 2010). However, "access" at this level may mean that a school is considered "connected" when it has only one computer dedicated to administrative functions involving e-mail or submitting state reports. The U.S. Department of Education's *National Educational Technology Plan* (2010) recognizes that equity at that level is insufficient for truly providing all students and teachers "access to a comprehensive infrastructure for learning when and where they need it" (p. 61), and sets that as a major goal. Similarly, the FCC's *National Broadband Plan* recognizes the limitations of the current e-Rate program and recommends lifting restrictions that prevent off-hours access to e-Rate-funded resources, expanding access to tribal libraries, and otherwise removing barriers to schools and specific populations.

Broadband access, a problem especially severe in rural areas, is an important starting point to provide sufficient access to information in all of its multimedia forms. Recent efforts by the U.S. federal government to facilitate broadband access and by media and telecommunications companies to reach more customers provide hope at this particular phase of our digital divide. As the chairman of the FCC stated in a video introducing the *National Broadband Plan*,

> We are lagging in critical ways: not everyone is connected, not everyone who has access subscribes, not everyone has the digital skills they need to participate in a 21st-century networked economy, and the speeds of our networks are not world class. (Genachowski, 2010)

Simply put, Americans must be provided affordable broadband at speeds sufficient for meaningful use, no matter where they live or how much money they make. Many areas of the country still lack broadband access that supports providing education leading to digital literacy for all students. Most schools in the country are at T1 (1.54 Mbps) connection speeds between school buildings, which is insufficient for accommodating the technology needs of concurrent users of emerging technologies. Bandwidth requirements per user can quickly compromise access for students and teachers engaged in digital learning activities, and administrators are wise to calculate bandwidth needs carefully (State Education Technology Directors Association, 2008). One such tool, the School 2.0 (n.d.) Bandwidth Calculator, may be particularly useful.

Another challenge to equitable access for students has been created by the very people charged with providing students with that access. Many well-intentioned administrators and technology coordinators in schools attempt to protect students from the perceived and actual evils online by deliberately limiting students' Internet access through school policies, firewalls, and filters. These actions may prevent students from accessing social networking sites, video services, or even sites that present extreme perspectives on controversial issues. These forms of censorship result in far more limited Internet access at school than many students have at home. Thus, a disparity is created between the types of information and resources available to the students who have access at home and those who do not. In terms of online courses, these same policies and practices can result in limited access to course resources at school, thereby creating disparities in the level of participation available to various students.

Schools justify censorship, sometimes legitimately and sometimes not, with concerns about computer viruses, bandwidth usage, potential student exposure to obscene material, cyberbullying, and other technical and safety reasons. Nevertheless, the result is still to create, rather than eliminate, disparities in the level of information available to various groups of students.

Access and equity to technology and high-speed broadband is now enhanced by the proliferation of portable devices. No longer must schools spend $1,500 on a computer when far less expensive smartphones, tablets, and other small portable devices are bringing the Internet into classrooms, homes, and many students' hands. Although many schools still ban the use or even possession of cell phones in school, more progressive and creative schools are tapping into the power of such devices to provide valuable educational experiences that go beyond the classroom walls. School administrators must still be cautious about assuming that all their students have access to such technologies, even if they have a population with high SES. There are parts of the country without cellular phone coverage, let alone 3G or 4G coverage. The *National Education Technology Plan* suggests that "schools can also solve the equity issue—concern that affluent students will have devices and others will not—by purchasing devices just for the students who need such financial support" (U.S. Department of Education, 2010, p. 54).

Creative use of such tools can clearly help address the digital divide. New generations of online courses that can be taken on portable devices provide lower costs, greater flexibility, and greater access to many more students.

Equitable Access to Online Courses

Our public education system has long reflected the racial, ethnic, and socioeconomic differences and divisions in our society. The undeniable intersections and overlaps among race, SES, and geography have been extensively documented, discussed, and analyzed. Many of the school busing programs that began in the 1960s following the landmark *Brown v. Board of Education* ruling (1954) were an attempt to provide equitable access to high-quality education. Despite the fact that remedies through busing have been very expensive and have had only mixed success in many areas, busing is still the primary tool that schools have as they attempt to blur the lines among SES, race, and educational quality that perpetuate disparities in opportunity. Achievement gaps—the difference in achievement between minority and nonminority students, particularly gaps between White students and Black students—continue to frustrate many school districts and our nation as a whole.

Fully online education removes the geographic boundaries that traditional on-ground education must face. Online education isn't the panacea for solving the educational equity problems in today's schools, but by blurring the geographic lines that have defined our system for so long, online education has the potential to be a stronger, more effective, and certainly less expensive solution to our nation's educational equity issues than busing has been. Toward this end, the *National Broadband Plan* (FCC, 2010) calls upon the U.S. Department of Education to "fund the development of innovative broadband-based online learning solutions" (p. 244).

The information regarding who is taking online courses is limited. Many part-time online programs do not feel they need to collect demographic data, and only a small number do so voluntarily. Even for public school programs, there is no requirement that online programs track data separately. While a survey of several hundred online programs in the country resulted in only 12 programs being willing or able to supply demographic data (Glick, 2010), a subsequent survey (Glick, 2011) drew responses from 139 U.S. programs. The 2010 survey suggests that minority students, particularly those self-identifying as African American, are taking online courses at higher rates than their White counterparts, relative to their representation in national K–12 populations. However, Glick's 2011 survey is probably more representative. It suggests that African American participation in online learning (16%) is slightly lower than in national K–12 populations overall (17%), while White participation (59%) is higher than in national populations (55%). However, this data is preliminary and does not include any related information on student achievement. This leaves a large hole in our knowledge about the effectiveness of online learning to bridge the relevant gaps (Rose & Blomeyer, 2007). Programs should watch for specific demographic patterns of enrollment or of student failures or withdrawals that could raise a flag of concern.

Administrators often feel that it takes a special student to take advantage of online education. In a situation where the available spaces in online courses are limited or incur additional cost, it's normal to want to see those courses used by students who will take advantage of the opportunity. This leads many programs to use initial surveys or assessments with a title like, "Is Online Learning Right for Me?" We believe this approach is misguided and may lead to unintentional biases in the online program.

Our opposition to the use of such pretests is not only because the question lacks the context of on-ground schools, but also because this is clearly the wrong question. Rather than "Is online learning right for me?" students should be asked, "What support systems do you need to be successful in online learning?" From the program or administrative perspective, the question should not be, "Will this student succeed?" but rather, "What do we need to have in place to ensure that this student *will* succeed?"

Of course, schools should be asking these questions for online as well as on-ground programs, and many are. These questions assume that all students can succeed if the right tools are in place, thus leading to programs that will be able to more equitably provide access to the opportunities that online education can bring to the students, without denying access based on preconceived notions.

Furthermore, instruments revised in the ways we are suggesting, rather than serving as gatekeepers, can help students assess their strengths, better understand their preferred learning style, and identify areas where they might have to work harder to be successful. Of course, this information would be beneficial for students' on-ground coursework as well. Schools might find on-ground students asking why they don't have access to that same type of information.

This approach is also safer from a legal perspective. A program that uses an assessment instrument as a hurdle to enrollment in online courses is risking serious legal problems. If instruments are used as admission criteria and the results of the assessment are used to deny students access to online courses, the program may face consequences if students in any protected group are denied access to public education. The existing instruments haven't been validated for use as entrance gatekeepers, and the instruments make assumptions about what an online course requires of students. While course prerequisites are acceptable, entrance exams or surveys used in this manner should be approached with intense skepticism and trepidation.

One Washington State school district was cited by the U.S. Department of Education's Office for Civil Rights after denying special-needs students access to the school's online education program (Special Ed Connection, 2007). Among other discriminatory practices, the school's unwritten criteria for admission screened out disabled students with documented inability to complete schoolwork independently or a documented reading-writing ability level below sixth or seventh grade. This practice eventually cost the district a great deal of time and money, and the negative publicity also had a detrimental impact on the school system. Ultimately, it had to reverse the policy as there was no justification for categorically denying special-needs students access to the school's online education courses.

Providing online learning courses that are not otherwise available can increase graduation rates, better prepare students for college, and increase college eligibility. In a study of the Digital Learning Commons (DLC) in Washington State, Baker, Fouts, Gratama, Clay, and Scott (2006) found that 76% of the classes that students enrolled in for online learning were not otherwise available at their local school. These courses consisted primarily of electives or advanced high school courses. Of the courses not available, 24% were taken because of scheduling conflicts with on-ground sections. Additionally, 33% of high school seniors in the study would not have graduated without taking an online course from the DLC during the study year of 2004–2005. Out of all the courses taken online, 32% were at the advanced high school level, and 26% earned dual high school and college credit, thus better preparing students for college. Furthermore, 5% of online courses taken resulted in increased college eligibility for students applying to a postsecondary institution upon graduation.

A recent survey conducted for the Sloan-C Foundation found administrators turning to online learning as a critical solution for rural districts that need to meet the needs of a wide range of students in small schools (Piccianno & Seaman, 2009). "The loudest and clearest voices were those of respondents representing small school districts where online learning is not simply an attractive alternative to face-to-face instruction, but increasingly is becoming a lifeline to basic high quality education," the report says. Without online learning, one survey respondent stated, "There may have been 40 fewer high school graduates in our small county last year" (p. 25).

Online programs can also provide opportunities for targeted programs designed to address particular learning styles or provide information on topics not available in traditional programs, making the curriculum more relevant and more accessible to particular student populations through instructional approach or cultural relevance. These programs can provide supplemental education or full programs. The number of special-focus programs is growing as these are now an accepted part of the online learning landscape. Online programs focus on Christian students, Native American students, urban students, and GLBTQ students. These choice schools provide an education customized to meet the needs of their particular target populations, while building communities from geographically dispersed areas where the numbers are so small that insufficient people are available to support such targeted programs locally.

The FCC (2010) referred to "digital exclusion" in the *National Broadband Plan* as an obstacle that marginalized groups must overcome if they want to compete for jobs, access

> The **Fort Washakie High School** on the Wind River Indian Reservation in Wyoming blends online courses with Native Ways of Knowing to achieve greater success with the Native American students who attend that blended online school.
>
> **GLBTQ Online High School** is designed specifically for students who are gay, lesbian, bisexual, transgender, or questioning their gender or sexual identity.

health information, receive 21st-century education, and have real-time information that is readily available in digital form. Our goal to reach all students challenges us to consider how marginalized groups such as low-income and minority students, English-language learners, and learners with disabilities interact with digital learning environments. The advances in language translation technology, alternative presentation formats (e.g., use of image, video, and audio), and new assistive technologies can improve opportunities to learn for these groups, as well as provide access to computers and networks in libraries, community centers, and after-school labs for those without these resources at home. Schools need to be aware of their responsibility to provide equal access to the necessary instructional materials, tools, and resources for all students to succeed.

There is a misconception that because students can't see each other, students don't experience discrimination in online courses. A small body of research reports on patterns of racial, ethnic, and gender equity issues in online courses at the higher education and adult professional development levels. An interesting study was conducted on services provided online by reference librarians (Shachaf & Horowitz, 2006). The study reported that library patrons were provided different levels of service based solely on the perceived ethnicity of the patron, centered entirely on the name of the patron. In the study, they made the same request for information with the only change being the name of the requestor. Differences were noted in speed of response, amount of information provided, and tone of the response. Unintentional biases based on stereotypes exist in society and impact the way we deal with people who are not like us. There is no reason to expect that K–12 online education is free from such biases. Thus, while online programs may eliminate some such issues, online programs need to maintain vigilance toward such unintentional biases that can discourage some learners and, in doing so, limit the desirability of an online program for the very students it was designed to reach.

Equitable Access to Quality Instruction

Equitable access to quality instruction implies that all students are receiving instruction from highly qualified teachers, as defined under the No Child Left Behind Act of 2001 (2002), and that the instruction addresses each student's learning needs on an individual or small-group basis, usually referred to as "differentiation." In the on-ground classroom, differentiation involves modification of curriculum and instruction for different learning styles, as well as a great deal of classroom management to handle the range of paces and abilities present in any typical classroom. The challenges of managing a classroom in this way, while maintaining the instructional pace specified by the school district to prepare students for high-stakes testing, has resulted, based on our own observations in schools, in a discouragingly small number of classrooms where instruction is truly and effectively differentiated.

In addition, on-ground teachers are expected to adapt their instruction as they integrate special-needs students into their classes. Due to competing demands, many students don't have access to *high-quality instruction* as we have defined it: instruction that meets each student's individual needs. A well-designed online course that incorporates effective online pedagogy can do more than just *allow* a natural differentiation; it can, in fact, encourage it and provide for an ease of management not possible in the typical on-ground classroom. Individualized pacing, multiple modes of learning for different learning styles, and the application of the principles of universal design for learning can ensure high-quality online courses that address equity and access issues.

A simple example of the instructional benefits of online learning can be found in the format of student-student discussions. In a traditional classroom, discussions are normally time-limited and can be fast-paced and intimidating for many students, especially those who are more reflective thinkers. As a result, it is often the case that a few personalities dominate the face-to-face classroom discussion. This outcome can also occur in online learning, where "some students will attempt to dominate the discussion" (Palloff & Pratt, 2001, p. 113). Online teachers may need to redirect this behavior at times. However, in an asynchronous online environment, the pace of discussion allows all students time to reflect on the issues before responding. This places the less assertive students on a more equitable footing and increases everyone's learning as more viewpoints are included.

Finding effective online teachers requires more than simply assigning the best on-ground teacher to put his or her course online. Online teachers need to understand online pedagogy and the unique challenges of teaching students they cannot see.

Training in online course design and instruction can also help to improve on-ground instruction. Research has found that on-ground teachers who participate in professional development to prepare them to become online teachers experience a transformation in their face-to-face teaching in terms of pedagogy, assessment techniques, and content (Lowes, 2008).

Equitable access to online education depends on having well-qualified teachers available to teach the courses. As reported in the *National Education Technology Plan* (U.S. Department of Education, 2010), "The least effective educators are most likely to be teaching in schools serving students from homes that are economically and educationally disadvantaged" (p. 47). Many schools struggle to find highly qualified teachers in every subject and to ensure that students have access to a wide range of courses. Almy and Theokas (2010) found fewer highly qualified teachers in high-poverty schools.

All school administrators face the problem of having the teacher and classroom resources available to offer all the courses students would like to have. The problem is more severe in smaller secondary schools, often in rural areas, where they have to make decisions about offering courses with limited enrollments. Some districts are also joining together to form regional online learning consortia to share teaching assignments and courses taught by qualified teachers.

Administrators wanting to create online educational programs rather than join an existing program have several options for staffing their program with highly qualified online designers and teachers. Programs can provide professional development for existing teachers, hire teachers who already possess the training and skills in online instruction and technologies, and even contract with online course providers for specific courses or seats in courses that the school is unable to offer. Administrators might then consider the creation of a locally staffed online and blended learning program as a component of a total school improvement plan.

Conclusion

The focus on equity and access is ultimately about improving student learning. Online education has been represented in this chapter as a tool to improve student learning by increasing opportunities, eliminating the constraints imposed on brick-and-mortar programs, and providing more opportunity for diversified teaching and individualized instruction.

Although online courses and programs will not solve all of our education woes, well-designed online courses and programs can provide far greater access to equitable education. If students are provided with sufficient access to computers, sufficient computing power, and broadband access, then geography and educational quality no longer have to go hand in hand. Students in the poorest rural district or most dilapidated urban school building can, through online courses, access the same courses and learning opportunities as those provided to the most privileged suburban kids with greater socioeconomic advantages.

School administrators need to ensure that their school has the appropriate ratio of computers to students and that all students can use these tools effectively. This matter cannot be left to chance or depend on an individual teacher's technology comfort level. Technology use in general and with online courses in particular is a 21st-century literacy. A school's technology plan should account for the increasing demand for greater high-speed Internet bandwidth, up-to-date computer hardware, current releases of software, and the skills and support needed to make optimal use of educational technologies to become literate in today's digitally connected world.

Administrators need to be prepared to counter the urban legend that only a special type of student is successful in online education, and only those students should be allowed to participate in online education. Another common myth is that online courses aren't as rigorous or effective as on-ground instruction, so only those students who aren't as valued should be placed in online courses. Online courses should hold the same credit value, class rank status, and cache as equivalent on-ground courses. If the perception is that online education isn't as good as the on-ground option, then the resources to ensure parity may not be provided, and can create a separate and unequal situation that will relegate those students taking online courses to second-class-student status.

Many online education skeptics make statements like, "Online education isn't for everyone." While this is true, the same is equally true for on-ground education. There is ample evidence that on-ground schools don't meet the needs of—and fail—many students. Online students and parents often comment on the welcomed rigor of online courses and students' improved attitudes about school.

Well-designed online courses can be highly personalized and can include a great deal of peer interaction and individualized support from the teacher. Effective online teaching requires special skills and training. Administrators have a variety of options for ensuring that online instructors are highly qualified and prepared to teach online.

Thomas Friedman's (2005) best-seller *The World Is Flat* pointed out that the workplace is no longer predominantly local. Students will enter a workforce where global teamwork and online training are the norm, and schools need to help students understand and prepare for that reality. One of the best ways to help students expand their awareness of the world is through exposure to the resources and tools available on the Internet and in online coursework.

References

Almy, S., & Theokas, C. (2010). *Not prepared for class: High-poverty schools continue to have fewer in-field teachers*. Washington, DC: Education Trust. Retrieved from http://files.eric.ed.gov/fulltext/ED543217.pdf

Baker, D. B., Fouts, J. T., Gratama, C. A., Clay, J. N., & Scott, S. G. (2006). *Digital Learning Commons: High school seniors' online course taking patterns in Washington State*. Seattle: Fouts and Associates.

Brown v. Board of Education., 347 U.S. 483 (1954).

Cavanaugh, C. (2009, May). *Getting students more learning time online*. Washington, DC: Center for American Progress. Retrieved from http://www.americanprogress.org/wp-content/uploads/issues/2009/05/pdf/distancelearning.pdf

Federal Communications Commission. (1934). *Communications Act of 1934*. 47 U.S.C. 214(e) Provision of Universal Service. Retrieved from http://www.fcc.gov/Reports/1934new.pdf

Federal Communications Commission. (2010). *National Broadband Plan*. Washington, DC: Author. Retrieved from http://www.fcc.gov/national-broadband-plan

Friedman, T. H. (2005). *The world is flat*. New York: Farrar.

Genachowski, J. (2010). *Julius Genachowski*. Washington, DC: Federal Communications Commission. Online video. Retrieved from http://www.broadband.gov/plan

Glick, D. (2010). *Survey of demographics of online programs*. Maplewood, MN: David B. Glick & Associates.

Glick, D. (2011). *The demographics of online students and teachers in the United States 2010–11*. Maplewood, MN: David B. Glick & Associates. Retrieved from http://glickconsulting.com/sites/default/files/images/Online_Demographics_Glick_2011.pdf

Hoffman, D. L., Novak, T. P., & Schlosser, A. E. (2000, March). The evolution of the digital divide: How gaps in Internet access may impact electronic commerce. *Journal of Computer-Mediated Communication, 5*(3). Retrieved from http://jcmc.indiana.edu/vol5/issue3/hoffman.html

Lowes, S. (2008). Online teaching and classroom change: The impact of Virtual High School on its teachers and their schools. *Innovate: Journal of Online Education, 4*(3). Retrieved from http://innovateonline.info

National Telecommunications and Information Administration. (1994). *Falling through the net: Defining the digital divide*. Washington, DC: U.S. Department of Commerce. Retrieved from http://www.ntia.doc.gov/ntiahome/fttn99

No Child Left Behind Act of 2001, 20 U.S.C. § 6301 et seq. (2002).

Palloff, R., & Pratt, K. (2001). *Lessons from the cyberspace classroom: The realities of online teaching*. San Francisco: Jossey-Bass.

Picciano, G., & Seaman, J. (2009). *K–12 online learning*. Newburyport, MA: Babson Research Group, CUNY, and the Sloan Consortium. Retrieved from http://sloanconsortium.org/sites/default/files/K-12_online_learning_2008.pdf

Rose, R. M., & Blomeyer, R. L. (2007). *Access and equity in online classes and virtual schools.* Vienna, VA: International Association for K–12 Online Learning. Retrieved from http://www.inacol.org/research/docs/NACOL_EquityAccess.pdf

School 2.0. (n.d.). *Bandwidth calculator.* Menlo Park, CA: SRI International. Retrieved from http://etoolkit.org/etoolkit/bandwidth_calculator

Shachaf, P., & Horowitz, S. (2006). Are virtual reference services color blind? *Library and Information Science Research, 28*(4), 501–520.

Special Ed Connection. (2007, November 16). *Case Report 108 LRP 17959, Quillayute Valley (WA) School District Office of Civil Rights, Western Division, Seattle (Washington), 10-06-1196.* Palm Beach Gardens, FL: LRP Publications.

State Education Technology Directors Association. (2008, June). *High-speed broadband access for all kids: Breaking through the barriers.* Glen Burnie, MD: Author. Retrieved from http://www.setda.org/c/document_library/get_file?folderId=270&name=DLFE-211.pdf

U.S. Department of Education. (2010). *National education technology plan: Transforming American education: Learning powered by technology.* Washington, DC: Author. Retrieved from http://www.ed.gov/technology/netp-2010

U.S. Department of Education, National Center for Education Statistics. (2006). *Internet access in U.S. public schools and classrooms: 1994–2005. Fast facts.* Washington, DC: Author. Retrieved from http://nces.ed.gov/fastfacts/display.asp?id=46

U.S. Department of Education, National Center for Education Statistics. (2010). *Educational technology in U.S. public schools: Fall 2008.* Washington, DC: Author. Retrieved from nces.ed.gov/pubs2010/2010034.pdf

Watson, J., Murin, A., Vashaw, L., Gemin, B., & Rapp, C. (2012). *Keeping pace with K–12 online & blended learning: A review of state-level policy and practice.* Durango, CO: Evergreen Education Group.

Appendix: Access and Equity Checklist

This checklist will help administrators ensure that the basic equity and access issues have been addressed as they design and supervise their online education programs.

Equitable Access to Technology

- Every classroom has access to broadband connections and sufficient computers to allow students access.
- There are sufficient computers with high-speed computer access, and are available in public spaces, to allow students to complete assignments even if they don't have a home computer or Internet access outside of school. These computers are available outside normal school hours.
- If necessary, a suitable number of computers are available to lend to students who do not otherwise have access to computers.
- Partnerships with public libraries, local colleges, businesses, or other organizations provide additional options for students without Internet access at home to engage in coursework outside the normal school day.

Equitable Access to Online Courses

Gatekeeping

- If initial applications or entrance surveys are in place, they are used to determine what support systems each student may need in order to be successful in online courses. There are no student assessments (formal or informal) that are used to deny student access to virtual education opportunities or reinforce preconceived notions about who can be successful in online courses.
- Guidance counselors, Individualized Education Plan (IEP) teams, and others who influence student enrollment in virtual education programs and courses are prepared to address the negative assumptions about online education that adversely impact student enrollment, and have identified the support systems possible and available to help ensure student success.

Home Access

- There are no requirements that students must have a home computer with Internet access in order to participate in online and blended education programs.

Design

- Course design standards based on Universal Design for Learning or other established practice are used in course design and selection to ensure that course material is accessible.

- The program trains course designers in the course design standards and monitors compliance with the standards.
- Multiple instructional approaches that address various learning styles are included in all courses.
- Culturally relevant content for a variety of student populations is included throughout coursework.

Demographics

- The virtual education program collects and publishes disaggregated demographic and special-needs information about student enrollment by program and course.
- Student success and information about student drops, withdrawals, and failures are reported by disaggregated demographics and special-needs categories.
- The program analyzes enrollment data as one element used for course and program modifications.
- The virtual education program has a special-needs policy or the existing special-needs policy includes a section on virtual education to ensure that special-needs students and students with handicaps can be accommodated.

Equitable Access to Quality Instruction

- All online teachers are highly qualified under federal No Child Left Behind standards.
- Teachers know how to differentiate online instruction as appropriate to meet individual learner needs.
- Teachers have the skills and training needed for effective online instruction.
- Administrators have options for staffing their online and blended learning program with teachers who are highly qualified and prepared to teach online.

PART THREE
Case Studies on Practice

8

A CASE STUDY OF EXTERNAL EVALUATION IN SUPPORT OF A NEW VIRTUAL SCHOOL

Kevin Oliver and Tracy Weeks

In this chapter we present a case study of the evolution of a new virtual school as informed by program- and project-level evaluation. Evaluation can help online learning providers improve their programs and encourage student success. In this chapter we introduce evaluation approaches and results specific to the North Carolina Virtual Public School (NCVPS) during its startup period (2007–2009), and discuss how the evaluation findings developed by teams at North Carolina State University helped the school reconsider its approaches to course design, teaching, policy, and more.

NCVPS is a state-funded organization providing well over 100 online and blended courses at no cost to in-state public school students, as well as students in Department of Defense or Bureau of Indian Affairs schools. The organization serves students who are unable to take a course at their regular school for any number of reasons (e.g., not offered at all, not offered when needed to meet graduation requirements, illness, homebound). State-licensed teachers lead all NCVPS courses, and students receive credit for completed courses on their regular school transcript. Current courses serve primarily high school and some middle school students. Courses are offered at several levels (e.g., occupational course of study [OCS], credit recovery, general studies, honors, and Advanced Placement) and in numerous content areas (e.g., arts, career and technical, English, health, math, science, social studies, test prep, world languages).

From its inception in summer 2007, NCVPS has forged partnerships with external evaluators to help solicit feedback from its stakeholders and review new pilot initiatives. Funds supporting evaluation work have largely come from the organization's own budget or from special contracts distributed by the state's Department of Public Instruction (NCDPI). NCVPS also staffs a small internal evaluation group that tracks progress on organizational goals with reporting to the state.

In this case study, selected findings are summarized from NCVPS evaluations led by faculty, staff, and graduate students affiliated with the Friday Institute for Educational Innovation at North Carolina State University. The case also includes reactions from NCVPS's executive director on the importance of external evaluation findings to the organization and decisions influenced by the findings. The partnership first began during NCVPS's start-up period and continues with new pilot efforts today. The following list summarizes completed and ongoing evaluation efforts along with reports and publications, where available, for each study:

- End of summer 2007, the first NCVPS term, program-level evaluation across all courses end of 2007–2008, program-level evaluation across all courses.
- Winter 2009, targeted project evaluation of course development teams building blended courses for the elementary and middle grades.
- End of 2008–2009, program-level evaluation across all courses offered.
- Summer 2009, program-level evaluation across all courses offered.
- Within summer 2009 survey, two survey branches target foreign language and math participants specifically to probe significantly lower ratings of these subject-area courses, while another targets credit recovery students.
- End of 2009–2010, targeted project evaluation of students exposed to a pilot freshman transition course (Oliver, 2010).
- 2011–present, targeted project evaluation of three local education agencies piloting new STEM courses and an instructional blend of online and face-to-face teachers.
- 2011–present, proposed, targeted project evaluation of NCVPS's OCS blended courses delivered to exceptional students, with teacher and parental surveys, classroom observations, and student focus group.

Methodological Summary

Participants

Across the varied evaluations, data were collected primarily from online students and teachers, teachers hired as course developers, and e-learning advisors (ELAs). ELAs represent existing school staff in each state high school who are paid a stipend to assist NCVPS with screening, registering, and advising online students at their schools. High school principals were also invited to complete surveys about NCVPS courses in their schools, but response rates were generally too low to summarize (~5%) and therefore are not emphasized in evaluation reports or publications.

General Design, Data Sources, and Questions

Most of the program-level evaluations discussed in this case were based on a mixed-methods concurrent triangulation design where quantitative data (i.e., multiple survey questions on a five-point Likert scale) and qualitative data (i.e., open-ended questions) bore equal weight and were used to corroborate one another (Creswell & Clark, 2007). Surveys were the most common data source across evaluations, with original questions developed in consultation with NCVPS staff to inform the organization's strategic goals (i.e., enrollment and assessment targets; trained teaching/advising professionals;

stakeholder satisfaction with academics and the online environment, including both content and teaching; and supportive systems). Surveys also probed student preparation for and barriers to online learning. Aside from surveys, teacher focus groups were also used in one evaluation of teacher course development efforts.

Many question items were first tested in summer 2007 surveys and then refined in subsequent iterations. Questions were aligned across survey groups where possible, to allow for comparison (e.g., students, teachers, and ELAs might all be asked the same question about student learning to see if one group differed from the others). In our surveys, we also found it useful to collect a variety of demographic data about students and teachers, as this enabled grouping participants to look for any significant differences in response (e.g., Do students at one course level report a different amount of course rigor compared to students at other levels? Do students with access to a computer in the home report more success in online courses than students dependent on computers in the school?). Demographics used for grouping purposes included

- Level of online course taken (or taught): credit recovery, regular, honors, Advanced Placement.
- Subject of online course taken (or taught): math, science, English, foreign language, social studies, and so on.
- Number of online courses taken (or taught) prior to a given semester: experienced with online versus nonexperienced.
- Year in school (or number of years teaching): academically experienced student/teacher versus nonexperienced.
- Self-reported grades typically received in school: mostly As, mostly Bs, and so on.
- Self-reported technology skills compared to other kids' (or teachers').
- Primary method of online connection to course: dial-up, cable modem, network at school, public wifi.
- Primary computer used for coursework: owned at home, loaned for home, in the school, in a public facility or library.
- Home zip code (rural versus urban low-income district versus median-income district).
- Ethnicity.
- Gender.

General Analytical Approaches

A variety of analytical approaches were used across the different evaluation studies. Descriptive statistics were computed for most survey results, reporting means for each question item on a five-point Likert scale ranging from strongly disagree to strongly agree. To compare group means, statistical procedures such as analysis of variance (ANOVA) were employed with post-hoc testing to reveal specific group differences. One study employed logistic regression to determine if group membership (e.g., credit recovery student) could be used to predict other variables (e.g., low technology proficiency). Open-ended comments on surveys and focus group transcripts were analyzed using qualitative approaches. These findings were imported into the NVivo qualitative analysis program and open-coded in a manner consistent with grounded theory. Preconceived coding schemes were not employed. In one evaluation of teacher course development teams, cross-case analysis was employed, looking across development teams for general trends.

Selected Evaluation Findings With NCVPS Reactions

Reviewing evaluation findings along with program responses to those findings provides an opportunity to learn about program challenges, best practices, and lessons learned. In this section we summarize key evaluation findings from various NCVPS studies, with NCVPS indicating how the findings were useful to help revise practice and develop new policies and procedures. Key findings have been sorted into the following topic areas: student preparation and advising, student strategies in online courses, differences in student groups, content and course development, logistical and technical issues, and teaching.

Student Preparation and Advising

Results

A variety of student preparation issues were reported to NCVPS, including lack of technical expertise, reading proficiency, and self-directedness/motivation in some students. Such findings could be useful to NCVPS to better screen students and to design appropriate support interventions. For example, in summer 2007, 18.7% of students rated their computer skills as fair or poor, illustrating the need to screen for appropriate technical skills when advising and enrolling students in online courses (Osborne, Oliver, Patel, & Holcomb, 2007). First, students recommended receiving technical requirements before enrolling in online courses, including computing and software requirements, and they recommended an orientation to course management systems. Second, a few teachers suggested students may require a certain reading proficiency to succeed in text-heavy online courses, indicating that reading ability may be another variable to screen for prior to enrollment. Third, many teachers believed that students lacked time management skills and could not handle the self-pacing required in online courses (Oliver, Osborne, Patel, & Kleiman, 2008). With limits in student self-direction, study participants suggested two potential interventions: more involved teaching through two-way conferencing tools and teacher reminders, and better orienting to course requirements and activities (Oliver, Osborne, Patel, & Kleiman, 2008).

Every high school in North Carolina has a designated staff member serving as the school's ELA. Only 27% of ELAs reported being in a full-time ELA position, however, suggesting these persons serve multiple roles and likely have divided interests (Oliver, Brady, Patel, & Townsend, 2009). ELAs reported on the tasks that consumed the majority of their time: counseling students to keep them on task (including communication with teachers and parents), monitoring student grades, and developing precourse activities such as orientation and registration (Oliver, Brady, Patel, & Osborne, 2008). More than a quarter of students reported that a lack of advising support at their schools was a barrier to taking NCVPS courses, indicating a need to set better expectations for the ELA role across the state (Oliver, Brady, Patel, & Townsend, 2009). Teachers recommended that NCVPS require ELAs to remain in contact with students and parents, and increase ELA professional development to better screen and support students (Oliver, Brady, Patel, & Osborne, 2008). ELAs recommended that NCVPS provide them with better teacher contact information, better registration procedures, better access to course management systems to monitor student grades (or auto-generated progress reports of advisees), a formal student screening process, standardized requirements for student or lab computers that would function with their courses, and a listing of websites and domains to unblock.

Reactions

NCVPS took this information on student preparation and advising and set out to provide students and ELAs with better tools for successfully taking and advising about online courses. To prepare students for the first day of their online course, the course is opened a few days before the scheduled start date for a "Meet the Teacher" experience. During Meet the Teacher, students can access a Getting Started Module that provides them with an orientation to the course and the technology needed to complete it. Additionally, teachers use these days to reach out and make an initial synchronous contact with each student in order to introduce themselves, make sure the student has been able to log into the course successfully, and answer any additional questions the student may have. Teachers continue to make synchronous contacts with students each week or more frequently if needed.

To prepare the ELA and other school staff to best support students in their online courses, NCVPS implemented several solutions. First, NCVPS developed a Getting Started module for the school-level ELA or the district level e-learning coordinator (ELC). This module helps the school contacts understand the registration process, the technology used in the courses, and the reporting cycles for NCVPS. Second, NCVPS now publishes all technical requirements for each course along with a master list of all websites that are necessary for each course. It encourages school technology staff to install all necessary software and plug-ins on student computers and ensure that required URLs will be accessible through local web filters. Third, NCVPS now provides a biweekly grade report for all students to the ELAs that notes the current grade and whether there are any missing assignments, which gives schools information they need to support students and catch them before they fall too far behind. Fourth, because of the growth in student enrollment over the past five years, interacting with each school-level ELA on an individual and regular basis became unscalable for NCVPS. Therefore, NCVPS asked each ELA to designate a district-level ELC who would be the primary point of contact for NCVPS. The ELC would receive contact and training from NCVPS and then work with each school-level ELA to train that person. Fifth, several updates to the NCVPS registration system have made it more user friendly and able to provide better data from the school to NCVPS. Most importantly, NCVPS now receives a statewide data export from the NC Wise data system each week that is uploaded into the registration system so that all the student information is present at the time of registration. ELAs no longer have to input all of the student information; they simply need to find their student in the system and then select the course(s) for registration. While improved integration with

NC Wise did not result from evaluation findings, the improved access to data should be useful in future studies. Finally, beginning with the 2012–2013 academic year, schools may register students for summer, fall, spring, and yearlong courses at the same time. This allows schools to plan student schedules for the entire year.

Student Strategies and Online Courses

Results

Most middle and high school students are entirely new to online learning. They have limited prior experience with the format and limited understanding of expectations (Oliver, Osborne, & Brady, 2009). Findings suggested that students commonly adopted specific learning strategies when taking online courses: most frequently, seeking one-on-one tutoring from adults and less frequently from peers, noting the importance of synchronous tools and to a lesser extent asynchronous tools; studying alone with note taking; reviewing teachers' notes, flash cards, and worksheets; and working with practice problems, exercises, and quizzes. Some online students preferred printed texts to online texts, as they found it difficult to simultaneously attend to online materials and an online text (Oliver, Osborne, Patel, & Kleiman, 2008).

In a focused study of the credit recovery program, students and teachers were asked if their courses might be improved by including 17 different strategies recommended for credit recovery programs (Kellogg & Oliver, under review). Two of the top six strategies involved teacher monitoring of student performance and helping students set course goals. Four of the top six strategies involved modular course designs and self-pacing through shorter mastery-oriented lessons. The least popular strategies involved on-site instruction as a supplement to the online course (e.g., tutors in labs, peer tutoring).

The importance that students placed on synchronous student-teacher communication highlights both the need to provide tools that functionally allow for such interaction as well as professional development for teachers so that they are prepared for and aware of the importance of regular teacher-student interaction. NCVPS online courses clearly contain a considerable amount of self-paced material for which students appreciate opportunities to review, practice, and receive feedback on progress.

Reactions

NCVPS took the information on common student strategies and used it to revise teacher expectations and teacher professional development, and to establish online professional learning communities. NCVPS teacher expectations are outlined in the teacher contract. However, based on this evaluation feedback, three major pillars of online instruction were outlined and communicated in a variety of ways to NCVPS teachers. The three pillars were synchronous contact, meaningful feedback, and instructional announcements. First, synchronous contact outlines the expectation that teachers will make some sort of contact with students each week using synchronous communication methods such as telephone, instant messaging, or the use of meeting tools such as Skype or Wimba Classroom. Teachers maintain a communications log where they track synchronous and asynchronous communications with students, parents, and school-level ELAs.

The second pillar, meaningful feedback, refers to the quality of feedback teachers provide to students on all assignments. Based on the concept of high-yield instructional strategies (Marzano, Pickering, & Pollock, 2001), teachers are expected to go beyond simply letting students know if items are right or wrong. They must provide coaching through the feedback so that students understand what they did wrong, or if they were successful receive encouragement on how to extend the knowledge to the next level.

Finally, the third pillar is instructional announcements. The term *announcements* is lingo specific to Blackboard, the initial learning management system used at NCVPS. With this Blackboard structure, teachers can push out traditional announcements such as upcoming due dates or other bits of information that students need to know. Additionally, teachers can use this construct to post video, images, text, or interactive tools that allow for teachers to reinforce the learning content or focus for the week, or to reteach content on which the class may need more instruction. Using the announcements for instruction rather than just information sharing engages the students and keeps them connected to the course.

To implement the three pillars, teacher professional development was delivered on these topics in multiple formats. In the fall of 2010, teachers were organized into content-specific professional learning communities. The purpose of the communities was to provide teachers with a platform to examine student data, discuss how to use the data to improve both the course and the instruction, and deliver common professional development when needed. Just-in-time modules were delivered on a variety of topics, including the three pillars. Additionally, the three pillars were written into the teacher expectations section of their contracts and reinforced each term during teacher orientation, and as new teachers were hired, they were trained on the pillars. Biweekly spot checks were performed to monitor how well teachers were adhering to the pillars and to provide coaching when needed. Additional 10-hour professional development modules have also been developed as an option for teachers who need to earn continuing education credits for licensure renewal. These PD10 modules often focus on one aspect or more of the three pillars.

Differences in Student Groups

Results

NCVPS evaluation studies revealed two interesting areas of student difference: credit recovery students often responded to surveys differently than students at other course levels, and students taking online courses in certain subject areas (e.g., math and foreign language) often responded to surveys differently than students taking other course types. These differences suggest that some online students face unique challenges that the virtual school may be able to address with specific interventions.

Across multiple studies, students in credit recovery courses were significantly less likely to possess strong technical skills—and significantly more likely to have technical issues that interfered with their coursework—compared to more advanced students (Oliver, Brady, Patel, & Townsend, 2009; Oliver, Osborne, Patel, & Kleiman, 2008; Osborne et al., 2007). Significantly more credit recovery students, between 26% and

30%, agreed that a lack of access to computers at their school was a barrier to taking online courses, and Internet connectivity at school and in the home were barriers. These findings suggest that school computers and networks may have been the primary source of access for some credit recovery students, while other students were better able to leverage technology in the home (Oliver, Brady, Patel, & Townsend, 2009).

Credit recovery students were also shown to possess lower motivation and less interest in taking additional online courses (Oliver, Osborne, Patel, & Kleiman, 2008; Osborne et al., 2007). In summer 2007, teachers of accelerated courses rated student learning significantly more favorably than teachers of credit recovery courses (Osborne et al., 2007). This trend continued through 2009, when 100% of Advanced Placement teachers agreed that students were succeeding online, while only 55.6% of credit recovery teachers agreed that students were succeeding online (Oliver, Brady, Patel, & Townsend, 2009).

In terms of subject-area differences, foreign-language and math students were less likely to agree with teacher quality variables in online courses compared to other subject areas, suggesting they may have held strong expectations for how teachers of these subjects are supposed to interact with students that did not match with the teaching style exhibited online (e.g., foreign-language teachers not modeling a spoken language as expected). Foreign-language and math students reported significantly lower learning online than students in other subjects, and significantly less course support for 21st-century skills (Oliver, Brady, Patel, & Townsend, 2009). In a follow-up survey probing these differences, foreign-language students recommended more teacher modeling of the language, more student-student and student-teacher interaction with opportunities to practice the language, and rapid teacher feedback on questions and assignments (Oliver, Kellogg, & Patel, 2009). Foreign-language students and teachers also suggested that content complexity could have led to reduced perceptions of learning.

In terms of math, students in a follow-up survey suggested that more teacher explanation of mathematical concepts was needed, along with opportunities to communicate with the teacher and peers, and collaborate on projects and assignments (Oliver, Kellogg, & Patel, 2010). As with foreign language, math students also suggested that the content area was particularly difficult and would require more teacher explanation and intervention than some other subject areas to overcome confusion. In addition to the suggested teaching limitations, some findings suggested that foreign-language and math content may have needed improvement as well. English/language arts students reported that their courses supported 21st-century skills the most, while foreign-language and math students reported that their courses supported the same skills the least among six subject areas queried (Oliver, Brady, Patel, & Townsend, 2009).

Reactions

NCVPS used the information on student differences as a driving factor in establishing professional learning communities. In the communities, which were organized by course, teachers were asked to look at data sets and use the information to improve both course content and instructional quality. The research data described previously were some of the earliest data used by the communities. In all areas, but particularly in math, science, and world languages, teachers were tasked with reviewing the number of assignments and the quality of assignments that students were asked to complete in a course. This activity resulted in the elimination of some assignments and the designation of some assignments as critical, while others could be optional or enrichment.

In the early iterations of the communities, teachers were asked to review their course monthly against a specific set of criteria. One month might focus on assignments, another on one of Marzano et al. (2001) high-yield strategies, then on the Web 2.0 tools used in the course, and so on. This focused discussion resulted in recommendations from the communities on how to revise the courses to improve each of those areas. However, because there were no funds for large-scale course revisions, the communities were largely responsible for implementing the revisions in the master version of each course. Unfortunately, the math and world-language courses were the most difficult to revise in this manner, as the content for those courses was purchased from an online vendor and had limited editing capabilities. Therefore, teachers in those areas looked for ways to improve synchronous interaction with their students through the use of Wimba Classroom and Skype.

As mentioned in a previous section, NCVPS also implemented a Getting Started unit for students in order to prepare them for the technical expectations of the course. Teachers began weekly synchronous contacts with students in order to develop relationships and provide encouragement to them. Quality feedback was given on all assignments, and schools were provided with biweekly grade reports and mastery charts so that they could better support their face-to-face students. In addition, NCVPS found that many of the students in the credit recovery courses had an individualized education program (IEP), which meant that the virtual teachers needed to contact the school to determine what modifications were needed for the student. In addition, NCVPS teachers come to an agreement with the local school on which modifications the online course can meet and which need to be met locally. The result is an IEP process that has been formalized and with which all teachers are expected to comply.

Content and Course Development

Results

Considerable comments were received regarding NCVPS course content quality, suggesting some initial problems at start-up in 2007. At start-up in summer 2007, students reported content issues such as spelling errors; assessments misaligned with content; and need for added supplements, including better instructions, detailed notes, sample problems, and/or more actual examples from teachers themselves in the form of virtual lectures or demonstrations (Oliver, Osborne, Patel, & Kleiman, 2008; Osborne et al., 2007). Teachers also reported issues working with a slow and cumbersome grade book, which was occasionally populated with duplicate assignments. In comparing 2008 and 2009 findings, significantly more teachers in 2009 agreed or strongly agreed that course content and assignments were rigorous and that course instructions were clear and helpful, suggesting improvements over time.

Students and teachers reported too many assignments in some courses (up to 150 in early course iterations). Many participants recommended less low-level busywork (e.g., vocabulary, worksheet, and quiz-type activities) and more authentic, real-world projects (Oliver, Brady, Patel, & Osborne, 2008; Oliver, Brady, Patel, & Townsend, 2009; Oliver, Kellogg, & Patel, 2009; Oliver, Osborne, & Brady, 2009; Oliver, Osborne, Patel, & Kleiman, 2008). Teachers recommended fewer assignments so that they could keep up with grading and provide prompt feedback to students.

Students, teachers, and ELAs were asked if NCVPS online courses were supportive of 21st-century skills. Participants generally agreed that courses supported group collaboration and technology literacy skills the most, and civic literacy and understanding of the global world the least (Oliver, Brady, Patel, & Osborne, 2008; Oliver, Brady, Patel, & Townsend, 2009). Possibly owing to the mastery-oriented format of credit recovery courses, significantly fewer credit recovery teachers reported that their courses were supportive of group collaboration and 21st-century collaborative tools such as wikis and blogs. While these findings were clearly content- and level-specific, if NCVPS wished to support a full range of 21st-century skills in each course, further examples and problems that introduced civic and global concepts could have been integrated across courses in general, and further activities and tools supportive of collaboration integrated into credit recovery courses in particular.

In one project evaluation looking less at content and more at the course development process, Oliver, Kellogg, Townsend, and Brady (2010) focused on eight teacher-led teams developing new blended courses for the elementary and middle school levels. Since its inception in 2007, NCVPS has moved toward a position of developing its own courses instead of purchasing courses from commercial entities or other states. Typically, a team of subject-area teachers work in consultation with a research, development, and innovation specialist (RDIS) to develop new offerings. Oliver, Kellogg, Townsend, and Brady (2010) discovered that teacher-developers required several levels of support: specific guidelines and expectations from NCVPS, an understanding of target learners' needs and prerequisite skills, regular feedback on course products, technical expertise from an RDIS to turn Web 2.0 and 3.0 visions into reality, professional development with opportunities for hands-on practice with new tools and concepts, and professional communities with opportunities to collaborate and see what other teams were doing. Further, teacher-developers requested more examples or models of online courses in general, Web 2.0 tools integrated into online courses in particular, and teacher documentation they would need to write to assist other teachers with deploying their courses.

Reactions

In 2011–2012 NCVPS had to prioritize the revision of all courses in order to comply with the new common core and essential standards adopted by the North Carolina State Board of Education, which led to organizational changes in several areas. First, the budget had to be examined and realigned in order to secure funds for these large-scale revisions. This was achieved by eliminating the RDIS contracts and moving from Blackboard to Moodle. The job duties previously assumed by the RDIS were redistributed to a new role, instructional leader, which also replaced the department chair positions. Courses were reviewed prior to revision to determine if the course would need minor, moderate, or major revisions based on how different the new content standards were from the old standards. In addition, a few courses, which had previously relied heavily on vendor-purchased content, really fell to the level of course development rather than course revision.

Second, a formal instructional design model was developed with clear standards in a number of areas for the revision of the courses. Training was provided to the course revision teams on a number of topics, including designing in Moodle, creating learning objects, universal design, quality assessments, and copyright compliance. The course revision teams comprised content developers and a person focused on placing content in Moodle. The teams were supported through a review process by the instructional leader for the course, the division director, a curriculum developer, and two additional staff members who supported Moodle and the development of learning objects. Teams were given a timeline and a cycle of revision that included developing a module, submitting the module for review, revising the module based on feedback, and then moving on to the next module to repeat the process. Future revision teams will also include an instructional reviewer who will review the module from the team for compliance with the instructional design model and copyright.

Course revision teams were allowed to focus primarily on content development rather than the look and feel of the course, as cascading style sheet (CSS) templates were developed for Moodle with a heavy focus on accessibility. Teams were also provided with templates and support for the development of learning objects. Teams could select the preferred learning object and provide the content to be included, and the NCVPS staff would develop the learning object for them to be included in the module. In addition, a small number of online subscriptions were purchased to allow the inclusion of additional objects and resources in the modules.

The research and evaluation results provided from the various studies heavily informed the instructional design model development as well as the support provided to the course revision teams. By taking the course revision process out of the professional learning communities, as described in an earlier section, in which revisions were done for free but lacked strategic guidance, the new revision process allowed for NCVPS to establish standards and hold all courses to the standards. Revision of all courses will take approximately three years to complete, at which time a regular cycle of revision will be implemented. Additional review and evaluation will be employed at that time to inform future revisions.

Logistical and Technical Issues

Results

Findings suggested a number of specific logistical issues to be resolved, primarily during NCVPS's start-up period in 2007 (Osborne et al., 2007). Some students and teachers reportedly did not receive course books and materials before their courses began, particularly credit recovery students, who were already academically challenged; and some students reportedly did not receive log-in information. Teachers reportedly received course rosters with incomplete or incorrect data, and some teachers reported that students were enrolled in course sections and working on assignments for several days before they received notification of the section and log-in information. Evaluation recommendations included ensuring enough time in advance of courses to ship any printed materials to students, to e-mail students and teachers course log-in IDs, and to provide course rosters to teachers. Also, it was recommended that NCVPS standardize course timelines, with teachers starting and stopping courses on a set schedule, to avoid unnecessary confusion.

At start-up in 2007, 25.6% of teachers did not believe that NCVPS provided enough technical support (Osborne et al., 2007). Similarly, 28.5% of students reported that technical issues interfered with completing their work. Continuing in 2008, a high percentage of students, teachers, and ELAs agreed or strongly agreed that technical problems affected students' course experiences and that further technical support was warranted (Oliver, Brady, Patel, & Osborne, 2008). Evaluation recommendations included adjusting help-desk hours and/or staffing, and considering additional nontraditional modes of support, such as peer tutoring. Findings suggest that NCVPS made improvements in technical support over time, since a comparison of 2008 and 2009 findings revealed significantly fewer students and teachers in 2009 reporting that technical problems affected their experiences taking or teaching online courses (Oliver, Brady, Patel, & Townsend, 2009).

Findings suggested that students relied primarily on their school infrastructure to take online courses (e.g., before- or after-school computer labs, wireless access), and to a lesser extent on computers or Internet in the home and in public places such as a town library (Oliver, Brady, Patel, & Osborne, 2008; Osborne et al., 2007). As noted, a small but significantly greater percentage of credit recovery students reported computer access at school and Internet connectivity at school and in the home were barriers to online course taking. Given the heavy reliance on school computer labs and networks to take NCVPS online courses, evaluation recommendations included preparing ELAs to establish a supportive school-based environment for online course taking, and providing lab facilitators with a standard lab setup scheme, listing any peripherals needed (e.g., headsets) and any websites in online courses that would need to be unblocked from campus filtering software (Oliver, Brady, Patel, & Townsend, 2009). It was also recommended that NCVPS establish some type of laptop loan program with schools to help facilitate equitable access to online courses.

Reactions

NCVPS took this information on logistical and technical findings and used it to justify the addition of several technical positions, both full-time and contracted. For several years, the NCVPS technical staff was limited to two positions: chief technology officer (CTO) and learning management system (LMS) administrator. The help desk was outsourced to a vendor. Recently, an additional full-time technical position has been added to include a coordinator of systems, research, and development. Also, two contracted positions have been established to support data needs and to host an in-house support desk.

To better understand and meet the needs of the schools and ELAs, a technology advisory committee was established and meets regularly to discuss the technical challenges that schools face as they support their students who enroll in NCVPS courses.

This committee is primarily made up of ELA and school technology directors. Feedback from this advisory group has resulted in changes to the registration system as well as the development of a list of technical requirements and necessary websites for each course. This feedback also led NCVPS to recommend that schools install all necessary software and plug-ins on student computers in advance, and adjust filter settings so that students can access websites cited in their courses.

Teaching

Results

Multiple studies indicated that students held expectations for their online teachers in at least three major categories—teaching, instructional design, and supporting communication (Oliver, Brady, Patel, & Osborne, 2008; Oliver, Kellogg, & Patel, 2009; Oliver, Osborne, & Brady, 2009;). First, students expected their teachers to actually teach, not just moderate or facilitate a prebuilt course shell. Students wanted teachers to actively lecture, explain, and answer questions, not simply distribute assignments and reading material. Second, many students held expectations for their teachers to supplement basic course shells with added materials and activities, which would place the teacher in more of an instructional design role than might be expected (e.g., lectures, examples of course content applied to relevant situations, quizzes, content interactions; Oliver, Osborne, & Brady, 2009). Third, students held several expectations for teachers to support communication in a course, including formal group-based assignments supportive of student-student communication, and rapid answers to their questions and feedback on projects in terms of teacher-student communication. Students also appreciated individualized attention and one-on-one tutoring through such means as virtual office hours and whiteboards. Teachers confirmed the need for added teacher-student communication, with some reporting less interaction with their online students compared to face-to-face settings (Oliver, Osborne, Patel, & Kleiman, 2008).

While teaching quality was generally rated as high across evaluation studies, teachers were more likely to agree with every teaching quality variable on the survey than students, further illustrating a possible gap between practice and student expectation (e.g., providing timely feedback, differentiating, using appropriate tools in the course, recommending student success strategies, encouraging questions, and providing clear instructions; Oliver, Brady, Patel, & Osborne, 2008). Differentiation was the teaching strategy that students, teachers, and ELAs all agreed was supported the least in online courses. Evaluation recommendations included defining roles and expectations for teachers (e.g., post biweekly lectures, hold three forums weekly) and clearly differentiating them from the complementary roles of school-level ELAs and content designers, so that each knows what is expected of him or her.

Teachers reported that several tasks consumed the majority of their time when teaching online: grading and providing feedback to students (particularly when the course includes an overwhelming number of low-level assignments and a cumbersome grade book), contacting students who fall behind on work as well as parents and ELAs when needed, and answering student questions via e-mail and phone (Oliver, Brady, Patel, &

Osborne, 2008). Only a few teachers reported that class discussions and content develop-ment took a lot of their time, suggesting that these types of communication and instruc-tional design activities were undertaken less than grading-management activities.

When asked how NCVPS could better support their teaching, the number-one sug-gestion from teachers was to communicate efficiently to stakeholders important dates, expectations, and contact information, and streamline communication so that it comes from one source rather than multiple persons (Oliver, Brady, Patel, & Osborne, 2008). Teachers also recommended further professional development on course management systems and time-saving administrative strategies, particularly summer sessions in subject-specific groups (e.g., all social studies teachers; Oliver, Brady, Patel, & Osborne, 2008). In comparing 2008 and 2009 findings, significantly more teachers in 2009 reported use of differentiation strategies in their online courses and Web 2.0 tools such as wikis and blogs, suggesting that teaching quality was improving, possibly as a result of experience or professional development intervention (Oliver, Brady, Patel, & Townsend, 2009).

Some differences were noted between teacher types. For example, teachers with prior online teaching experience rated their experience significantly more favorably than teachers lacking online experience (Osborne et al., 2007). In terms of retention, teach-ers with more online experience also expressed significantly more interest in continu-ing to teach for NCVPS (Osborne et al., 2007). Also, teachers who taught only credit recovery courses rated their experience significantly less favorably than teachers who taught both accelerated and credit recovery courses, perhaps because teaching only credit recovery students proved more challenging and possibly frustrating and perhaps because the mastery-oriented model in credit recovery courses did not match with a preferred teaching style (Osborne et al., 2007). Teachers who taught only credit recovery courses also rated their preparation from NCVPS significantly less favorably, perhaps because they perceived being less prepared to support credit recovery students with the many challenges already noted (technical, motivational, learning; Osborne et al., 2007).

Findings showing reduced learning in foreign language and math suggest that teach-ers in different content areas may need to learn specialized methods and tools in profes-sional development to maximally reach their audience (Oliver, Kellogg, & Patel, 2009, 2010). For example, foreign-language teachers should benefit from advanced knowledge of written discussion forums in support of reading and writing skills, synchronous tools in support of oral proficiency, and authentic projects that encourage conversations with native speakers. Math teachers should benefit from advanced knowledge of supporting student practice online through tutorials or problems, utilizing authentic data in sup-port of projects, explaining mathematical concepts to students through asynchronous or synchronous tools, and supporting collaborative work and peer support through Web 2.0 tools.

Reactions

As mentioned earlier, NCVPS used this information on teaching to establish clear teacher expectations centered on the three pillars of synchronous contact, meaningful feedback, and instructional announcements. In addition, implementing the spot-check process ensures that the adoption of the three pillars is seen in the instruction from all teachers, not just a few highfliers. Professional development on these pillars is seen in the teacher orientation as well as just-in-time modules available to teachers.

Establishing these clear teacher expectations begins before teachers are hired to teach for NCVPS. Teachers interested in teaching with NCVPS must complete the Teaching Online Courses training available through the LearnNC organization or show that equivalent training at another organization has been completed. This training must be finished before a teaching application will be accepted. Teacher candidates who meet all application requirements are interviewed based on need in a content area. After a successful interview, they are enrolled in the NCVPS Teacher Assistant Process. The TA Process takes a full semester to complete and is similar to a student teaching experience. The first 10 weeks include a facilitated online module in which candidates are trained in the expectations for online teachers developed by NCVPS along with the three pillars and technology skills. Upon completion of the TA module, the candidates are paired with a veteran teacher whom they shadow for the remaining weeks of the term. The TA takes over the grading, feedback, and communication with a small number of students in the course, supervised and coached by the veteran teacher. They also develop several instructional announcements for the course. Once candidates have completed the TA process, they are eligible for hire based on need.

NCVPS also developed specific guidelines on the number of sections and students that teachers could carry per term in order to provide high-quality student support rather than simply the management of learning. As all NCVPS teachers are adjunct instructors, most also teach full-time for a face-to-face school or work in some administrative capacity for an ELA. These teachers who are otherwise employed full-time with another organization are limited to a maximum of two sections per term with no more than 30 students per section. Teachers who do not have other full-time employment may be considered for a maximum of three sections per term with no more than 30 students per section. New teachers are limited to one section of 20 students during their first term with NCVPS. Teachers who work for an NC ELA must get permission from both their local principal and superintendent to teach with NCVPS, and they can be limited by their ELA on the number of sections they are allowed to teach outside the school day. Finally, based on spot checks and response to coaching, teachers may be limited in sections or section size in order to allow them the opportunity to master the three pillars and demonstrate their ability to support students with high-quality instruction.

Conclusion

The design and underlying questions of a given evaluation will ultimately drive the information generated to help an organization make changes. Thus, information generated by other evaluations of virtual schools will no doubt vary from that summarized in this chapter. However, the described partnership between NC State and NCVPS, across a range of studies, serves to illustrate by example how evaluation findings can be put to use by online and blended learning programs to inform practices, procedures, and policies. It also illustrates how program challenges identified through evaluation can lead to lessons learned by the organization—and more effective programs.

Evaluation findings served to influence NCVPS practices in a key area: improving the training and preparation of teachers and ELA support staff. NCVPS designed new student orientation experiences and provided new training for district-level ELCs and school-level ELAs. NCVPS also established a train-the-trainer model whereby ELCs are a readily accessible, single point of contact who disseminate information and training to their ELAs. NCVPS also delivered teacher professional development in a variety of forums—a standard online teaching course with follow-up shadowing of an existing NCVPS teacher before assigning new teachers to their own courses, professional development modules tied to continuing education credits, and trainings targeted at professional learning communities.

Further, evaluation findings served to influence NCVPS procedures in three other key areas: efficiency, quality, and technical issues. Efficiency procedures were adopted to streamline registration procedures for ELAs, to assist ELAs with monitoring their students via biweekly grade reports, and to assist NCVPS teachers with developing IEP agreements with schools via a formalized process. Also, quality procedures were adopted to develop a standardized instructional design model for better control over course quality with training of course developers on key quality components, to spot-check teachers and determine how well expectations are being met, to establish professional learning communities by content areas to examine student data and continuously improve course content and instruction, and to initiate a course revision cycle. Finally, procedures were adopted to identify the technical needs of students enrolling in NCVPS courses via a technical advisory committee, document and provide to ELAs technical requirements on a course-by-course basis, and develop CSS templates for course development to address issues of accessibility.

Finally, evaluation findings served to influence NCVPS policies in two key areas: teaching and organizational priorities. In terms of teaching policy, NCVPS established teacher contracts with explicit expectations to better meet the three pillars of synchronous contact, meaningful feedback, and instructional announcements. NCVPS also developed policies on the number of courses and students an online teacher could serve per term. In terms of organizational priorities, NCVPS prioritized courses for revision, targeted new populations that the findings demonstrated could be served by the organization (e.g., OCS students), created new positions based on identified needs (e.g., technical staff), and reassigned old positions to better target organizational priorities (e.g., RDIS, instructional leaders).

The partnership of NC State and NCVPS is continuing. The state's Department of Public Instruction collaborated with NCVPS to develop blended courses for students enrolled in the state's OCS program. This model of learning was used to help secure Race to the Top grant funding awarded to the state of North Carolina. Through the grant funds, blended STEM courses will be developed and piloted to at-risk students in three North Carolina ELAs. The ongoing evaluation of this grant will provide NCVPS with additional feedback to further improve these instructional models.

References

Creswell, J. W., & Clark, V. L. P. (2007). *Designing and conducting mixed methods research*. Thousand Oaks, CA: Sage.

Kellogg, S., & Oliver, K. (under review). *Credit recovery in a virtual school: Student needs and the affordances of online learning.*

Marzano, R. J., Pickering, D. J., & Pollock, J. E. (2001). *Classroom instruction that works: Research-based strategies for improving student achievement.* Alexandria, VA: ASCD.

Oliver, K., Kellogg, S., & Patel, R. (2009). An investigation into reported differences between online foreign language instruction and other subject areas in a virtual school. *CALICO Journal, 29*(2), 269–296.

Oliver, K., Kellogg, S., & Patel, R. (2010). An investigation into reported differences between online math instruction and other subject areas in a virtual school. *Journal of Computers in Mathematics and Science Teaching, 29*(4), 417–453.

Oliver, K., Kellogg, S., Townsend, L., & Brady, K. (2010). Needs of elementary and middle school teachers developing online courses for a virtual school. *Distance Education, 31*(1), 55–75.

Oliver, K. M. (2010). *Success 101: Preliminary evaluation report.* Raleigh, NC: William and Ida Friday Institute for Educational Innovation.

Oliver, K. M., Brady, K., Patel, R., & Osborne, J. (2008). *2007–2008 evaluation report: North Carolina Virtual Public School.* Raleigh, NC: William and Ida Friday Institute for Educational Innovation.

Oliver, K. M., Brady, K., Patel, R., & Townsend, T. (2009). *2008–2009 evaluation report: North Carolina Virtual Public School.* Raleigh, NC: William and Ida Friday Institute for Educational Innovation.

Oliver, K., Osborne, J., & Brady, K. (2009). What are secondary students' expectations for teachers in virtual school environments? *Distance Education, 30*(1), 23–45.

Oliver, K., Osborne, J., Patel, R., & Kleiman, G. (2008). Issues surrounding the deployment of a new statewide virtual public school. *Quarterly Review of Distance Education, 10*(1), 37–50.

Osborne, J. W., Oliver, K. M., Patel, R., & Holcomb, L. (2007). *Summer 2007 evaluation report: North Carolina Virtual Public School.* Raleigh, NC: William and Ida Friday Institute for Educational Innovation.

9

BOISE STATE'S JOURNEY TO A K–12 ONLINE TEACHING ENDORSEMENT PROGRAM

Dazhi Yang and Kerry Rice

The key to successful K–12 online learning may rely more on the quality of instruction than the medium used to deliver that instruction (Rice, 2012). The quality of online instruction and teachers' professional development concerning teaching online remains a critical issue, as well as a challenge, in the field of K–12 online teaching (Fisk, 2011). Higher education institutions are beginning to address this issue by providing teachers with K–12 online teaching certificate or endorsement programs. Boise State University (BSU) is one such institution.

Currently, policies that guide the practice of K–12 online education lag behind in terms of what states are doing or are planning to do to ensure that online teachers have the necessary qualifications and skills to teach online (Fisk, 2011). As the topic of online teaching preparation increases in visibility, more and more states and organizations have become involved in setting quality standards for K–12 online education and now are adopting specific requirements for online teachers (Vander Ark, 2010). The *Idaho Standards for Online Teachers* (Idaho State Board of Education and Idaho State Department of Education, 2010) and the Idaho K–12 Online Teaching Endorsement are a good example. The essence of these standards and endorsement efforts is to guide online education practice and ensure that teachers have the necessary qualifications and skills to be effective in online education environments. They recognize that successful online teaching requires a unique set of knowledge and skills, which is similar in nature to the types of specialized skills required in subject areas such as special education or reading.

Questions have been raised as to whether there is a need for K–12 online teaching endorsements at all. A teaching endorsement is usually a process demonstrating that a teacher possesses certain competencies and is endorsed by the state to teach in a certain subject area, while a licensure only demonstrates a teacher has the permission to teach in that state. Relevant literature would suggest that knowledge and skills developed in order to be qualified to teach in face-to-face settings are not adequate preparation for teaching online (Deubel, 2008). The need for licensed teachers to be certified or endorsed in teaching online has been acknowledged by both researchers and educational organizations (Kennedy & Archambault, 2012; National Education Association [NEA],

104

2012). The NEA recommended that "teachers who provide distance education should in addition be skilled in learning theories, technologies, and teaching pedagogies appropriate for the online environment" (NEA, 2012, para. 10).

The reality is that few teacher education programs in the United States offer any training in learning theories or teaching pedagogies appropriate for online environments (Kennedy & Archambault, 2012; Patrick & Dawley, 2009). This is disturbing considering that in the *Going Virtual!: 2010* report, Dawley, Rice, and Hinck (2010) reported that 12% of brand-new teachers had never taught face-to-face. About 25% of new online teachers received no training in online teaching methods. However, that percentage decreased dramatically after five years of online teaching (12%). About 81% of online teachers reported receiving ongoing professional development in online instruction, typically through the organizations in which they were employed.

The state of Idaho is one of four states (along with Florida, Minnesota, and Wisconsin) that stand out in providing a wide variety of full online programs and supplemental options for students across most grade levels (International Association for K–12 Online Learning, 2012). Idaho has been at the forefront of K–12 online learning since 2006 with the inception of its state supplemental online program, the Idaho Digital Learning Academy (IDLA). As of 2012 Idaho had eight approved cyber charter schools that primarily deliver full-time K–12 online learning. Steady growth in enrollments in Idaho's virtual schools has further highlighted the need for online teacher training as the next immediate step in Idaho's K–12 online learning development (Watson, Murin, Vashaw, Gemin, & Rapp, 2010, 2011, 2012).

In 2008 the Office of Teacher Certification in the Idaho State Department of Education appointed a committee to consider the viability of a state endorsement in K–12 online teaching. The committee included respective stakeholders from Idaho, including higher education representatives from private and public institutions, representatives from state colleges of education, advocates for publicly funded K–12 online schools and programs, practicing teachers, and State Department of Education and State Board of Education members. The committee reached a consensus on the need for establishing a K–12 online teaching endorsement in the state of Idaho. A subcommittee of education experts was subsequently created to develop the Idaho State standards, which would inform the criteria for the endorsement.

In the following section we describe the overall picture of national and state standards that guided the development of Idaho's standards for K–12 online teaching. Idaho's standards for K–12 online teaching are the foundation for Idaho's journey to a K–12 online teaching endorsement.

Idaho Standards for Online Teachers

The Idaho standards for quality online teaching were developed from extensive research and synthesis of previously recognized online standards provided by state, national, and international organizations. In 2006 the NEA published its *Guide to Online High School Courses* (2006a) and *Guide to Teaching Online Courses* (2006b). The *Guide to Teaching Online Courses* recommended that colleges of education should train every new teacher to teach online. In general, NEA's standards proposed recommendations for highly facilitated courses that were student-centered, collaborative, and flexible, and that actively fostered the development of 21st-century skills.

The International Society for Technology in Education (ISTE)'s National Educational Technology Standards (NETS) for students, teachers, and administrators also informed the development of Idaho's standards for online teaching as well as the development of the endorsement (International Society for Technology in Education, 2007, 2008, 2009). The ISTE NETS for Teachers (NETS•T) had four different levels (i.e., beginning, developing, proficient, and transformative) for directing and measuring teachers' use of technology. The first three levels' standards were viewed as more appropriate and timely for traditional teachers using technology in Idaho schools. Although not specific to online teaching, the ISTE NETS standards addressed the creative and intellectual skills necessary to live, interact, learn, and teach in a 21st-century global and digital world. In particular the committee consisting of respective stakeholders from Idaho was interested in aligning the online teaching endorsement with ISTE's transformative (i.e., creative and innovative use of technology) standards for teachers.

Finally, in 2008 the International Association for K–12 Online Learning (iNACOL) released its *National Standards for Quality Online Teaching* (updated in 2011; International Association for K–12 Online Learning, 2011). These standards highlighted teaching skills and methods (in both online and blended classes) in the following areas:

- Knowledge of online instruction (including concepts, structures, and instructional strategies).
- Knowledge and competencies to use technologies to support online learning and engagement.
- Knowledge and competencies to implement interactive and collaborative strategies.
- Knowledge of online classroom management, student online learning assessment, and online communication skills.
- Knowledge and competencies to deal with legal, safety, and ethical issues in online learning.

Each of these earlier initiatives informed the development of the *Idaho Standards for Online Teachers*. In 2010 a proposal to include these standards in the Idaho Standards for the Initial Certification of Professional School Personnel was filed and approved by the Professional Standards Commission. In 2011 the standards were approved by the Idaho legislature. The *Idaho Standards for Online Teachers* required that all teacher candidates for the endorsement meet the standards specific to their discipline area(s) in addition to the Idaho's Core Teacher Standards, which were basic standards for any licensed teacher in the state. The *Idaho Standards for Online Teachers* consisted of the following 10 standards:

Standard #1: Knowledge of Online Education—The online teacher understands the central concepts, tools of inquiry, and structures in online instruction and creates learning experiences that take advantage of the transformative potential in online learning environments.

Standard #2: Knowledge of Human Development and Learning—The teacher understands how students learn and develop, and provides opportunities that support their intellectual, social, and personal development.

Standard #3: Modifying Instruction for Individual Needs—The teacher understands how students differ in their approaches to learning and creates instructional opportunities that are adapted to learners with diverse needs.

Standard #4: Multiple Instructional Strategies—The online teacher understands and uses a variety of instructional strategies to develop students' critical thinking, problem solving, and performance skills.

Standard #5: Classroom Motivation and Management Skills—The teacher understands individual and group motivation and behavior and creates a learning environment that encourages positive social interaction, active engagement in learning, and self-motivation.

Standard #6: Communication Skills, Networking, and Community Building—The online teacher uses a variety of communication techniques, including verbal, nonverbal, and media, to foster inquiry, collaboration, and supportive interaction in and beyond the classroom.

Standard #7: Instructional Planning Skills—The online teacher plans and prepares instruction based upon knowledge of subject matter, students, the community, and curriculum goals.

Standard #8: Assessment of Student Learning—The online teacher understands, uses, and interprets formal and informal assessment strategies to evaluate and advance student performance and to determine program effectiveness.

Standard #9: Professional Commitment and Responsibility—The online teacher is a reflective practitioner who demonstrates a commitment to professional standards and is continuously engaged in purposeful mastery of the art and science of online teaching.

Standard #10: Partnerships—The online teacher interacts in a professional, effective manner with colleagues, parents, and other members of the community to support students' learning and well being.

The full standards can be viewed at http://www.sde.idaho.gov/site/forms/augDocs/Online_Teaching_Standards_OSBE.pdf.

Each of the standards is associated with a list of statements related to detailed knowledge and performance statements that K–12 online teachers should possess, as well as the competencies needed to implement their knowledge in the online environment (Idaho State Board of Education and Idaho State Department of Education, 2010).

Development of Idaho's K-12 Online Teaching Endorsement

The online teaching endorsement committee members agreed that their desired outcome was to develop a voluntary competency-based, K–12 online teaching endorsement. Teacher candidates should be able to choose to demonstrate their competencies in K–12 online teaching with required coursework or by supplementing required coursework with evidence of meeting competencies that had been aligned with the new standards for online teaching (e.g., through artifacts resulting from professional development activities). Throughout the process, the committee considered how the endorsement might be structured, challenges that might be encountered in developing endorsement programs that met the endorsement requirements, the actual implementation process for such a program, and how to keep the endorsement current in terms of emerging knowledge and technologies in online learning.

The structure of the endorsement requires that it be specific to the K–12 learning environment, crossing over into online instruction while maintaining Highly Qualified Teacher (HQT) standards (Information for Financial Aid Professionals, 2004). Participant teacher candidates should also be required to demonstrate the acquisition of knowledge and skills for online teaching and learning, which could be done by providing evidence such as an e-portfolio rather than being evaluated solely based upon completion of endorsement program course requirements. The committee discussed issues such as how competency-based evaluation can be paired effectively with credit-based courses for effective skill building, how to consider and include a variety of competencies in the endorsement requirements, and how to make the endorsement broad enough in scope to address all contingencies.

The state endorsement first needs to acknowledge the differences in skill sets required for teaching in online environments compared to face-to-face classrooms. Although the two instructional delivery mediums are not mutually exclusive, the K–12 online teaching endorsement must reflect consideration of the possibility that a teacher could excel in one environment and not the other. Thus, the endorsement structure needed to consider an endorsement candidate's experiences as a teacher and learner in online environments, rather than in face-to-face environments. Use of a range of technologies, especially emerging technologies and associated strategies for using such technologies, needed to be considered during the development of the endorsement. Last but not least, the development of a K–12 online teaching endorsement needed to take into consideration the human elements (e.g., online communications and managing online classrooms).

Discussion of implementation challenges faced by endorsement programs revolved around how to effectively and efficiently evaluate teacher candidates seeking a competency-based endorsement. For example, a model was discussed where artifacts from professional development activities (e.g., forum discussion posts produced in an online K–12 professional community of practice) could be counted toward meeting the competency requirement. A competency-based endorsement also presents challenges in monitoring progress and outcomes, as it usually took multiple iterations to evaluate artifacts claiming to meet certain competencies. Finally resource issues and technological access across variable social-economic groups were seen as influential factors in the successful implementation of any K–12 online teaching endorsement program that met the endorsement requirements.

Technology is in a state of constant change in today's 21st-century educational landscape. Online teaching requires knowledge and skills that should keep pace with this ever-changing landscape. Therefore, a state that offers a K–12 online teaching endorsement must be prepared to implement innovative and forward-looking educational technologies and pedagogical methodologies. In order to keep best practices updated, requirements for the endorsement need to be frequently reviewed and revised as needed. Endorsement programs might be permitted to consider factors such as professional development experience, relevant coursework, and action research in assessing the level of contemporary expertise in candidates for the endorsement, thereby helping to keep the state's endorsement current (Dawley et al., 2010).

More importantly, states should be flexible as to how universities integrate standards into teacher education programs as they develop curriculum, best practices, and evidences for the evaluation of teacher candidates. Each university or college should be allowed to have its own curriculum and program standards for quality control while the state education agency evaluates the endorsement program as they do for any other teacher education program. However, the state should require that the quality standards used to evaluate teacher candidates for the K–12 online teaching endorsement be research-based, taking into consideration the latest research and development in an ever changing field.

To be eligible for an online teacher endorsement (Pre-K–12), the Idaho State Board of Education requires all teacher candidates to satisfy the following requirements:

- Meets states' professional teaching or licensure standards and is qualified to teach in his or her field of study.
- Provides evidence of online experience or course time both as a student and as a learner and demonstrates online learning and teaching proficiency.
- Has completed (Completes) an eight-week online teaching internship in a Pre-K–12 program, or has one year of verifiable and successful experience as a teacher delivering curriculum online in grades Pre-K–12 within the past three years.
- Provides verification of completion of a state-approved program of at least 20 semester credits hours of study in online teaching and learning at an accredited college or university or a state-approved equivalent.
- Demonstrates proficiency in the *Idaho Standards for Online Teachers*.

As we can see, the endorsement program requires evidence of academic qualifications, evidence of experience in online environments as both a learner and a teacher, and proficiency in the methods and tools of online instruction as outlined by the *Idaho Standards for Online Teachers*.

BSU's K–12 Online Teaching Endorsement Program: A Case Study

In August 2011 the Department of Educational Technology at BSU became a state-approved K–12 Online Teaching Endorsement program provider in the state of Idaho. BSU is a metropolitan research university located in Boise, Idaho, whose Department of Educational Technology offers various fully online programs at both the doctoral and master's levels. The Department of Educational Technology is somewhat unique in that it has been preparing K–12 teachers to teach in online environments since 2006. In the process of becoming the program provider, the Department of Educational Technology developed an Endorsement Competency Checklist (2011) for evaluating teacher candidates' competencies and their alignment with the *Idaho Standards for Online Teachers*. This checklist was intended to be updated and revised periodically. It is excerpted in Appendix A and is available online from the program's home page.

An endorsement matrix was also developed in which performance indicators for the *Idaho K–12 Standards for Online Teachers* were illustrated with example artifacts. The matrix is not intended as a sample portfolio but instead is intended to illustrate how course-related artifacts could be used to demonstrate competencies. An excerpt from this matrix is reproduced in Appendix B.

BSU's program can be described in terms of three stages: admission requirements and procedures, overall program requirements, and evaluation and recommendation process.

1. *Admission requirements and procedures.* For students who were currently enrolled or had graduated from the Department of Educational Technology programs at BSU after 2006, no additional admission procedure was required. The rest of the candidates must first apply to the Graduate College of BSU as non-degree-seeking students in order to be placed in the endorsement program.

2. *Overall program requirements.* The endorsement program at BSU is competency-based and requires teacher candidates to demonstrate their competencies through a combination of course completions and artifacts. Specific program requirements include

   • Courses/competencies—all candidates must complete 20 credits of required or equivalent courses. Alternatively, all candidates must demonstrate competencies of online teaching and learning through submitted artifacts from relevant coursework or professional development experiences.
   • Minimum grade point average of 3.00 for all courses or equivalent courses.
   • At least one-year of online teaching experience in grades Pre-K–12 within the past three years.
   • Evidence of Idaho teacher certification.

3. *Evaluation and recommendation process.* The Department of Educational Technology at BSU evaluates teacher candidates and recommends them for endorsement to the Idaho State Department of Education if they meet all the program requirements. A support letter or report of professional online teaching experience from a school administrator or an online field teaching experience class can be used to satisfy the online teaching experience requirement.

More information about BSU's K–12 Online Teaching Endorsement can be found on the program's home page (http://edtech.boisestate.edu/idaho-K-12-online-teaching-endorsement-program).

Challenges and How They Were Resolved

All program providers face challenges in getting required courses in place, building partnerships with K–12 online schools that can host the online teaching field experience for teacher candidates, and deciding appropriate artifacts for demonstrations of required competencies.

Beginning any new program of study can be a challenge, and in the case of an online program, those challenges can be intensified. BSU had the advantage of being able to build upon existing Department of Educational Technology certification programs (e.g., Technology Integration, Online Teaching, and School Technology Coordination). All required courses had been previously offered, except the online teaching field experience course. In spring 2012 BSU's University Curriculum Council approved EDTECH 524, a two-credit graduate-level online teaching field experience designed to provide hands-on experience for teacher candidates in a fully online K–12 environment.

Despite preexisting curricula, a great length of time elapsed from conception to implementation of the endorsement program. Discussions about preservice and in-service teacher placement in online school environments had been occurring among BSU's College of Education, the Department of Educational Technology, and various online schools in Idaho for more than five years. Development of teaching standards and an endorsement by the state were also necessary preconditions for endorsement program development.

Placing teacher candidates or interns in an online K–12 school was more challenging than placing them in a face-to-face school. First, generally speaking, there are fewer virtual schools available for placement. Partnerships with virtual schools are not only critical for teacher placement but can also serve as a resource for research and process exchanges. For example, online schools are often very interested in increasing their pool of qualified teacher applicants. The Department of Educational Technology at BSU had a long history of partnering with virtual schools within the state as well as with IDLA, the state online supplemental program. IDLA agreed to host teacher candidates for the Department of Educational Technology at BSU's online teaching field experience as part of a pilot program.

In addition to hosting teachers, IDLA served as a valuable resource for the development of the student teacher placement processes as well as our new *K–12 Online Teaching Endorsement: Online Field Experience Guide* (EDTECH, 2012). IDLA also helped organize orientation activities, such as introducing students to mentor teachers and creating online tutorials for the teacher candidates to become familiar with their online course management system.

During the process of forming a partnership with this host online school, a series of new issues emerged. One such issue was how to fairly compensate online mentor teachers. During the process of setting up the field experience, we became aware that the honorarium for compensating traditional mentor teachers was not going to be sufficient for teachers in an online environment due to the higher time commitment involved. BSU thus offered to pay mentor teachers via IDLA an amount four times the typical rate for a public school teacher who agrees to supervise traditional teacher candidates or interns.

Another challenge occurred in obtaining background checks for potential intern teachers. In the state of Idaho, online schools do not accept background clearances from other states and required that all teacher candidates receive clearance in the state of Idaho. The Department of Educational Technology at BSU is an online graduate program, serving students from around the globe. The department was required to assist students located in other states and countries with fingerprint and background checks. This resulted in more financial expenses and logistical issues for those teacher candidates who lived outside of Idaho.

Competency-based evaluations also presented challenges, primarily in the time and effort it took to review candidates on a case-by-case basis. To simplify the evaluation process of the required competencies for meeting the K–12 Online Teaching Endorsement program at BSU, all competencies could be articulated through the BSU Endorsement Competency Checklist, which aligned with the *Idaho Standards for Online Teachers* in terms of their performance indicators. Using the checklist, artifacts could easily be evaluated on each performance factor.

Despite the many challenges faced, program implementation has been successful to date. During the spring 2012 semester, two teacher candidates successfully obtained their Idaho K–12 Online Teaching Endorsement through the Department of Educational Technology at BSU. In the fall semester of 2012, the online field experience course (i.e., EDTECH 524: Field Experience in Online Teaching) was offered for the first time to teacher candidates who had the desire to obtain hands-on teaching experience in an online Pre-K–12 program. IDLA teachers served as the mentor teachers for participating students.

Conclusion

The development of the Idaho K–12 Online Teaching Endorsement program at BSU provides a viable example of how colleges and universities can prepare teachers to teach in online environments, building on state standards and endorsement requirements designed to ensure that online teachers have the necessary qualifications and skills to be effective. The competency-based evaluation framework developed by BSU for its K–12 Online Teaching Endorsement program is highly flexible and adaptable. The framework's flexibility permits teacher candidates to substitute professional development experience for required coursework. Our experience has been that this not only saves time and resources for teachers, schools, and organizations but also motivates teachers to update their knowledge and skills for online teaching in a variety of ways, such as participating in online professional community discussion forums.

Following BSU's example, university teacher education programs could partner with local schools and institutions to provide teacher candidates with professional development workshops and internships in fully online K–12 environments and create a competency checklist as a developmental framework for online teacher evaluation and recommendation purposes.

Competency-based programs such as this can be updated on an ongoing basis, thus ensuring the ongoing evaluation of teacher candidates' competencies and skills in a changing 21st-century educational landscape. State adoption of competency-based requirements could also facilitate multistate use of distance education resources, such as mutual recognition of the K–12 Online Teaching Endorsement program for teachers who resided and had been licensed in other states.

The process of developing BSU's online teaching endorsement program was not without its challenges. Although most courses needed were already in place for the endorsement program, several years elapsed from conception to implementation. Student placements in virtual schools were necessary. An existing partnership with IDLA proved invaluable, but placement still presented challenges, such as determining appropriate compensation for teacher mentors. Another barrier was the need for background checks of out-of-state program participants. Evaluation of teaching artifacts presented challenges in terms of the time and effort required, but the development of a competency checklist with artifact examples linked to standards-based performance indicators made this process easier. Despite the challenges we faced, our state-approved K–12 Online Teaching Endorsement program has been a success to date. We hope that others can learn from our experiences.

References

Dawley, L., Rice, K., & Hinck, G. (2010). *Going virtual! 2010: The status of professional development and unique needs of K–12 online teachers.* Vienna, VA: North American Council for Online Learning.

Department of Educational Technology. (2011). *Endorsement Competency Checklist.* Pocatello: Idaho State University. Retrieved from http://edtech.boisestate.edu/docs/programs/k12endorsement/K-12OnlineEndorsement_Checklist.docx

Deubel, P. (2008, January 8). K–12 online teaching endorsements: Are they needed? *T.H.E. Journal, 1.* Retrieved from http://thejournal.com/Articles/2008/01/10/K12-Online-Teaching-Endorsements-Are-They-Needed.aspx?Page=1

EDTECH. (2012). *K–12 Online teaching endorsement: Online field experience guide.* Boise, ID: Boise State University. Retrieved from http://bit.ly/YtvBel

Fisk, C. (2011). *Teaching in the world of virtual K–12 learning: Challenges to ensure educator quality.* A final report prepared for the Educational Testing Service. Retrieved from http://www.ets.org/s/educator_licensure/ets_online_teaching_policy_final_report.pdf

Idaho State Board of Education and Idaho State Department of Education. (2010). *Idaho standards for online teachers.* Boise: Authors. Retrieved from http://www.sde.idaho.gov/site/forms/augDocs/Online_Teaching_Standards_OSBE.pdf

Idaho State Department of Education. (2012). *Common core state standards.* Boise: Author. Retrieved from http://www.sde.idaho.gov/site/common

Information for Financial Aid Professionals. (2004). *Definition of a highly qualified teacher.* Washington, DC: Author. Retrieved from http://ifap.ed.gov/dpcletters/GEN0414.html

International Association for K–12 Online Learning. (2011). *National standards for quality online teaching, version 2.* Vienna, VA: Author. Retrieved from http://www.inacol.org/research/nationalstandards/iNACOL_TeachingStandardsv2.pdf

International Association for K–12 Online Learning. (2012). *Fast facts about online learning.* Vienna, VA: Author. Retrieved from http://www.inacol.org/press/docs/nacol_fast_facts.pdf

International Society for Technology in Education. (2007). *ISTE's NETS for students (NETS•S).* Washington, DC: Author. Retrieved from http://www.iste.org/docs/pdfs/nets-s-standards.pdf?sfvrsn=2

International Society for Technology in Education. (2008). *ISTE's NETS for teachers (NETS•T)*. Washington, DC: Author. Retrieved from http://www.iste.org/docs/pdfs/nets-t-standards .pdf?sfvrsn=2

International Society for Technology in Education. (2009). *ISTE's NETS for administrators (NETS•A)*. Washington, DC: Author. Retrieved from http://www.iste.org/docs/pdfs/nets-a-standards.pdf?sfvrsn=2

Kennedy, K., & Archambault, L. M. (2012). Offering pre-service teachers field experiences in K–12 online learning: A national survey of teacher education programs. *Journal of Teacher Education, 63*(3), 185–200.

National Education Association. (2006a). *Guide to online high school courses*. Washington, DC: Author. Retrieved from http://www.nea.org/assets/docs/onlinecourses.pdf

National Education Association. (2006b). *Guide to teaching online courses*. Washington, DC: Author. Retrieved from http://www.nea.org/assets/docs/onlineteachguide.pdf

National Education Association. (2012). *NEA policy statements: Distance education*. Washington, DC: Author. Retrieved from http://www.nea.org/home/34765.htm

Patrick, S., & Dawley, L. (2009). *Redefining teacher education: K–12 online–blended learning and virtual schools*. Austin: University of Texas.

Rice, K. (2012). *Making the move to K–12 online teaching: Research-based strategies and practices*. Saddle River, NJ: Pearson Education.

Vander Ark, T. (2010). States adding mandatory cert for teaching online. *Getting Smart*. Retrieved from http://gettingsmart.com/news/states-adding-mandatory-cert-for-teaching-online

Watson, J., Murin, A., Vashaw, L., Gemin, B., & Rapp, C. (2010). *Keeping pace with K–12 online learning*. Boulder, CO: Evergreen Education Group. Retrieved from http://www.kpk12.com/ cms/wp-content/uploads/KeepingPaceK12_2010.pdf

Watson, J., Murin, A., Vashaw, L., Gemin, B., & Rapp, C. (2011). *Keeping pace with K–12 online learning: An annual review of policy and practice*. Evergreen, CO: Evergreen Education Group. Retrieved from http://kpk12.com/cms/wp-content/uploads/KeepingPace2011.pdf

Watson, J., Murin, A., Vashaw, L., Gemin, B., & Rapp, C. (2012). *Keeping pace with K–12 online and blended learning: An annual review of policy and practice*. Evergreen, CO: Evergreen Education Group. Retrieved from http://kpk12.com/cms/wp-content/uploads/KeepingPace2012 .pdf

Appendix A: K-12 Online Teaching Endorsement Competency Checklist (Excerpt)

BSU's Department of Educational Technology developed an Endorsement Competency Checklist (2011) for evaluating teacher candidates' competencies and their alignment with the *Idaho Standards for Online Teachers*. This checklist will be updated periodically. It is excerpted here and is available online from the program's home page.

Standard #1: Knowledge of Online Education—The online teacher understands the central concepts, tools of inquiry, and structures in online instruction and creates learning experiences that take advantage of the transformative potential in online learning environments.

Performance Indicator		Checklist	Points
The online teacher utilizes current standards for best practices in online teaching to identify appropriate instructional processes and strategies.	☐	Applications of online instructional principles/strategies/guidelines • Classroom practice examples • Synthesis of standards into best practice	_/10
The online teacher demonstrates application of communication technologies for teaching and learning.	☐	Applications of online teaching, learning, and communication technologies/tools • LMS (learning management system) • CMS (course management system) • E-mail • Discussion • Videoconference (Minimum # of one tool needed to pass)	_/5
	☐	Planning for communication in online course design • Checklist for what to do before the class begins • Checklist for things planned during the first week of class	_/5

Standard #2: Knowledge of Human Development and Learning—The teacher understands how students learn and develop, and provides opportunities that support their intellectual, social, and personal development.

Performance Indicator		Checklist	Points
The online teacher utilizes current standards for best practices in on-line teaching to identify appropriate instructional processes and strategies.	☐	• Multiple forms of delivery of the same content addressing multiple learning styles (text, audio, video, graphic) • Synchronous and asynchronous delivery of the content • Individual and group learning • Digital communities for extended learning activities • Applications of learning theories and instructional principles to provide multiple learning opportunities	_/10
The online teacher uses communication technologies to alter learning strategies and skills (e.g., media literacy, visual literacy).	☐	• Multiple representations of the same content (text, audio, video, graphic) • Multiple forms of delivery of the same content addressing multiple learning styles (synchronous and asynchronous modes)	_/10

Appendix B: K-12 Online Teaching Endorsement Matrix (Excerpt)

The following matrix excerpt illustrates multiple ways in which students can provide evidence to meet competencies for performance indicators in the *Idaho K–12 Standards for Online Teachers*. It should be noted that courses in this matrix are offered by BSU's Department of Educational Technology to provide students with opportunities to meet these competencies.

Framework for Teaching Domain #1: Planning and Preparation

Standard #1: Knowledge of Online Education—The online teacher understands the central concepts, tools of inquiry, and structures in online instruction and creates learning experiences that take advantage of the transformative potential in online learning environments.

EDTECH Course	Performance Indicator	Example Artifacts/Evidence
EDTECH 523: Advanced Online Teaching Methods	The online teacher utilizes current standards for best practices in online teaching to identify appropriate instructional processes and strategies.	• Principles of effective online instruction
EDTECH 512: Online Course Design EDTECH 521: Teaching Online in the K–12 Environment EDTECH 523: Advanced Online Teaching	The online teacher demonstrates application of communication technologies for teaching and learning (e.g., learning management system [LMS], content management system [CMS], e-mail, discussion, desktop videoconferencing, and instant messaging tools).	• Online course site • Netiquette consensus-building project • Adobe Connect recorded lesson • Adobe Connect live lesson
EDTECH 523: Advanced Online Teaching EDTECH 597: Social Network Learning	The online teacher demonstrates application of emerging technologies for teaching and learning (e.g., blogs, wikis, content creation tools, mobile technologies, virtual worlds).	• Virtual icebreaker project development wiki • Adobe Connect live lesson • Social network mind map
EDTECH 502: Internet for Educators EDTECH 597: Social Network Learning	The online teacher demonstrates application of advanced troubleshooting skills (e.g., digital asset management, firewalls, web-based applications).	• 502 website http://edtech2.boisestate.edu/sabaa/502/homepage/portfolio.html • Social network wiki: Troubleshooting the PLC

(Continues)

EDTECH Course	Performance Indicator	Example Artifacts/Evidence
EDTECH 512: Online Course Design	The online teacher demonstrates the use of design methods and standards in course/document creation and delivery.	• Online course site, message, and visual design guidelines
EDTECH 521: Teaching Online in the K–12 Environment EDTECH 502: Internet for Educators	The online teacher demonstrates knowledge of access, equity (digital divide), and safety concerns in online environments.	• Netiquette lesson • Netiquette rules for the online classroom • Accessibility lesson

10

BUILDING BLENDED CHARTERS

A Case Study of the Nexus Academies, U.S.

Mickey Revenaugh

From the flowering of state online high schools to the emergence of virtual charters, the first 10 years of the 21st century in North American K–12 education could reasonably be called the Decade of Online Learning.

It was around 2010 that thought leaders in K–12 online learning began turning their attention to innovative combinations of virtual and face-to-face instruction. These efforts were spurred in part by promising early research, such as a meta-analysis indicating that students in blended learning environments achieve at higher levels of mastery than students in either purely face-to-face or purely virtual settings (Means, Toyama, Murphy, Bakia, & Jones, 2010), and in part by new tools such as the Apple iPad and smartphones that blurred the line between online and offline endeavors. New blended combinations have emerged and evolved very quickly: Innosight Institute's original typology of blended learning models was put forth in the seminal *The Rise of K–12 Blended Learning* (Horn & Staker, 2011), which was refined less than 18 months later with the publication of *Classifying K–12 Blended Learning* (Staker & Horn, 2012). Meanwhile, interest in blended learning skyrocketed among districts and providers. According to the 2012 edition of *Keeping Pace With K–12 Online and Blended Learning*—which added "blended" to this annual report's name for the first time—blended programs are the fastest-growing in the sector (Watson, Murin, Vashaw, Gemin, & Rapp, 2012). The second decade of the 21st century has emerged as the Age of Blended Learning.

For a company like Connections Education, founded in 2001 and quickly taking its place as a leader in fully virtual education for students in grades K–12, this Age of Blended Learning has posed a unique challenge and opportunity. From two schools serving a total of 400 students, the company's Connections Academy division had grown to support more than 20 multidistrict public online schools—most of them statewide—serving more than 50,000 full-time students. These virtual schools, most of them charter schools, reinvented the education experience during the Decade of Online Learning by establishing that "school" is not a place but a set of relationships between teachers and students structured around mastery of a body of knowledge and personalized for each learner. In a Connections Academy virtual school, those teacher-student and student-student relationships are mediated via technology, focused on a deep standards-aligned curriculum, and individualized by a steady stream of data from that curriculum. In addition to their highly qualified teachers, with whom they interact both synchronously and asynchronously, Connections Academy students benefit from face-to-face support and assistance provided by a *learning coach*, typically a parent or extended family member. The entire school experience is delivered and organized via Connections' proprietary platform, an education management system known as Connexus, which does everything from tracking student data to delivering curriculum, from facilitating communication to managing physical assets such as the thousands of computers delivered to participating students across the United States.

In approaching blended learning, Connections wanted to have an equally profound definitional effect, combining face-to-face and online learning in ways that go beyond simply defaulting to the lowest common denominator of each—undifferentiated lecture-based instruction on the one hand, and disengaged computer drills on the other. What might a physical school look like if one started from scratch and structured the entire experience around data-driven personalized learning for every student? This essential question guided the development of what would become the Nexus Academy model.

Nexus in Context

As it began conceptualizing its blended learning approach, Connections faced a competitive field that was rapidly taking shape. According to foundational typology work, there are four primary blended learning models: rotation, flex, self-blend, and enriched virtual (Staker & Horn, 2012). Of these, the rotation and flex models dominated among full-time, full-school blended models, particularly in the charter/contract school sector, and the existing implementations fundamentally resembled one another.

Early dominant players in full-school blended implementations included

- *Carpe Diem*, which essentially created the blended secondary school template with its successful and groundbreaking charter school in Yuma, Arizona. Carpe Diem students work in office-style cubicles using the E2020 online curriculum, rotating out into seminar rooms for face-to-face teacher-led instruction and project activities. Beginning in 2012, Carpe Diem has begun expanding its network with schools in Indiana, Ohio, and elsewhere.
- *Flex Academies*, the blended learning brand launched by K12 Inc. in the Bay Area of California. Despite its name, the flex model follows the online/offline rotational approach pioneered by Carpe Diem, with similar cubicles and group instruction rooms but using the K12 curriculum originally developed for K12-affiliated virtual charter schools around the country. The flex model is proposed for replication in Washington, DC, and elsewhere.
- *Rocketship*, a K–5 rotational model that uses blended learning explicitly as a strategy to allow fewer but better-paid licensed teachers, since students spend part of the day in a learning lab doing computer-based math and English language arts practice supervised by an aide. Rocketship's goal is to have thousands of schools across the nation and has begun expanding in Tennessee, Indiana, and Louisiana, among other states.

As these models were taking shape, Connections implemented a series of pilots to shape and distinguish its own approach to blended learning. It conducted internal evaluations of each pilot, gathering and analyzing data. Findings and conclusions informed subsequent pilots and the development of the Nexus Academy initiative.

Matthew Henson Elementary Summer Program, Baltimore, Maryland

Conducted during summer 2008, this pilot provided one blended classroom each for third, fourth, and fifth grades as an option to the traditional classrooms in these grades during mandatory summer school. The pilot was staffed by face-to-face classroom teachers employed by Matthew Henson working with Connections virtual teachers, and focused on language arts and math along with enrichment activities such as sign language and yoga. This pilot made clear that blended programs for elementary-age students would require intensive face-to-face support, especially for struggling readers, while the set up of the room—with desktop computers lining the walls and students with their backs to the room—was convenient for the adults but did little to allow for community building or project-based instruction. Nonetheless, the pilot results were promising: The students in the blended classrooms were significantly more likely to attend school, and they made average pretest to posttest gains of 16 points in language arts (compared to 0 points for the control group) and 21 points in math (compared to 24 points for the control group).

Vision Academy, Houston, Texas

Pro-Vision Charter School is an established boys-only brick-and-mortar middle school that found that its graduating students floundered at traditional high schools and often dropped out. Pro-Vision turned to Connections to develop a blended high school center on its campus so that its students could continue with the school in ninth grade and beyond. Called Vision Academy, the blended program served approximately 15 at-risk ninth graders in 2009–2010 and a total of approximately 40 at-risk ninth and tenth graders the following year. Vision Academy ultimately occupied three Pro-Vision classrooms that had been converted into labs and that students occupied all day; in Year 1, the labs were staffed by paraprofessional coaches. Although Vision Academy students had a median course pass rate of 92% in Year 1, scores on the state's Texas Assessment of Knowledge and Skills lagged, especially in math, leading to a shift to inclusion of a face-to-face math teacher for Year 2. In addition, student feedback indicated that requiring students to work at static desktop computers all day without varying their activities and setting was not ideal. Many of the ultimate Nexus Academy innovations on use of space and time were inspired by the Vision experience.

ACCESS Online Program, Prince George's County, Maryland

Launched in fall 2010 this blended credit recovery/credit enhancement program serves nearly 300 simultaneous course enrollments for students who travel to the ACCESS center from throughout Prince George's County, Maryland, a geographically large and demographically diverse district outside of Washington, DC. The program is specifically focused on 11th and 12th graders who are one or more credits short of those needed for graduation. The ACCESS center is staffed by certified teachers—one math, one English—who serve as coaches to the students and coteachers with the online staff. Although the overall 85% pass rate in Year 1 was acceptable, a lag in math pass rates led to more intensified face-to-face interventions based on performance. By Year 2, the overall pass rate had increased to 91%, and there was a 10% improvement in passing rates among students taking Algebra I, Geometry, and Algebra II. ACCESS staff are proud to report that more than 20 seniors taking ACCESS courses who would not otherwise have been eligible for graduation did graduate in 2010–2011, and that number increased in the following year. The ACCESS program was renewed for 2012–2013 and is on track for further renewal. This pilot was the subject of a case study (Connections Learning, 2012).

Commonwealth Connections Academy, Philadelphia, Pennsylvania

The Commonwealth Connections Academy (CCA) in Philadelphia was created to serve struggling Philadelphia-area high school students who are enrolled in the CCA statewide cyber charter school. The center is located in an office building in downtown Philadelphia. Students attend during a morning or afternoon shift. Part of their time is spent in lounge-style rooms working on electives, social studies, and science supervised by paraprofessionals, and part of their time is spent in small-group face-to-face instruction with certified teachers in math and English. The center opened in January 2012, and early results have been encouraging. Before coming to the center, students' fall semester pass rate was at 55%. In mid-March, 66% of center students were passing, and the center ended the spring term with student pass rates increasing to 74%. For 2012–2013, the center has also implemented a pre- and posttest that should provide critical growth data.

Based on what it learned from its pilot programs, as well as observation of other schools in the field, Connections focused on developing a full-school blended approach that would meet the following imperatives:

- Preserve the intimacy and personalization of virtual schooling while leveraging the social power of place.
- Provide a physical space that inspires learning, allows flexibility and freedom of movement for students, and makes the most of the fact that students are together.
- Leverage the Connections digital curriculum and Connexus education management throughout the school day.
- Use individual student learning data—as opposed to the rotational clock—to drive the mix of face-to-face and online instruction.
- Provide an innovative staffing model with altogether new roles for teachers and others focused on academic and emotional success for each student.

These imperatives became the hallmarks of the Nexus Academy blended school model.

Nexus Up Close: The School Design Process

Beginning in late 2011 the Connections team began prototyping the Nexus Academy model in earnest. Key questions facing the team are described in the following sections.

What Is the Vehicle for School Creation?

While public school districts across the nation are beginning to embrace blended learn-ing, and Connections ultimately hopes to help them practice it effectively, the most immediate opportunity for full-school implementation with fidelity was to create start-up charter schools. Connections has a very positive 10-year track record in working with local nonprofit boards to develop and manage charter schools, so it launched discus-sions with high-quality charter authorizers in Ohio and Michigan to initiate the first five Nexus Academy schools in fall 2012.

Which Students Will the Schools Serve?

The blended pilot implementations persuaded Connections that the greatest need and greatest potential impact would be in high school. Not only are high school students better able to move through the school day somewhat independently, but also the modu-larity of the high school curriculum—with its clearly defined and separately taught sub-jects—lends itself well to a differentiated blended approach. More urgently, the need for additional high-quality high school options was evident everywhere in the United States. Across the country, the graduation rate is hovering at about 75% (Agus, 2010). Many districts offer only large comprehensive high schools, averaging more than 700 students and quite often topping 1,000 (Agus, 2010), or alternative schools aimed at students with serious behavior or academic issues. Fewer than 20% of all charter schools in the United States are high schools (National Alliance for Public Charter Schools, 2012). Furthermore, the sharpening national focus on college and career readiness convinced Connections to ensure that the blended school program would be college preparatory.

How Big Will the Schools Be?

Connections has paid close attention to the emerging research on high school size and efficacy, including recently published longitudinal work from New York City showing that small high schools (400 students or fewer) produced high school graduation rates 8.6 percentage points above large schools (1,000+ students) serving the same demographic (Bloom, Thompson, & Unterman, 2010). As a result, the design team determined that Nexus Academy would be an intentionally small school, and they began experimenting with variables to see just how small it could be and still be sustainable. Given that the Connections digital curriculum and online teachers would allow a comprehensive edu-cational program regardless of the number of students, the sweet spot in terms of staffing model, physical footprint, and budget was determined to be 300 students. This would make Nexus Academy radically more intimate than any other high school in most com-munities (Agus, 2010).

What Will Be Taught Face-to-Face—and How?

Once the college-prep high school focus was selected and the small-school imperative embraced, these conditions framed the essential design question. The Nexus team knew that it wanted to use the Connections digital curriculum as the foundation for all courses, thus leveraging a decade of investment in quality and data-producing power. In terms of instruction, though, the design team wanted to deploy face-to-face teaching where it would be most likely to maximize academic outcomes, while preserving the flexibility and personalization offered by online teaching approaches. While all four core curriculum areas were considered essential—along with the richest possible array of electives—literacy and numeracy were recognized as gateways for all other study.

In addition, the emergence of Common Core Curriculum Standards in English language arts (ELA) and math provided a renewed focus. Connections had already aligned its curriculum and assessments with the Common Core and developed the capability of monitoring student progress with the Common Core objective level in both math and ELA. What if Nexus Academy students worked with face-to-face teachers on mastery of Common Core objectives, and what if their work with these teachers was driven directly by individual performance data from the curriculum? In essence, the school's expert ELA and math teachers would focus their instructional time not on curriculum delivery—because students would "self-serve" the curriculum via their computers—but instead on intervention, remediation, acceleration, and enrichment.

Commitment to this approach would allow Nexus Academy to fulfill the ambitions of the flex model in the blended learning taxonomy: Rather than rotating between online and face-to-face, Nexus Academy would truly blend both together in the highest-priority core areas. From there, the team determined that, in this small school setting, science and social studies would be best delivered online—allowing for the broadest and deepest choices for students—along with elective and enrichment courses. Allowances were made for hands-on/face-to-face activities in science and the arts, perhaps involving guest instructors, and for physical education. Throughout all of their courses, students would have access to online LiveTutors who could get them unstuck with on-demand, just-in-time assistance.

What Will the School Schedule Look Like?

The Nexus team turned to focusing on the school schedule. Since students would have 24/7/365 access to all of their courses, the team's first goal was to structure students' on-site time to maximize the impact of their face-to-face teachers and success coaches. A second goal was to allow flexible time for jobs, internships, college classes, and "personal passion" activities such as sports or the arts, as well as accommodating individual needs regarding sleep patterns and peak attention. The team also believed that the positive impact of the small school size could be multiplied by having even smaller numbers of students on campus simultaneously. The decision was made to serve students in two shifts of more than 150 students each, one in the morning (8:30 a.m.–12:30 p.m.) and the other in the afternoon (1–5 p.m.). This created a real student-to-adult ratio of 12.5 to 1. Furthermore, face-to-face sessions with on-site teachers would be scheduled in increments of 25 to 35 minutes, allowing staff to mix and match time blocks to meet students' individual needs.

How Will the Program Be Personalized for Students?

As in the Connections Academy virtual schools, each student at Nexus Academy would have a Personalized Learning Plan (PLP). Developed collaboratively by the staff with input from the student and his or her parents, the PLP guides the tailoring of both curriculum and instruction to meet that student's needs. Special attention would be paid to meeting the needs of students with disabilities and students who are English-language learners, PLPs the would reflect necessary modifications and accommodations. Beyond the PLP, Nexus Academy would practice "dynamic differentiation" to ensure that its teaching resources were targeted most efficaciously. As students work in their digital curriculum, data is generated on their mastery of underlying objectives—the Common Core in math and English, and national/state standards in other subjects. This objective mastery data is used to dynamically group students for intervention, enrichment, project work, and individual study. At the Nexus Academy campus, the school team would formulate new math and English groups every one to two weeks, with struggling students meeting with the face-to-face teachers daily or multiple times per day, focusing on mastery of targeted objectives. The online teachers would likewise schedule synchronous LiveLesson sessions for intervention and enrichment in all other subjects.

What Technology Will Be Used?

The Nexus design team agreed that students should have ubiquitous access to the Connections digital curriculum, Connexus platform, and online instructional resources, including teachers and LiveTutors. To do so, the school would provide all students with a mobile computing device (laptop or tablet) to use throughout the school day to access their powerful and engaging online curriculum, which they could also take home to continue their work beyond the school day. Each school would also explore a Bring Your Own Device approach that makes use of students' own smartphones and other computing devices they may bring to school.

What About Students' Physical Needs?

The Nexus design team keyed in on research about exercise/fitness and academic performance (Medina, 2008) and determined that wellness should be an integrated part of the daily Nexus experience. This goal would be facilitated through creation of on-site fitness centers with dedicated staffing and personalized fitness planning, plus use of community options from martial arts to spinning to yoga. Rather than a traditional lunch program, the school would plan for healthful packaged food and snacks available to students on demand.

How Will the Schools Be Staffed?

Intertwined with questions about school size and instructional design were variables relating to staffing. Based on the documented importance of effective school leadership (Leithwood & Riehl, 2003), having a principal was a given—with the caveat that for a school of 300 the principal would be a hands-on instructional leader. The college-/career-ready focus also created an imperative for a guidance counselor, while the on-site fitness center would be staffed by a personal trainer (who might also be a licensed PE teacher). Having determined that ELA and math would be "face-to-face driven," the design team further built out the staffing model by assuming two on-site teachers in each of those subjects to permit adequate planning/grading time for each, as well as a bit of specialization by grade range (e.g., one math teacher would teach consumer math while the other might do precalculus). For all of their other courses, students would have highly qualified online teachers, but the Nexus design team wanted to ensure that students also had on-site support that went beyond a mere lab facilitator; the team created the role of the success coach. Drawing on research from coaching in higher education (Bettinger & Baker, 2011), the team defined the *success coach* as a specially selected and trained paraprofessional wearing two hats: academic—focusing on ensuring that students are on track and motivated in their online courses—and guidance—focusing on future goals, college readiness, and self-management skills. The Nexus school staff would be rounded out by a school secretary who would help facilitate data handling as well as outreach and recruitment activities, plus shared special services staff (e.g., special education coordinators or English-language learning specialists) as needed. Each school's face-to-face staff would number no fewer than 12, supplemented by hundreds of online teachers and Connections "headquarters" staff responsible for school business services, enrollment services, grant writing, high-level reporting, and so on.

How Will the Space Be Designed?

In thinking about the physical school setting, the Connections team wanted to take a very different approach than some of the other leading blended-school models. Rather than cubicles like Carpe Diem or a combination of traditional classrooms and computer labs like Rocketship, the Nexus design group wanted to create a singularly open school environment resembling a college lounge or high-tech start-up. Students would work on their online courses in a casual seating area with couches and high-top tables to which they'd be assigned to dedicated team cohorts under the supervision of a success coach; within their team zones they could sit where they wanted and move when they chose. When meeting with their face-to-face teachers, students would work in glass-walled seminar rooms in small flexible groups rather than in closed classrooms with forward-facing rows of desks. The principal, guidance counselor, and school secretary would not be sequestered in offices but instead would work in cubicles with visual access to students at all times. Even the fitness center would be integrated into this open floor plan. Connections conducted a request for proposal (RFP) process to select a leading school architect to bring this vision to life; see the accompanying illustration (Figure 10.1) and floor plan (Figure 10.2) developed by Godshall Kane O'Rourke Architects, working in partnership with the Nexus design team.

With a footprint of 15,000 square feet, this design could easily be implemented in nontraditional school settings such as office buildings, former industrial spaces, and retail areas. The goal would be an entirely different kind of high school for the different world that today's students inhabit.

Putting It All Together: A Typical Nexus Student Day

Travis is a typical Nexus Academy freshman. Travis takes the city bus to arrive at school at 8:30 a.m. for the school's morning shift. He swipes his key card at the door, greets the principal, and reports directly to his Team Zone to claim his spot at the high café table where he does his best work. Travis pulls his laptop out of his backpack and logs in to

Figure 10.1: Nexus Academy open floor plan illustration

review his class schedule for the day and check to see if he has any new WebMail messages. He sees that his biology teacher scored the lab report that he submitted on Monday and he got a 93. He quickly clicks on his Grade Book to check his overall course score and is excited that it is up to 89. Travis's day officially begins with a brief team meeting led by his success coach, Mr. Johnson. Every Wednesday, during first period, Travis and his classmates participate in a structured small-group program called Success Highways that helps them think about the skills necessary for academic success. Today's lesson is on career ideas. Travis's journal assignment is to write down three jobs that he might enjoy doing and to share with a partner how success in school will prepare him to succeed in the jobs that he listed. During the next two class periods, Travis stays in his Team Zone and completes work in his online Spanish and biology classes. He gets to choose which online classes to do when—and which ones he'd rather tackle at home on any given day.

At 10:10 a.m., as noted in his online schedule, Travis logs into his American Government teacher's LiveLesson web conference, "How a Bill Becomes a Law." He enjoys collaborating via audio and text chat with classmates from other Nexus Academy schools and likes when the teacher breaks the students into virtual groups to answer questions about the lesson in different chat pods. Participating in the LiveLesson polls helps Travis learn how his classmates are feeling about the lesson.

When Travis hears the music to indicate it's time to change classes, he grabs his laptop and heads to his Algebra I classroom. The objective of the class is "rewriting expressions involving radicals and rational exponents using the properties of exponents." This is a skill that he has been working on in his algebra course. His teacher reviews the skill with the class and then asks the students to work in small groups to solve a problem and justify their answer. After the small-group activity, Travis and a few of his classmates log into Study Island to complete an assignment to assess concept mastery. Other students are assigned a Khan Academy video about properties of exponents for review, and the teacher works with a few students at a small table. Travis has an 84 in math and is only scheduled for face-to-face class

Figure 10.2: Nexus Academy floor plan

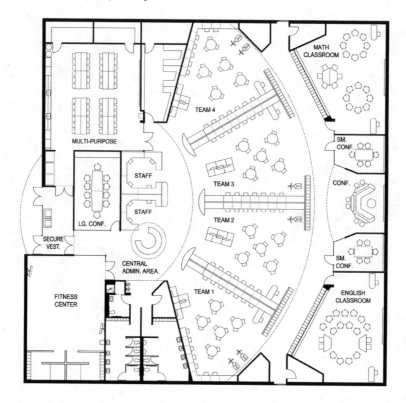

twice this week. That allows him to accelerate through his online class while the teacher spends more time with students who need additional help with the concept.

At 11:20 a.m. Travis goes to the Fitness Center, where he is working on a personal fitness goal to improve his endurance. He thinks it's great that he has a personal trainer at school who can help him meet his goals and develop a fitness plan just for him. Next month a guest instructor is offering kickboxing classes!

Travis's last class is English 9. He has been struggling with *Animal Farm* and is scheduled to attend face-to-face small-group sessions with his English teacher every day this week. At 12:30 p.m. Travis grabs a healthy snack from the vending kiosk and meets his friend in the multipurpose area to walk back to the bus stop. He heads to his part-time job at a local marketing firm until 5 p.m. After dinner, Travis works on another two hours of schoolwork, including his favorite class, Game Design. He also sends a webmail to his success coach and the guidance counselor with his burning question of the day: What does it take to get into Stanford?

Nexus Rollout: Fall 2012

While the school design team worked to rapidly prototype the Nexus model, the Connections school development staff was in negotiations with charter authorizers about establishing the first schools. The roster for fall 2012 emerged as five Nexus Academy charter schools, one each in Cleveland, Ohio; Columbus, Ohio; Grand Rapids, Michigan;

Lansing, Michigan; and Toledo, Ohio. All would open on September 4, 2012, following six months of space negotiations, renovations, furniture sourcing, and staff recruitment and training. Student recruitment processes kicked in during summer 2012, with the result that first-year enrollment in all five schools was well below the 300-student cap, allowing time and staff attention for fine-tuning the model on a daily basis.

The challenges that emerged during the Nexus Academy launch and first year of operation are instructive. The newness of the blended concept and the very short recruitment window—especially for campuses that were still under construction throughout the summer—made it difficult to attract large numbers of targeted college-prep students who typically have made their school choices many months in advance. Deploying the right staff for any innovative educational approach is always a challenge, but the Nexus Academy team found that the face-to-face teachers especially needed additional training to move away from whole-class instructional techniques to data-driven intervention strategies focused on small groups. Finally, uneven enrollment patterns and last-minute zoning struggles made clear to the team the importance of site choice, setting in motion a much more data-driven predictive model for selecting the locations for future Nexus academies.

Imagining the Blended Future

Nexus Academy's first-year challenges were more than counterbalanced by excitement about this intentionally new approach to schooling. Bloggers tagged Nexus as the cutting edge of blended learning, calling out the combination of the flex model with unique features like the success coach and the integrated wellness program (Vander Ark, 2012). Organizations such as the Thurgood Marshall College Fund, which supports public historically Black colleges and universities (HBCUs) around the country, stepped up to partner with Connections to develop Nexus-style early college schools on or near HBCU campuses. The Nexus design team is at work on the next proposed Nexus Academy charter schools opening in Indiana, Michigan, Washington, DC, and beyond, while school districts throughout the United States are considering whether the Nexus approach—with its efficient use of space, targeted staffing pattern, and commitment to data-driven differentiation—could provide an effective alternative for students who might otherwise have left the district rolls for virtual charters, private schools, or no school at all.

Meanwhile, all eyes will be on the results generated by the first Nexus Academy schools. The goal is for Nexus Academy students, compared to their demographic peers, to outperform on state exams, the SAT/ACT, and Advanced Placement tests; graduate in greater numbers; and make a more successful transition to postsecondary education. If the initial wave of Nexus academies produce results as expected, they will help transform blended learning from a trend to a true path for the future of American education.

References

Agus, J. (2010). *High schools in the United States*. Washington, DC: American Institutes for Research, National High School Research Center.

Bettinger, E., & Baker, R. (2011). *The effects of student coaching in college: An evaluation of a randomized experiment in student mentoring*. NBER Working Paper No. 16881. Cambridge, MA: National Bureau of Economic Research.

Bloom, H., Thompson, S. L., & Unterman, R. (2010). *Transforming the high school experience: How New York City's new small schools are boosting student achievement and graduation rates.* New York: MRDC.

Connections Learning. (2012). *Blended learning: How brick-and-mortar schools are taking advantage of online learning options.* Baltimore: Author. Retrieved from http://www .connectionslearning.com/Libraries/Institutional_Sales/Blended_Learning_Primer__ FINAL_1.pdf

Horn, M. B., & Staker, H. (2011). *The rise of K–12 blended learning.* San Mateo, CA: Innosight Institute.

Leithwood, K., & Riehl, C. (2003). *What we know about successful school leadership: A report by Division A of AERA.* Washington, DC: American Educational Research Association and National Council for School Leadership.

Means, B., Toyama, Y., Murphy, R., Bakia, M., & Jones, K. (2010). *Evaluation of evidence-based practices in online learning: A meta-analysis and review of online learning studies.* (Rev. ed.). Washington, DC: U.S. Department of Education, Office of Planning, Evaluation and Policy Development.

Medina, J. (2008). *Brain rules: 12 principles for surviving and thriving at work, home, and school.* Seattle: Pear Press.

National Alliance for Public Charter Schools. (2012, January 11). *The public charter schools dashboard: Schools by grade configuration.* Washington, DC: Author. Retrieved from http:// dashboard.publiccharters.org/dashboard/schools/page/conf/year/2012

Staker, H., & Horn, H. B. (2012). *Classifying K–12 blended learning.* San Mateo, CA: Innosight Institute.

Vander Ark, T. (2012, November 4). What's next? A flex plus school model by Connections Education. *Education Week.* Retrieved from phttp://blogs.edweek.org/edweek/on_innovation/ 2012/11/whats_next_a_flex_plus_school_model_by_connections_education.html

Watson, J., Murin, A., Vashaw, L., Gemin, B., & Rapp, C. (2012). *Keeping pace with K–12 online and blended learning.* Durango, CO: Evergreen Education Group.

11

A CASE STUDY OF CLARK COUNTY SCHOOL DISTRICT'S VIRTUAL HIGH SCHOOL

Jhone M. Ebert and Allison Powell

I n this chapter we trace the evolution of the Clark County School District (CCSD) Virtual High School from its origins as a supplemental course provider in the late 1990s to a mature program that informs policy and practice, setting the stage for online and blended learning to become a key district strategy for implementing choice, innovation, and productivity today.

Overview of CCSD Virtual High School

Clark County is one of the most diverse districts in the nation. Although the majority of the student population has always been in the Las Vegas metropolitan area, the district covers almost 8,000 square miles in total and enrolls over 309,000 students, making it the fifth-largest school district in the country. The community is urban, suburban, and rural. With this unique demographic, the CCSD has been providing learning at a distance for over 40 years. Learning packets, videotapes, and lessons delivered on the local public broadcast station have all been part of providing access to a quality education for all students.

In 1998 CCSD began the transition of its distance learning courses to the Internet and created the Cyber Schoolhouse. The goal was to create engaging courses that allowed for flexibility of the learning environment while providing highly qualified teachers for hard-to-fill positions and for schools where low enrollment in a course prevented a student from having access to the course. With little research to rely on and scant resources available, the Cyber Schoolhouse was started with just a handful of motivated teachers and students who wanted to explore this new learning environment. Within four years it had grown to serving more than 4,000 part-time students and 30 part- and full-time teachers while also providing coursework for school districts across the state of Nevada.

In 2004 the Cyber Schoolhouse shed its title to become the CCSD Virtual High School. Students were now able to enroll in the school full-time and earn a high school diploma without attending a traditional brick-and-mortar building. Even though students did not have to attend a face-to-face class five days a week, they were assigned to attend a synchronous (i.e., live online) session once a week. Students were also required to pick up textbooks and other supplemental materials as well as take all course final exams and state-mandated tests face-to-face. The first graduating class in 2005 had eight seniors.

Over the years, CCSD Virtual High School has created more online courses and stopped publishing video classes. Students are no longer issued physical textbooks. Today e-texts are more common; the availability of course authoring tools removed this requirement. Part-time enrollments have been fluid and in flux as virtual labs[1] were established in brick-and-mortar schools and the course fee/tuition structures were changed over time to make enrollment tuition-free, except for nondistrict residents. Full-time enrollment has remained somewhat constant over the years, hovering at around 200 students for the 2012 school year.

Enrollment at CCSD Virtual High School grew over 60% between 2010 and 2012. More comprehensive schools are hosting virtual labs. The course catalog continues to grow, offering a wide range of core classes, electives, honors, and Advanced Placement courses for students to take for original credit or credit retrieval. In 2012 CCSD Virtual High School was proud to honor its largest graduating class of 56 seniors, prepared for today's technology-driven society.

Although the CCSD has not mandated online or blended courses as a requirement for high school graduation, the district does believe that all students should have the opportunity to engage in this 21st-century learning environment. The district believes that it has the obligation, opportunity, and capacity to make online and blended learning universally available for all CCSD students. In 2012 the district created the Innovative Learning Environments Department within the Technology and Information Systems Services Division. This department is charged with building and supporting a districtwide learning environment where at least 100,000 students will participate in an online or blended learning course by 2015.

To this end, current district-level courses are now being aligned to the Common Core State Standards (CCSS)[2] and built in modules so that they may be implemented in blended classroom instruction throughout the district. This approach will increase access and use of high-quality instructional materials to students and families beyond the traditional school day. Establishment of district-level CCSS courses ensures that the courses meet district standards and are approved for internal credits, for original credit, credit recovery, or both. All of this increases opportunities for young people.

To ensure that teachers will be able to implement these courses and course modules, the district developed an online teacher certification program. Content including online and blended learning pedagogy, the use of appropriate tools, and other aligned topics, such as flipping the classroom and using mobile devices, is being developed to provide teachers, administrators, and staff with the knowledge and skills necessary to deliver high-quality online and blended teaching and learning to CCSD students. The program includes foundational courses aligned to nationally recognized models of blended learning as well as to standards for online teachers, courses, programs, and content. These courses support the various blended learning environments, from flipping the classroom to hosting virtual labs, and the deployment of online courses in the brick-and-mortar schools. In addition, a catalog of approved vendors for purchased or leased content will be established after a thorough alignment to district standards and the CCSS. District-owned courses reduce the cost of leased seats or annual maintenance fees of outside vendors. When content is purchased/leased, it is reviewed through a rigorous evaluation process by a team of content and online learning experts, in order to maintain the district's high expectations.

Challenges and Lessons Learned

CCSD Virtual High School began as a three-course program for concurrently enrolled students; transitioned to an accredited, diploma-granting high school; and now has been challenged to serve over 100,000 students in a blended and online learning environment. CCSD made the determination in 2000 to build and offer courses via the Internet: a bold move at that time. Not until December 2000 did the Congressional Web-Based Education Commission publish its report *The Power of the Internet for Learning: Moving From Promise to Practice*, urging that "the nation should embrace an 'e-Learning' agenda as a centerpiece of our federal education policy."[3]

Four people supported the CCSD program. Jhone Ebert, Karlene McCormick-Lee, Allison Powell, and Tom Stanley would gather around a table in the back room of a high school library to make a determination on how to move forward. There was little research and only a handful of other online programs across the country to look to as resources. With *Designing and Teaching an On-line Course* (Schweizer, 1999) as a primary resource, the team began to plan the Cyber Schoolhouse. Three teachers were hired on a part-time basis to build and deliver health, U.S. government, and Advanced Placement (AP) geopolitical economics courses. These courses were chosen for a variety of reasons. Health was a one-semester course that interfered with scheduling for students who wanted to take yearlong electives. U.S. government was a required course for seniors, and several students failed the first semester with no way of recovering the credit in order to graduate on time. The AP course was offered at only one school in the state; inclusion would give students across the district the opportunity to access the course and teacher.

Using the research and information from *Facilitating Online Learning: Effective Strategies for Moderators* (Collison, Elbaum, Haavind, & Tinker, 2000) and the lessons learned from the creation and first year of offering the three courses, a professional development program was developed. We offered training on the pedagogy of teaching online, the use of asynchronous and synchronous tools, and developing an online course, in addition to ongoing professional development for facilitating discussions and creating assessments; other topics identified as teachers' needs were also brought to our attention and addressed. Each year new teachers were trained and courses built based on the needs of the district. AP, foreign language, algebra, and an English-language learners (ELL) program were established in the first three years of the Cyber Schoolhouse.

As the Cyber Schoolhouse began to grow, other programs across the country were also developing. Our team went on site visits and attended the Virtual School Symposium and other conferences related to online learning in order to network and learn from and share our best practices with other practitioners. From these travels, a relationship with the Florida Virtual School (FLVS) was established. The district purchased an AP

Economics course from FLVS to better understand how others were developing courses. Both organizations learned from this experience, which improved how we developed new courses.

The field of K–12 online learning was still in its infancy when the Cyber Schoolhouse began. Because of this, we were forced to develop almost everything from scratch, including policies, content, and professional development. We also realized that in moving to this new learning environment, we would need to change the perceptions of our community. Implementing the Cyber Schoolhouse brought many challenges and lessons learned.

Policy and Funding

Building an online school where teachers and students were not required to come on campus required CCSD to develop policies and procedures for ensuring the best and most appropriate experience for all. Teachers and course developers had to sign off that they fully understood intellectual property and copyright laws. They also had to establish and maintain office hours during which time students could contact them through purchased web tools or by phone. Attendance and grade reporting opened up its own set of challenges.

Established laws and policies presented a challenge in content design at the beginning of the online endeavor in the district. When the district started to build online courses, Nevada law stated that each and every student was required to have a textbook for each core course. CCSD Virtual High School had to build courses with assignments and readings aligned to the adopted textbook, also ensuring that the district was covering the state's newly developed content and process standards. Such laws and policies have changed over time. Nevada law now recognizes the validity of online content without the requirement of textbooks, but maintains an assurance of quality by requiring that the Nevada State Department of Education approve all content delivered online.

Competency-based education is currently a hot topic. The CCSD is in full agreement that a student must be able to demonstrate proficiency, so much so that the state requires students to be able to pass four different proficiency exams before receiving a high school diploma. Delivering the full curriculum in a comprehensive manner is critical; the question has always been whether seat time equates to content competency. When CCSD Virtual High School was established, there was no allowance for competency-based courses in Nevada law. Recently, legislation was passed that allowed for state-approved, computer-based courses to be offered in a competency-based format. That is, once a student has demonstrated that he has met the standards for the course curriculum, he may be issued a grade for the course, without consideration of the Carnegie Unit. CCSD continues to work with the International Association for K–12 Online Learning (iNACOL) and the National Collegiate Athletic Association (NCAA) to ensure that CCSD and all other entities can demonstrate that learning can, and should, take place beyond the constraints of a bell schedule and four walls, which equates to seat time.

Funding for CCSD Virtual High School is allocated through four main systems. The school receives standard per-pupil funding for each full-time student, as every comprehensive high school does. A self-funded model is in place for part-time students, who utilize CCSD Virtual High School to extend their school day beyond the six-period day at their home school. These students pay a fee per semester course. CCSD Virtual High School receives a small allocation to assist in paying for the learning management system (LMS), technology support, and central support functions provided to other CCSD schools. Finally, CCSD Virtual High School has been awarded allocations from a number of competitive state and federal grants.

Implementation

In order to bring course offerings to scale, the district made the determination to put together a distance learning task force. The district had just passed the 1998 bond to build 88 new schools. To support the understanding that the population growth was moving at a much faster rate than schools could be built, Cyber Schoolhouse was established as a timely and cost-effective means of educating CCSD students. Utilizing the district's network infrastructure and a combination of multiple technologies, students were able to experience online learning. The district also merged existing credit-bearing video courses and called the program Video Schoolhouse.

Implementation at a larger scale brought with it some very significant challenges. Teachers with varying backgrounds would come to CCSD Virtual High School with preconceived notions of what online learning should be. A brand-new teacher, for example, would take right to online learning processes and functions, utilize the tools to their highest capacity, and find success in the achievement of students. An experienced classroom teacher, however, may struggle with the use of technology tools, especially those available at the time, to replace the valuable face-to-face interaction with students. One teacher covertly drove all across the Las Vegas valley to meet with students face-to-face. He also found great success in the achievement of his students. It was as if these teachers were trying to put into practice blended learning models that we had not yet defined or even considered.

Another challenge to the early success of CCSD Virtual High School was the dependence on the decision making of comprehensive high school guidance counselors. Established enrollment systems and practices put the counselor in the role of gatekeeper to CCSD Virtual High School courses. Especially in the early days, only through the decision of a counselor would a student be able to enroll in an online course. The administrative team made it a priority to educate and support counselors across the district in order to earn their trust to enroll students in the Cyber Schoolhouse. In presentations and professional development opportunities we provided for counselors, we used student data (e.g., completion rates, course evaluations from students and parents, AP exam scores, as well as state exam scores) in addition to the student and teacher voice to show that students were receiving educational experiences equal to—if not better than, in some cases—those students in a face-to-face classroom. Although it took a lot of time to earn their trust, counselors across the district began enrolling more students in Cyber Schoolhouse courses as they saw the benefits for students, in addition to making their jobs easier by reducing scheduling conflicts, providing credit recovery options to graduate more students on time, and providing access to more courses for their students.

Perceptions of Online Learning

In the early days of Cyber Schoolhouse, there were times when the district's central office would state how we had "messed everything up" because students meeting only once a week left blanks in the Student Information System, designed to document daily seat time. Students—sometime parents—would come to the school's office demanding to know why they earned a D and have to be shown the records that indicated the number of times the student logged in to complete coursework. The team will never forget the meeting when a principal turned to us and said with disdain, "You mean you are going to issue students a course credit and they are never going to set foot in a classroom?" Those were the days when we knew we were on the right track, but had a long road to travel.

The team needed to reestablish perceptions of central office, school staff, parents, and students—essentially, every major stakeholder—in order for this project to succeed. We needed to capitalize on early successes and the clear benefits of online learning that would help to persuade our community. We found that some of our colleagues were ready for the online revolution and some were not, but not too many were on the fence. Those who were not ready required only some conversation and some education. When the distance learning task force was formed, the inclusion of experts from around the field of online learning as well as representatives from across the district, both those in favor of and opposed to online learning, allowed for the sharing of expertise. In some instances, the task force visited schools to meet and talk with administration and counselors individually. The team embarked on major marketing campaigns, placing ads in newspapers and movie theaters, to increase visibility and acceptance across the community as well.

Content

The CCSD team worked very closely with FLVS to capitalize on lessons already learned by the Florida team. Julie Young, president and CEO of FLVS, and her team freely provided guidance on to how to build online courses and deliver them to thousands of students. Based upon their guidance, we were also able to select an appropriate LMS.

Because the CCSD was already standards-based and had established course syllabi, online course development was less of a challenge than it could have been. We had only to apply current online learning best practices based on the literature and our experiences to already developed course objectives.

The biggest challenge in creating digital content was in assisting teachers to use the tools to create the content. In the early days of the Cyber Schoolhouse, teachers had to learn to use web design tools such as Dreamweaver and Photoshop in addition to some HTML, as the tools available were not as easy as dragging and dropping content into the LMS as they are today. We learned very quickly after changing LMSs three times in three years the importance of writing all of the content in HTML so that it could be easily accessible and edited within any tool on the Internet.

Today, the development of an online course by CCSD is a collaboration of a team of teachers, curriculum specialists, administrators, technical support personnel, and web designers and curators. District administrators and curriculum specialists worked hard on the Cyber Schoolhouse plan from its inception, understanding the use of distance learning as a teaching tool and how to evaluate the use of the tools and pedagogy for online courses.

Providing accessible content was another challenge. All students across the district were eligible to enroll in online courses. When content was first created, teachers used text, images, videos, and simulations in addition to the live audio from Centra, the school's synchronous tool. When a student who was deaf enrolled, we had to find ways for him to participate in Centra, which was a totally audio-based tool. We brought someone in to sign the conversation and speak for him during the course. A student who was blind also enrolled, which taught us how to tag every picture with a description and add subtitles to all of the videos with the courses. These were huge challenges we learned from in developing our own content, but in the end they made our courses more engaging for all students.

Some specific content objectives did not apply to or were not easily applicable to an online environment. For example, one of the English language arts Nevada content standard strands indicated that students should be able to use public-speaking techniques to deliver presentations with appropriate prosody, volume, eye contact, enunciation, posture, expressions, audience, and purpose. Eye contact, posture, and expressions could not be demonstrated in the audio-only synchronous environment established for live classroom sessions. The choice was to change the standard or find a tool that would meet those specific needs. Over time, those tools have become available.

Teacher Professional Development

Teacher evaluation was the one area with few challenges for the district. Because the coursework was available online 24/7, administrators always had the opportunity to view content and support the teachers. The administrators could watch a live or recorded lesson from Centra or review the content in the LMS and have a professional discussion on how students were engaging with the content and teacher, as well as how well they were meeting the expected outcomes.

From the very beginning, teachers have received professional development in the delivery of online instruction. During the first few years, the courses were taught face-to-face with an online component. Today, they are delivered exclusively online. When teachers are hired, they are enrolled in and paid to take the 140-plus hours of professional development courses required to teach and develop an online course. In addition, for a semester teachers are provided an experienced online teacher as a mentor. Teachers assist their mentors with synchronous and asynchronous lessons, grading, and working with students.

The professional development program was built with guidance from experienced faculty at the University of Nevada Las Vegas (UNLV) College of Education in addition to what the team had learned in taking courses from the Concord Consortium's Virtual High School (later VHS Inc., now VHS Collaborative). There were some studies and books on best practices in developing asynchronous online courses, but to the best of our knowledge, we were the only program in the country using a synchronous tool to enhance our asynchronous content. Our staff was able to learn about some best practices in using the tool for learning and to build community among students from the corporate community. We had to develop this aspect of professional development on our own, trying to use the asynchronous tool for more than lecturing purposes.

Effective Practices

As the Cyber Schoolhouse expanded and grew into the CCSD Virtual High School, we continuously documented, revisited, and updated our policies, content, and professional development based on the data and experiences of the team and stakeholders.

The policies of the state and district have evolved over the past 14 years, making it possible for the CCSD Virtual High School to provide better support and access for all students. A move to competency-based learning has removed the challenge of attendance requirements that did not apply to students in online courses. District technology infrastructure policies have been updated as well, enabling the school's technology to integrate across the district's systems, making it easier to capture student data as well as offer courses across the district, both in student's homes and in the school buildings.

As one of the earliest content developers in the country, CCSD Virtual High School has developed several promising practices in the curriculum development area. The district has chosen to build some of its own courses but has also purchased and leased courses from content providers when local content experts were not available, or courses could not be built quickly enough.

In 2000 CCSD hired IBM consultants to assist in documenting and improving our course development process in order to streamline it and our professional development program (see Fig. 11.1). In a 10-step process, courses were developed through small- and whole-group collaboration. A design team was developed with specific roles for each member, and a timeline was set for the development process. Existing technologies and available course content were reviewed. Standards were considered with which the course needed to align. The course was outlined, outcomes were determined, and the course was mapped. Training was developed for instructors in use of tools, content, and pedagogy related to the course. Each course unit was developed through a cyclical process, including objectives, activities, assessment, consideration of learning styles and real-world connections, related resources, and unit design, ending with development of an end-of-unit survey and pretest. The module was then built online. Design team reviews occurred at regular intervals during the process.

In addition to the creation of the course development and professional development processes, an advisory team developed curriculum design and development guidelines. The first set of guidelines focused around general course design. These guidelines ensured that courses had a consistent look and feel in addition to similar navigation and instructions. This allowed for students taking multiple courses to focus on learning rather than how to navigate the course. Instructional design guidelines were developed to ensure that the courses were dynamic, engaging, and of high quality. A process was developed within these guidelines for reviewing the content, assignments, and assessments to ensure that they were aligned to content standards and provided opportunities for students to learn the content in a variety of ways. A summary of these guidelines is listed in the following section.

Figure 11.1: Development process (as developed by CCCS teacher/trainers, June 12, 2000)

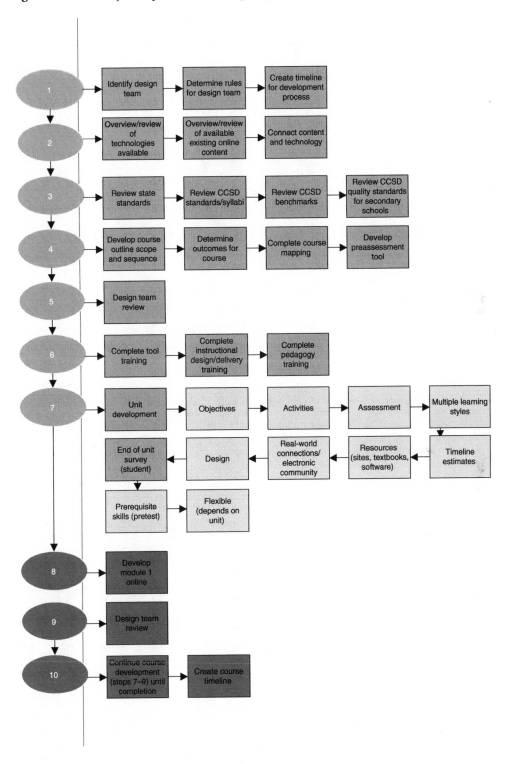

General Design

- Incorporation of asynchronous and synchronous learning objectives and units of instruction
- Organization format and structure

  o Easy to navigate and use
  o Consistency of presentation
  o Consistent instructions and directions

- Standard "Start Here" module/unit
- Course map with activities, assignments, time-to-complete estimates
- Relevant use of graphics—graphics that add instructional value
- Ancillary resources supporting online instruction

  o Textbooks, CDs, web links

- Consistent use of tools

  o Centra, Macromedia Tools, and Learning Space

Instructional Design

- Built upon CCSD Secondary Course Syllabi
- Developed collaboratively by CCSD Design Team

  o Teacher—master of content
  o Content specialist
  o Cyber Schoolhouse trainer

- Formalized peer review process for continued enhancement and improvement
- Collaborative, interactive, and engaging
- Project-based activities
- Multiple assessments
- Incorporates multiple learning styles and multiple intelligences
- Incorporates CCSD Standards of Quality

With the development process chart and these guidelines, content development teams were better able to streamline and benchmark their process to ensure that deadlines were met in the creation of high-quality and engaging courses. Although these processes were developed in 2000, several of the pieces are still applicable to the course development process today.

As the field has become more advanced, so has the research and technology. Teachers no longer need to learn HTML programming code and can develop their content with easy-to-use online drag-and-drop tools. National organizations such as iNACOL (2011a, 2011b) have developed national standards for quality online courses and teaching, providing a more detailed framework for the development of online courses within the district.

Another example of effective practice is our professional development program. Professional development has also been a district priority for teaching in the online environment. As the field has evolved, the need for updating the training for teachers has as well. While the pedagogy has stayed consistent in the CCSD Virtual High School, evolving technologies and policies create a continuous need for updating professional development. In the beginning, teachers were required to hold weekly synchronous sessions with students, and all students were required to stay on a semester timeline. Synchronous sessions are no longer required, although most teachers continue to offer them, and competency-based learning policies now allow for anytime, any-pace learning. "Lunch and Learn," 30-minute synchronous professional development opportunities, were developed to share quick tips and new tools and ideas during teachers' lunch hours. These sessions were recorded so that those who could not participate live could watch them at any time from the archives.

Another example is our continuing work to change perceptions of online and blended learning among stakeholders. As online learning becomes more mainstream, it has been easier to get buy-in from administrators, teachers, counselors, parents, and students in the district and across the state. CCSD Virtual High School team leaders continue to educate the state and district stakeholders about the benefits and opportunities that online and blended learning provide students. While this takes time as personnel is continually changing, the CCSD Virtual High School leadership has found this to be an effective practice in earning the confidence and trust of the district and community, in addition to getting feedback on how to continually improve the school.

Future of Online and Blended Learning in CCSD

CCSD believes that every student should have access to high-quality teachers and a high-performing school (online, charter, or other) and should graduate with the knowledge, skills, and behaviors needed to succeed in a competitive global society. To this end, CCSD presented a vision for the development of a new model of schooling in a recent report, *A Look Ahead Phase I* (Jones, 2011). Key elements described include moving toward competency-based education, providing diverse pathways to high school completion, and taking advantage of online and computer-based solutions for personalized learning. In setting forth principles for ensuring that students are "ready by exit," CCSD superintendent Dwight Jones states the need to recognize that choice and innovation are the engines driving needed school reform (Principle #5). To achieve this, he proposes that the district leverage technology to alter instructional processes and improve efficiency and effectiveness, and expand the use of "anywhere anytime learning."

To accomplish this, an Innovative Learning Environments Department has been established within the Technology and Information Systems Services Division, which includes new online and blended learning programs that build upon the Virtual High School and its effective practices. The position of chief innovation and productivity officer has been created in the superintendent's office to lead development of online and blended learning as well as data-driven management processes.

The blended learning initiative is being executed as a collection of subprojects in three categories, using a modular approach to program development and implementation:

- Innovative Learning Environments Online Resource Development—The purchase, development, and alignment of online instructional materials; professional development; online systems integration; and district support to schools.
- CCSD Graduation Pathways—Providing online courses and consultation from credit recovery to advancement.
- Grow Your Own Blended Learning School—Working with elementary, middle, and high school staff to shift to blended learning strategies in traditional school.

In the future, continued efforts will be required in the area of reshaping policy and statute. We are working with the Nevada state legislature to implement the Digital Learning Act, which will remove obstacles currently inhibiting the district from providing certain innovative solutions for students who want to participate in digital or blended learning. One of the requested amendments would provide an exemption to a current requirement for a licensed educator to be in every classroom where instruction is occurring. The exemption would allow a class or group of students who are participating in a program at a distance to be supervised in a computer lab or classroom by an unlicensed employee, with the online or blended teacher who is delivering the course serving as the licensed teacher of record.

CCSD has the obligation, opportunity, and capacity to make online and blended learning universally available for students through thoughtful and ambitious reform. In developing its districtwide vision, CCSD has incorporated the four models of blended learning (Staker, 2012). By leveraging technology and expanding anywhere, anytime access, the district will support all schools in implementing choice and innovation in instruction.

Notes

1. Participating schools had the option to utilize a virtual lab on-site designed for student participation in Virtual High School courses during the school day. The home school identified a teacher to monitor students in the computer lab as they completed VHS coursework.
2. For more information on the CCSS, visit http://corestandards.org.
3. www2.ed.gov/offices/AC/WBEC/FinalReport/WBECReport.pdf.

References

Collison, G., Elbaum, B., Haavind, S., & Tinker, R. (2000). *Facilitating online learning: Effective strategies for moderators.* Madison, WI: Atwood.

International Association for K–12 Online Learning. (2011a). *National standards for quality online courses, version 2.* Retrieved from http://www.inacol.org/research/nationalstandards/iNACOL_CourseStandards_2011.pdf

International Association for K–12 Online Learning. (2011b). *National standards for quality online teaching, version 2*. Retrieved from http://www.inacol.org/research/nationalstandards/ iNACOL_TeachingStandardsv2.pdf

Jones, D. D. (2011). *A look ahead phase I: Preliminary reforms report*. Las Vegas: Clark County School District. Retrieved from http://www.ccsd.net/district/superintendent/resources/pdf/a-look-ahead-05-2011.pdf

Schweizer, H. (1999). *Designing and teaching an on-line course: Spinning your web classroom*. Needham Heights, MA: Allyn & Bacon.

Staker, H. B. (2012). *Classifying K–12 blended learning*. San Medro, CA: Innosight Institute. Retrieved from http://www.innosightinstitute.org/innosight/wp-content/uploads/2012/05/ Classifying-K-12-blended-learning2.pdf

12

VIRTUAL HIGH SCHOOL (ONTARIO)

A Case Study of an Online Private School

John Smallwood, Jennifer Reaburn, and Stephen Baker

In the spring of 1995 Stephen Baker, a staff member at Goderich District Collegiate Institute within the Huron County Board of Education (now the Avon-Maitland District School Board in Ontario, Canada), took a board-sponsored course on the fundamentals of HTML. The natural fit of education and the Internet was immediately apparent. In the fall of 1996 Baker used Notepad to construct an 11th-grade biology course, which was posted via wsFTP onto an Odyssey Network Inc. server housed in the back room of a jewelry store in Clinton, Ontario, under the HuronWeb.com domain (WHOis.com, n.d.-a). The biology online course was viewable to anyone connected to the Internet. In the spring of 1996 Baker posted a second course, Canadian Literature, written by John Smallwood. This course won a North American award for course development (Hall, 1997). On January 2, 1997, the fledgling school was moved to the VirtualHighSchool.com domain (WHOis.com, n.d.-b). During these early years, Baker pieced together a rudimentary learning management system (LMS) to run the two online courses, providing a log-in so that students could gain access to their courses, a secure testing site, and a rudimentary role structure for students, teachers, and administrators.

Over the next couple of years, Baker continued to refine the curriculum writing, content development, and instructional design processes for the Virtual High School (Ontario; VHS) courses. However, just before the millennium, the business relationship between VHS and the school board began to unravel. At issue were the ownership rights to the courses already developed, ownership of the VirtualHighSchool.com domain, and the board's desire to run the courses in a CD production environment rather than through the Internet. Five years after it started, VHS was sent back to the starting line with two courses and the VirtualHighSchool.com domain. This restart would turn out to be significantly more challenging, as there was no longer any support from the school board. Further, the online school could not grant any form of acceptable credit.

Around the same time, Baker helped his son John establish another company, Desire-2Learn, which used the structure of VHS's two existing online courses as a template to construct its LMS. By the end of August 2002, Desire2Learn had continued its evolution, and VHS had six courses developed. However, despite extensive marketing, VHS had only seven students, none of whom earned a credit as they finished their courses. In Ontario, only inspected private schools have the ability to grant Ontario Secondary School Diploma (OSSD) credits (Education Act, 1990). Without accreditation from the Ministry of Education, the online courses would have no particular appeal apart from the courses serving as supplemental or extra-help study offerings for students in conventional school settings.

Baker subsequently applied to the Ontario Ministry of Education for recognition as an accredited private school (Ontario Ministry of Education, 2012). In 2002 the process of establishing a private school in Ontario was still mired in the physical world. For example, the online school had to supply a fire inspection report with its application. Despite these traditional regulations, the Ministry of Education also looked at factors related to online school quality. It performed a number of in-depth inspections on the six courses of study, resulting in VHS becoming a fully accredited, inspected private school in Ontario in April 2003 with the BSID #665681. OSSD credits could now be offered to students.

Despite its new role as an inspected private school, Baker felt that many people in the province were still not ready for a *virtual* high school, so the online school was called the Kitchener-Waterloo Private School.

Following the granting of private school status, student credits that year reached 46. There were 157 enrollments in 2004 and 292 in 2005. Obviously, there existed a student need for online schools that offered courses that met the ministry's standards. In 2006 Baker hired two additional staff members to look after the administration of the school. By 2008 the staff totaled six, still operating out of Baker's basement. In the fall of 2010 Baker began to look for a commercial property that might serve the needs of the rapidly expanding school, as it now had eight full-time administrative staff.

Physical Space

Baker purchased an existing, historically significant landmark (i.e., the old Ritz Hotel in Bayfield, Ontario) and redesigned it into three stories of usable space totaling some 8,100 square feet that served as the administrative and teaching hub for students and teachers. One floor contains administrative offices. Like all schools, VHS is required by the ministry to keep hard-copy files for all students. These Ontario School Records are audited in detail by officials during their regular inspection visits. Students and school counselors from around the world routinely communicate with VHS administrative staff regarding equivalent credits, prerequisites, financial matters, and the daily concerns in attending a school. Such activities require a physical space in which to collaborate on the day-to-day operations of a successful school, making VHS in some ways quite traditional in its approach to serving a student body.

Another floor of the building is occupied by curriculum coordinators, content developers, instructional designers, and department heads who meet often to discuss changes in the Ontario Ministry requirements, how those changes will be implemented in the courses, and other matters such as plagiarism, course design, and effective teaching strategies. Also, a considerable amount of discussion and mentoring ensues among curriculum developers on how to most effectively deliver courses to the entire student body.

Such interaction creates a strong team atmosphere in which all faculty members in the office work together.

Thus, the physical space that VHS occupies and the building are a blend of the traditional and the modern in the same way that the instruction combines entirely contemporary and innovative trends in online learning with a powerful emphasis on student-teacher interaction, the latter of which has been the timeless hallmark of successful instruction. VHS is now an established private online school in the province of Ontario, Canada. The school currently offers 71 distinct high school courses in the asynchronous mode of delivery to students from grades nine to 12. Expecting more than 4,600 student credit registrations in 2012, VHS has succeeded in becoming the largest nondenominational private online high school in Canada (Bennett, 2012).

Asynchronicity as a Philosophy of Education

Like their teachers, students lead more varied and often more demanding lives than at any time in the past. Within a class of 30 students, individual learning needs and styles are readily apparent to every instructor. In an online "classroom" the student body is just as or even more varied than in any other situation. Over the past several years VHS students have been training on national ski teams in Colorado, competing with the Canadian Olympic team in fencing, attending the Juilliard School in New York, traveling with their parents—the activities are as unique as the individuals who undertake them. Justin Bieber studied English at VHS while on tour, and other students who had suffered from health concerns and physical challenges that prevented them from attending traditional schools studied online during their convalescence.

In addition to serving the young, online courses also suit the growing needs of adults. Adult learners who never completed high school and who are seeking employment will find that without a diploma they will have no chance of gaining an interview. These adults, many of whom have young families, benefit from policies that allow students up to 18 months to complete courses.

Hence, the mobility and unique characteristics of many learners have created a demand for a classroom structure to differ radically from the traditional classroom method of handling synchronized batches of students. Not having a school year, nor semesters, but instead having every class always in session relieves the pressure on the student to fit his or her schedule to that of the school. The course content, the tests, the assessments and evaluations, and even the final exam can be accessed at a time convenient to the student. The benefit of this asynchronous environment to students in different time zones is immediately apparent and may be the most appealing feature of VHS for international students.

The Courses

The courses that are offered online must consist of much more than the easily built and often seemingly endless slabs of content and pages of questions that require routine answers. Because students today have sophisticated expectations of any material that is online, course design at VHS is of primary importance. An online course must provide effective, challenging material that is attractive and enthusiastically received by the student. This curriculum design not only meets the requirements of the ministry but also teaches the student in a manner that promotes authentic learning. Students, like all other learners, are motivated to learn when they find the work appealing.

Writing a course can be a daunting task. Increasingly, we question how to teach the required concepts while making the material attractive to students who have a wealth of exciting information on their phones, laptops, and tablets. Teachers are invited to write each course VHS develops, but the development of those courses requires help from a team of other teachers and curriculum coordinators. When individual teachers create courses, they are naturally inclined to emphasize the topics that interest them. While such autonomy is desirable, teachers within a curricular area share the courses, so their feedback is invited on all parts of newly launched courses.

The appropriate curriculum coordinator works closely with the teacher or teachers writing the content of the online course, carefully editing the work so that the course will have wide appeal among students and general acceptance by all of the teachers who are involved in the instruction. In the past, buying hard-copy texts was problematic because teachers preferred one text over another. VHS teachers and coordinators now create their own texts, bringing their own unique approaches to topics.

Having a number of contributors ensures that the texts and examples that are chosen for instruction are suitable for all students. This does not mean that the courses lack interest or variety; it does mean that every student feels comfortable with the subject matter and that the teachers' sensitivity to their students' needs is evident. The matters of writing, topics, items for evaluation, the exam, and the distribution of marks, to name only a few, are dealt with by the teacher who has taken the lead in course creation, but the process is entirely democratic and participatory under the direction of curriculum coordinators who, in turn, work with instructional designers and content developers from other departments. Simulations, theatre productions, language labs, quizzes that are immediately graded with feedback—all of these elements are combined to provide courses that are limited only by the expertise, innovation, and creativity of effective online teachers and their course and content developers.

While a broad consensus among teachers in a department may exist regarding a particular course and its content, taking the process up a pedagogical rung, curriculum coordinators often exchange information on how their teachers are doing their work. By having this close connection, coordinators arrive at common policies regarding turnaround times in grading, protocols regarding e-mails from students, plagiarism, and other matters of common interest. Hence, students who take several courses with VHS have the feeling that they are treated in a consistent, respectful way by all members of the faculty.

The Online Teaching Environment

Online teaching with VHS affords opportunities for veteran and newly graduated teachers alike. Teachers with considerable experience in conventional classes may, at first, doubt that their work in the e-classroom can be as effective. However, committed educators find that they can be just as successful online in an asynchronous environment as they are in traditional settings. VHS teachers and students interact frequently. Students share as much information as they choose with their teachers and peers in discussion forums, blogs, e-mails, chats, and the ePortfolio tools within the LMS. Teachers respond within 24 hours to the students' requests for clarification, respecting at all times the students' needs for privacy. Far from being isolating, online learning can provide better individual attention and stronger relationships than those that exist in many physical classrooms. We have found that those students who seldom volunteer ideas in the physical classroom because they are self-conscious, fear or wish to avoid criticism, or have not done their homework feel much freer to volunteer information to the teacher or classmates in the online environment. VHS has had students from major city school boards enroll with them in order to avoid the intimidation existing in traditional settings. The teacher has no knowledge of the student's history apart from what the student has chosen to divulge. Furthermore, the unfortunate biases that may exist based on prior teaching experience with a student or on other grounds do not arise, leaving the student able to continue his or her work without any preconceived notions on the part of the teacher about the student's ability. As a result, every course marks an entirely new beginning in the students' academic experience.

Competition among students for the teacher's attention is similarly reduced. The Socratic ideal of one teacher per student operates when communication takes place. Within the Desire2Learn LMS, teachers track the student's work and provide individual feedback on student performance and progress. Because the students use a system of drop boxes, students and teachers have immediate access to all of the work that the student has done previously in the course.

Assessment and Evaluation in a Fully Online Environment

Recently the Ontario Ministry of Education has attempted to improve student learning by issuing a document concerning changes that would be implemented in the province's classrooms with respect to assessment and evaluation. These changes aligned the province with trends that had evolved elsewhere when the emphasis shifted to less summative work being submitted and more of the assessment being done with the focus on process. This trend has been ongoing for decades, but it was the Ontario Ministry of Education's (2010) *Growing Success: Assessment, Evaluation, and Reporting in Ontario Schools* that fully outlined different types of assessment, assessment *as* learning and assessment *for* learning. Assessment *as* learning entails self- and peer assessment by students of their own progress, while assessment *for* learning provides feedback to students about their work.

The real challenge for the VHS department heads, course developers, and instructional designers has been to develop online courses that fulfill the assessment and evaluation expectations of the ministry when those expectations had been tailored with brick-and-mortar institutions in mind. VHS has made the new accommodations to ministry policy the dominant focus. The inspectors from the ministry showed great support and, frankly speaking, considerable surprise that the curriculum coordinators and instructional designers had so convincingly and so innovatively reworked the approaches to assessment and evaluation to conform to government mandates.

In a fully online and asynchronous environment, teachers have particular challenges when it comes to assessment and evaluation. How can instructors create a supportive and collaborative learning environment in which students have opportunities to practice skills and receive ongoing feedback on their progress in a situation in which students can begin or finish on any day and are logging in from all over the world? VHS uses a variety of methods to ensure that students are nurtured to become aware of and responsible for their own learning through self-assessment (i.e., assessment *as* learning), and have multiple opportunities to receive constructive feedback on work that is not formally assessed (i.e., assessment *for* learning), in addition to being formally evaluated on summative assignments (i.e., assessment *of* learning).

VHS uses the Desire2Learn tools—such as the Rubric Tool, ePortfolio, Forms, and Discussions—to design instruction in such a way as to meet the challenges and to incorporate all aspects of effective assessment and evaluation. The goal of assessment *as* learning is to nurture students to be aware of expectations, understand what is necessary in order to meet those expectations, and self-monitor and self-assess throughout the course. To this end, designers have created Unit Introductions that clearly communicate unit expectations and explain how students will be assessed. Learning Goals are stated in student-centered language, and students are cued to reflect on these goals throughout the unit. At the end of each unit, Unit Exit Cards lead learners to examine their progress, strengths, and next steps. VHS has also made extensive use of ePortfolio, a tool that provides students with a personal online space within the LMS to store, organize, reflect on, and share work that demonstrates their learning. This manner of communicating curriculum expectations and supporting student awareness works equally well for Canadian and international students; Canadian students are accustomed to the vocabulary and practices, while international students find comfort in having expectations clearly delineated.

Assessment *for* learning activities give students the chance to apply concepts, experiment, check their learning, and receive constructive feedback from their teachers before handing in work to be formally evaluated. There have been challenges to getting students to participate in such activities and preventing them from simply skipping ahead to hand in work to be graded. VHS teachers have found that clearly detailing the benefits and connections increases student buy-in. In some cases, summative assignments have even been designed to include marks for using teacher feedback in revisions. VHS has multiple methods of presenting assessments *for* learning. For example, some work is handed into a drop box to be assessed, some work is posted to a discussion forum to receive peer comments and teacher feedback, and students may also invite their teachers to give comments on work they have posted to their ePortfolios.

Assessment *of* learning refers to formally evaluated student products, which can be tests or student assignments of various kinds. The Desire2Learn system has allowed VHS to create and install drop boxes and tests that are accessible at any time, from anywhere, allowing students all over the world to complete and hand in work at times that are convenient for them. Teachers, likewise, have flexibility; tests and assignments may be graded at any time from anywhere. The Rubric Tool is fully integrated into the system. To provide maximum functionality and improve the student experience, VHS curriculum coordinators have created specific, detailed rubrics for each assignment. Rubrics integrate the four categories of knowledge and skills (i.e., knowledge and understanding, inquiry/thinking, communication, and application; KICA), with specific curriculum expectations and learning goals from the curriculum documents.

The assessments and evaluations are fair, transparent, equitable, and reliable because the student knows exactly what is expected, as the content standards are clearly delineated and the performance standards are precisely laid out in the achievement chart for each course. The teachers can then evaluate with confidence and consistency, providing clear and specific feedback to the students.

Ensuring Consistent, Effective Teaching

In addition to the procedures mentioned previously, teachers in an online environment must at all times be respectful and constructive in the tone of their communication with each student. All of the cues that students pick up on in the classroom are obviously missing in an online environment. Effective online teachers refer to the students by name in their communication; the grading becomes a conversation with the student. Through tools such as Track Changes in Microsoft Word, the teacher coaches and corrects, elaborates and encourages as the feedback on the work continues. A final note at the end of the assignment recaps the student's work in a meaningful way. The days of "Good work! B+" accompanied by no other comment are decidedly over in successful online education.

The result of quality teacher-student communication is that the students and their parents both demonstrate a high degree of satisfaction with the instruction the students are receiving in online courses. In a comment responding to the online article "Report: Online Learning Nearly Doubles Among High School Students," one parent (susan104 from India) responds, not uncharacteristically, on her daughter's experience with online learning:

> An Online Tutor may not be there physically, but they do a wonderful job. . . . I feel that they are often more persistent, understanding and sometimes even more demanding than a traditional tutor. They did wonders for my daughter's reading capability and now she not only actually looks forward to sessions with her online tutor but her performance in class has improved drastically. (Nagel, 2010)

As mentioned at the end of the blog, online classes can supplement and enhance student learning. In a time of large class sizes and busy teaching schedules, additional instruction online can benefit teachers in conventional schools who have limited time in which to provide additional help. Highly qualified online teachers who are entirely aware of the governing bodies' expectations interact with students and are even better prepared to cope with the increasing demands of upper levels of education than many busy teachers are in brick-and-mortar schools. As the parent indicates,

> They [the company she has registered with] have a vast tutor bank for all subjects and grades, have a "tutor search" box which enables one to choose the right tutor, get the same tutor each time (as compared to others which assign whoever may be on shift at that time), and they post tutor reviews too on their site which helps you to decide. What's more, they are affordable and suit your pocket! It seems that online tutoring is here to stay. (Nagel, 2010)

While this comment refers to tutoring, consider the greater impact that full teaching will have on students when positive, continual feedback is provided.

A further note on evaluation: Often, due to the pressures of everyday teaching, students receive marks on assignments and little feedback regarding how the mark was produced. In conventional settings, teacher performance, as in every other vocation, can vary widely. Such disparities among teachers are particularly obvious in situations where strong collective agreements limit the roles of administrators. In some situations teachers resent any input from administrators; such teachers often resist change and see any recommendations as interference. Even more concerning are those teachers who strongly object to departmental changes mandated by provincial or state-run boards of education. Such resistance can surface in the classroom and disadvantage the program, the morale of the students, and the overall effectiveness of the school. As a consequence, teachers may feel beleaguered and dissatisfied when others air their frustrations.

Teachers at VHS are members of the Ontario College of Teachers (OCT), an organization mandated by the Ontario government. To become a member of OCT, a designation of the college, teachers must have a bachelor of education degree in addition to a bachelor's in their disciplines. Additionally, teachers are required to submit documents provided by police departments indicating that the instructors have committed no offenses that would in any way compromise the safety and security of the students. In this way, teachers meet or surpass all of the requirements that teachers in conventional schools do. These credentials are updated every year when the teacher files a document attesting to the fact that no offenses have been committed.

Academically speaking, VHS teachers also surpass the requirements set out for instructors in traditional schools. Of the 71 teachers, 39 have earned graduate degrees, either a master's of education or a master's in a discipline area, while five teachers have earned doctoral degrees. Further, two additional teachers are currently enrolled in their master's program. While graduate degrees do not necessarily improve teaching performance, the statistics do reinforce the fact that VHS teachers are sufficiently motivated to do additional work in their disciplines, and presumably the degrees make for more informed, more interesting courses. Most of the graduate degrees have been earned by younger teachers, and while this may reflect the paucity of work in education available to the young, it may also indicate that a particular type of teacher teaches online. Research into the qualifications of teachers in online environments and in conventional settings could certainly be worth doing.

VHS has structured its school so that each department head routinely checks the communication and evaluation of the teachers in the various departments. The marking of each assignment can be seen, as well as the feedback the teacher provides to students. Department heads, who have decades of experience in education, can ensure that the marking is complete and at an appropriate level, that students are encouraged at all times to do their best work, and that the communication is constructive. Each teacher is made aware of this agreed-upon procedure when joining VHS. Following these reviews, commendations or recommendations are made by the coordinators. Guidance and exemplars are provided to the teaching staff as required. Fortunately, teachers have been entirely compliant in accepting constructive criticism from their department heads.

When teachers plan holidays, they e-mail their students letting them know the dates when instruction and marking will not take place. Students may prepare for these periods by submitting work before the teachers' breaks or have teachers clarify what is required in upcoming assignments when the teacher will be absent. Students can thus continue their work asynchronously and maintain their momentum in the course by working ahead of where they might otherwise be. Occasionally, when emergencies arise, teachers take over the marking for other instructors, allowing for the continual marking of the students' work and providing for a seamless experience for students who diligently plan their work. Because the teachers have been guided by a department head on standards and on quality of feedback, students have prompt (within five days) returns on their assignments with no disruptions.

On extremely rare occasions, when a teacher's performance does not meet expectations, the teacher receives no more registrations in his or her courses, but this happens only after a three-step process to improve the teacher's performance. In this way, the consistency and quality of instruction are maintained. Students indicate their general approval of their experience in their studies at VHS.

International Online Students

School populations have become increasingly diverse with changes in demographics. Classrooms today bear little resemblance to those even a few decades ago as immigration patterns have changed and increasing numbers of immigrant families have settled in North America and elsewhere. The diversity seen in traditional schools is reflected in online schools and has been made possible through the use of new technologies. For these reasons, 17% of VHS's enrollment is now made up of students who are not residents in Ontario. In addition to students from the various provinces, VHS instructors have worked with learners in 64 countries ranging from Antigua to Zimbabwe. The school has working agreements with schools in Singapore, Nigeria, several Caribbean islands, Switzerland, mainland China, and Hong Kong. Such arrangements facilitate the teaching when language difficulties arise, and proctoring for the final exam is made easier when teachers in the schools can work with VHS teachers should questions arise during the exams.

The demand for online courses, particularly those offered by Ontario schools, is driven by the attractiveness of the Ontario Secondary School Diploma, which all major postsecondary institutions in North America recognize. On a national level, Canada is well regarded on the world stage with respect to its educational system. The provinces of Ontario and Alberta consistently rank first or second nationally in terms of student achievement on standardized testing, so it is little wonder that international students are drawn to Canadian schools, and in this case to courses offered by VHS.

Plagiarism

Plagiarism continues to be an important topic for educators in every setting, leading many to question the ability of online schools to deal effectively with the problem. In reference to the previous paragraphs, VHS teachers have found that cultural differences exist among students from different countries, and instructors have determined that some students simply introduce copyrighted material without citing it. This approach may be permissible in some contexts, but certainly not in North America. VHS has implemented a stringent plagiarism policy that distinguishes between negligent and dishonest plagiarism. Teachers may at all times work with students who may not be familiar with North American standards when doing their assignments. A personal, supportive approach is taken, and every effort is made to inform rather than to penalize the student who has made the error, but as the policy indicates, if a student is consistently remiss in either negligent or dishonest plagiarism, he or she is removed from the course, and no refund is provided.

The proctoring of exams is likewise a concern for many. Administrative staff work with proctors whose names and qualifications are provided by the student. The proctors are vetted carefully and their credentials checked. Proctors are given a password that enables the student to take the exam, and the supervisor remains with the students to ensure that the exam is completed without outside assistance. Because the student body is international, VHS is examining other possibilities to ensure that oversight of exams is conducted properly. In the future, the use of established test centers is a possibility, as is an even more intriguing option: an online electronic proctoring program. This type of online proctoring program is currently widely used in American and Canadian universities and, having proved successful, seems to hold real promise for students who do not have easy or immediate access to a qualified proctor.

Conclusion

VHS-Ontario has established a clear niche as an accredited private school and online course provider that follows an individualized learning model, offering asynchronous anywhere/anytime learning, rolling enrollment, and extended course completion times. This model allows VHS to serve students who lead varied and demanding lives, such as athletes and entertainers, students with health challenges and other concerns, adult learners seeking to complete high school, and students from around the world.

Teachers establish strong partnerships with students who take responsibility for their own education in a supportive, creative environment. Teachers and students use a variety of online tools to interact frequently. Students who seldom volunteer ideas, who feel intimidated, or who have suffered from bias or preconceived notions in prior school experiences may find a new beginning to their academic experience in an individualized VHS course.

Attaining accreditation as a private school from a highly regarded provincial education ministry and remaining aligned with its evolving standards has allowed VHS to issue course credits recognized by all major postsecondary institutions in North America. This has been one of the key factors in VHS enrollment growth over time. Colocation of administrators and teachers in a single building has allowed VHS administrative staff to interact effectively with provincial officials, and facilitated the development of a collegial faculty approach to course development and instruction.

Working in collaboration with other teachers and a curriculum coordinator in a collaborative and creative atmosphere, teachers develop unique courses and texts that reflect their interests and talents while ensuring wide appeal among students and general acceptance among VHS teachers. VHS also has made great strides in ensuring consistent, effective teaching practices. Department heads routinely check the online communication and assessment work of their teachers, an agreed-upon procedure for teachers joining VHS. Teachers have clear expectations and support structures to ensure effective instruction.

Responding to evolving provincial standards, VHS has developed effective practices for providing a supportive and collaborative assessment environment for students taking its individualized asynchronous courses. VHS students are nurtured to become aware of and responsible for their own learning through self-assessment and to receive constructive feedback in a positive manner, leading them to be successful in summative assessments. VHS has developed effective approaches for dealing with perennial issues in online education, such as plagiarism and proctoring of exams, but is always interested in exploring new approaches to ensuring educational quality and accountability.

Thus far, the response to courses and to the teaching at VHS has been positive, and students have gone on to excel in universities both in North America and abroad. University officials have responded enthusiastically to the work being done by VHS students. Government officials, who can be less than supportive of private schools, and, even more often, skeptical of online private schools, are right to examine closely the content as well as the degree to which ministry provisions have been met in online schools. Once the officials see that official requirements have been met, great opportunities exist for partnerships between public and private schools when students require individual credits. Closer working relationships will result in greater opportunities for teachers; administrators; and, most importantly, students.

For nearly two decades, VHS has been a pioneer in its student-centric approach to online education. Today, the asynchronous nature of VHS accommodates students who need to access their learning 24/7/365. This personalized style of education, combined with a curriculum that is highly challenging, a responsive teaching staff, and a robust learning environment, continue to be the essential ingredients that make VHS a successful online school.

References

Bennett, P. (2012). *The sky has limits: Online learning in Canadian K–12 public education.* Toronto: Society for Quality Education. Retrieved from http://societyforqualityeducation.org/parents/theskyhaslimits

Education Act. Government of Ontario, R.S.O. (1990).

Hall, R. (1997). *Guided surfing: Development and assessment of a World Wide Web interface for an undergraduate psychology class.* Paper presented at the North American Web-Based Learning Conference Series, Shortening the Distance to Education Conference, Fredericton, NB. Retrieved from http://www.uvm.edu/~hag/naweb97/papers/hall.html

Nagel, D. (2010, June 29). Report: Online learning nearly doubles among high school students. *T.H.E. Journal.* Retrieved from http://www.icyte.com/system/snapshots/fs1/c/e/d/f/cedf157c95d2af66dd55f557d4c82d3de1f115f9/index.html

Ontario Ministry of Education. (2010). *Growing success: Assessment, evaluation, and reporting in Ontario schools.* Toronto: Queen's Printing for Ontario.

Ontario Ministry of Education. (2012). *Private elementary and secondary schools.* Toronto: Queen's Printing for Ontario. Retrieved from http://www.edu.gov.on.ca/eng/general/elemsec/privsch/index.html

WHOis.com. (n.d.-a). *WHOis.com huronweb.com.* Author. Retrieved from http://www.whois.com/whois/huronweb.com

WHOis.com. (n.d.-b). *WHOis.com virtualhighschool.com.* Author. Retrieved from http://www.whois.com/whois/virtualhighschool.com

13

BARRIERS TO ONLINE LEARNING IN DEVELOPING NATIONS

The Case of Nepal

Cathy Cavanaugh

In many nations, e-learning for elementary and secondary students is seen as a solution to several educational problems, including crowded schools, shortages of secondary courses needed by remedial or accelerated students, lack of access to qualified teachers in a local school, and students who need to learn at a pace or in a place different from a school classroom. A fundamental challenge in this relatively new educational field is building upon successful practice and research. In this chapter I seek to address this need for guidance from prior research and practice through application to the case of one of the world's least developed countries, Nepal.

The UN Millennium Development Goal of Education for All indicated in 2011 that over 160,000 children are still out of school in Nepal. Traditional reasons for non-participation in schooling include lack of toilets for girls, the cost of books and supplies, the preference to keep children at home to work for the family, unsafe and long walks to school, and lack of employment opportunities after completing school. To add to these long-standing concerns, new fears have arisen as a result of government instability, bombings, and attacks around the country from political and personal conflicts. Because Nepal's population has wide disparity in education attainment and literacy, as well as language and culture, the type of personalization afforded by e-learning is critical to increasing access to appropriate education opportunities, thereby improving participation in the emerging democracy and economy.

Nepal's Education Context

Nepal is unique in several respects that make it a strong candidate for development in virtual education. Specific characteristics of its demographics and national governance demonstrate both the need for increasing access to education and the relative advantages of adoption and implementation of virtual programs. Nepal had a secondary school

This work was supported by the U.S. Department of State Fulbright Commission.

gross enrollment rate of 56% as of 2007, according to the United Nations Educational, Scientific and Cultural Organization (UNESCO; 2010). Recent figures show that each school in the country serves an average of fewer than 150 students, contributing to a high potential per-student capital investment in management, teachers, land, construction, and maintenance (UNESCO, 2010).

The country was united from 59 different ethnic groups (Sherpa, 2005). It has an emerging democratic government with diverse representation in a congress of 601 members from across geographic and cultural groups. Nepal has an ambitious national education plan that prioritizes technology. Education is viewed as a step toward its national economic goals, which include diversifying from agriculture to reach economic independence. The country has an established national school curriculum and exam system that extends to centralized university teacher preparation and licensure programs. So far, low numbers of qualified teachers have stalled expansion of traditional schooling. Nepal is one of many countries worldwide that face similar challenges: UNESCO estimated that 10 million teachers will be needed to meet the world's needs in coming years (Bokova, Clark, Lake, & Somovia, 2010). Solving the educational access problem with virtual schools in one country provides a model for others.

In Nepal, most schools are open five and a half to six days per week, a calendar that supports the provision of adequate learning time. However, that time is eroded by lengthy examination periods, vacations, and as many as 80 public holidays during the year to accommodate civil and religious observances. Add to that number missed school due to childhood illnesses, including the common condition of diarrhea resulting from a shortage of clean water. In recent years, dozens of strikes have brought school, work, and travel to a standstill around Kathmandu. It does not take many unanticipated days out of school to amount to a significant proportion of the school year, and it does not take many missed school days to noticeably impact student academic performance. American researchers recently studied this impact by investigating the effect of snow days on student learning outcomes, finding that as few as four days of school missed in a year because of snowstorms reduced student exam scores (Marcotte & Hemelt, 2008). In the United States, several schools and districts have implemented online snow days for continuity of education and to expand learning time in a cost-effective and educationally sound way (Cavanaugh, 2009). Around the world, most notably in Singapore, schools have implemented online lessons and teaching in the event of epidemics, natural disasters, and other events that temporarily close schools (Murphy, 2006). A robust communications infrastructure in Nepal, coupled with low-cost computing devices now available, could make online school days a reality.

Nepal's Economic and Environmental Context

Nepal's geographic, environmental, and cultural characteristics are such that increasing access to virtual education has advantages over attempting to physically place all students in school buildings with teachers. Climate change in the Himalayan area has had real impacts in recent years on daily life. Water supplies, agriculture, electric power, and tourism are just a few of the ways that billions of people in and around Nepal depend on the Himalayan glaciers. Partly in response to climate change, Nepal began to reduce its dependence on agriculture and move toward a more diverse economy. Developing a more diverse workforce requires that a larger proportion of the population complete secondary and higher education.

Travel of even a short distance to school can be perilous where roads are narrow, often unpaved, and occupied above their designed capacity with vehicles driven by the increasing middle class. Even in the city, where travel is easier than in rural areas, there are other environmental hazards. In the Economics Intelligence Unit 2010 ranking of livability in the world's 140 largest cities, the capital city, Kathmandu, ranked 132 based on several factors, including safety, education, hygiene, health care, culture, environment, recreation, political-economic stability, and public transportation. The air quality and noise associated with the traffic impact student health and ability to learn. Recent and historic studies by the U.S. Environmental Protection Agency and National Institutes of Health, the World Health Organization, and health scientists have established links among pollution, noise, and learning (Lee & Fleming, 2002). Adverse effects of noise on humans that impact learning include hearing impairment, adverse influences on communication, increased stress, cardiovascular disturbance, impaired memory and attention, delayed cognitive development, and negative social behavior (Evans & Lepore, 1993). Increases in aggression are associated with prolonged exposure to noise of 80+ dB. My own sample of noise levels on a fairly small one-way street on a weekday afternoon not far from the center of the city showed noise levels up to 90 dB (Stansfeld, Berglund, Clark, et al., 2005). With children arriving regularly in Kathmandu from their rural homes for boarding school, the problem is acute. Virtual education programs could reduce the relocation of students to the city for education and could reduce the exposure of students in the city to its hazards.

Basic infrastructural limitations can result in high costs and logistical hurdles for expanding participation in traditional schooling. At the domestic level, participation in school-based education requires time for learning, basic clothing and supplies, and space and support for learning at home. Many homes of Nepalis who participate in government schooling have limited electrical power, water, and space. Electricity has been available as few as eight hours each day during the dry season, when hydropower cannot keep up with growing demand. Limited refrigeration necessitates daily shopping, and carrying water means that much labor is involved in daily living. Children are needed in many homes to assist in tasks to support the family.

Fuel shortages in the country in 2011 brought to light the tenuous dependence of people on transportation to school and the high cost of fuel for many families. Online education could alleviate the fuel-related education problem by reducing or eliminating travel to and from classes. Daily attendance in school amounts to hundreds of kilometers of travel for villagers to campuses on a weekly basis, and the school terms can exceed 22 weeks. This distance can be expensive by bus, and if students travel by motorbike, the pump cost was nearly $6/gallon for gas when available, or closer to $8/gallon on the black market, as of 2011. These costs can exceed tuition at the public university over the course of the year.

Adults who have not had access to adequate education often leave their homes and families to work in homes of other families abroad. The number was 300,000 as of 2010 (Amnesty International, 2011). The funds returned to Nepal by migrant workers constitute up to a quarter of the national GDP, ranking it third in the world for percentage of GDP from remittances (World Bank, 2013). With higher levels of education, more Nepalis could fill some of the professional positions in the cities now held by people who have come from outside the country. In addition, investment in the communication infrastructure for virtual education would enable the crafts and culture that are abundant in villages to be exported in physical and virtual forms.

Information Technology Context in Nepal

Once children are in school, the potential of technology to increase their access to educational materials is great, but will require solutions tailored to conditions. Nepal had in 2010 a mobile phone adoption rate of 30% with no subsidy for education use of cell phones, and cellular service is nearly ubiquitous in the country (Nepal Telecommunication Authority, 2010). Nepal Telecomm began installation in 2011 of 500 new mobile communication towers around the country. Mobile phones are an economic development strategy that can be co-opted for educational development: "For every additional 10 mobile phones per 100 people in a developing country, GDP rose 0.6% to 1.2%" (Perry & Wadhams, 2011, para. 6). The advent of inexpensive and pervasive "more than mobile" communication systems and handsets may be changing the traditional education paradigm. The many advantages of such systems to the general population in developing countries include direct access to personalized instruction, according to the *Economist* (2011). The technology could even lead to leapfrogging of learners in developing countries into personalized learning as a norm before such a shift happens in developed countries. Developed countries have a much higher investment in school-based learning and a much higher school participation rate, making such shifts more cumbersome.

Potential for Virtual Education in Nepal

Countries like Nepal have opportunities to capitalize on unique features and assets to become leaders in specific domains of education. For example, students around the country can become involved in project-based learning related to alpine health, climate change, local ecosystems, indigenous cultures and arts, and the political system by collecting data, stories, histories, and media artifacts that they contribute in physical or digital form to an open online repository. They can also do data analysis in quantitative and qualitative form with the materials in the repository. The repository can serve as a portal to open education resources, experts within and beyond Nepal, and mentors to build interest and knowledge for a broad range of careers. Teacher education students at the university can design these projects in collaboration with university students in the content areas and computer science.

These projects require little in the way of technology infrastructure beyond a cellular signal and inexpensive handheld devices that can be charged using solar, wind, or mechanical power. A Nepali organization that is leading in virtual education is Open Learning Exchange (OLE) Nepal, which sponsors ambitious and well-planned initiatives in public primary schools. The OLE program is systemic, including teacher professional development in technology integration and coordination with the national curriculum officers to bring digital resources to students that fill needs in each grade's educational materials. The program attends to the practical aspects of implementing mobile computing devices through the One Laptop Per Child program, evaluation, sound instructional design practices, ongoing support for participating schools, and an immense online repository of open activities and books at E-Pustakalaya. This program is a laudable model for blended education with benefits to the teachers and students. Teachers learn new strategies and instructional design thinking, students learn the national standards and 21st-century skills, and the public has access to high-quality materials. University teacher education programs can use the materials and possibly become involved in review and production; university faculty could become research and evaluation partners. Businesses and other entities could be supporters. Universities and businesses are likely to benefit from the increased population who are college and career ready.

The OLE Nepal program is an exemplar of the type of blended e-learning program that has been shown to successfully increase the capacity of all schools to educate all citizens (Ferdig, Cavanaugh, & Freidhoff, 2012). It includes several of the success factors for K–12 blended programs: clear purpose and direction, support for changes in pedagogy, collaboration at multiple levels in the education system, and structured professional development. With modest investment of technical and human resources, this program can expand more rapidly. For example, until the teacher education universities prepare adequate teachers within the country, cadres of on-site and virtual volunteer teachers might augment the teaching force, working through organizations such as the Peace Corps, Fulbright, and Teachers without Borders that already send many short-term volunteers to Nepal annually. In addition, these teachers can support expansion of OLE Nepal's curricula and computing devices to adult learners in the communities where it operates school programs.

Changing Outcomes Through Virtual Education in Developing Countries

Expanding options for schooling in the developing world is a critical issue. UNICEF's (2011) *State of the World's Children 2011* report states that 88% of the world's 1.2 billion adolescents live in the developing world. The report adds that nearly half of secondary-school-age children will not be able to attend. Add to that number the adults who have not completed primary and secondary education, and the result is an audience of billions in need of education in areas where physical schools with classroom teachers cannot quickly accommodate them. An effort to unite the research and development communities focused on technical infrastructure, digital content, teacher education, and public education could jump-start access to personalized flexible education and resulting opportunities for the undereducated in these regions. Nepal and neighboring South Asian countries are home to the largest group of adolescents, 335 million, followed by another 329 million in east Asia and Pacific countries. In these areas, investment in mobile education is most crucial. Through its human development rankings, the United Nations tracks Nepal's status in key education indicators, which include mean years of schooling for adults, expected years of schooling for children, adult literacy rates, national education expenditures, enrollment in education, and Internet use. Inclusion of the Internet indicator in the education rankings makes an important statement about the nature of education and the accompanying role of information.

- In the composite of these indicators, Nepal ranks 99 of 117 countries.
- In years of schooling, Nepal ranks 152 of 173 countries.
- In literacy, Nepal is 123 of 141.
- In expenditure, Nepal is 112 of 171.
- In enrollment, Nepal is 139 of 183.
- In Internet use, Nepal is 167 of 189.

Given a modest increase in expenditure alongside partnerships among Internet service providers, alternate micropower services, and mobile communication device makers, Internet use will dramatically increase. That is a key to increasing all of the other education indicators. Such partnerships have succeeded in Africa to open routes to communication, literacy, education, and commerce. Today, 20 times more Africans access the Internet via mobile phones than by networked computers (West, 2012).

A primary and secondary e-learning program has numerous requirements, many of which are in place in Nepal:

- Digital curriculum and references have been developed by OLE Nepal.
- Teacher professional development in technology use is being provided by the National Center for Education Development.
- Research and leadership in e-learning has begun at Nepal's universities.
- Mobile communications technology is widely distributed among citizens.

What remains? National vision and leadership are needed to bring the components of a program together into a system. The Ministry of Education, individual schools, and entrepreneurs have begun moving in this direction. In addition to the resources and educators in the country who can participate in this program development, Nepal has a rich pool of expatriates abroad who may be enlisted to support the system or serve as mentors and teachers online.

The initiatives of neighboring countries offer models for Nepal in many of these directions. While not a developing country, Singapore provides an example of effective collaboration for setting a national e-learning framework led by the Ministry of Education and the information and communications authority (Powell & Patrick, 2006). India has embarked on a public-private partnership for digital resources and low-cost computing devices (Powell, 2011). The United Arab Emirates has launched a national K–20 mobile e-learning program with all government education entities working together (Cavanaugh, Hargis, Munns, & Kamali, 2013).

UN secretary general Ban Ki-moon issued a statement marking May 17 as World Telecommunications and Information Society Day, emphasizing the importance of providers of information and communication technology (ICT) as "enablers of modern society." ICT offers access to cultures, economic opportunity, health care, and education, all of which are especially critical in rural areas, according to the secretary.

He specifically mentions transforming lives by connecting village schools to the Internet. One of UNESCO's newest education efforts is guiding mobile learning as a strategy for reaching the *Education for All* goal, given that the vast majority of mobile phone subscriptions are located in the developing world and seizing on the growth of low-cost tablet computers (Vosloo, 2012). The guidelines echo the need for partnerships, quality open education resources, and educator professional development (West, 2012).

As exciting as it is to see the United Nations and many participating countries speaking on behalf of K–12 e-learning and even sponsoring special programs around this date, sustained access to quality educational resources and experiences requires a permanent systemic commitment on the part of collaborating governments and agencies. The United States has taken steps in the right direction with recent initiatives such as the National Broadband Plan for Education. Education, as a lifelong enterprise, involves families, governments at all levels, K–adult education organizations, education material publishers, support systems, and infrastructures. Coordinating all of these entities requires vision and leadership that can unite learners, providers, and supporters around the goal of education as a path to social advancement.

The literature related to e-learning programs for K–12 students dates to the mid-1990s and builds upon a century of research and practice from K–12 distance education (Allen & Seaman, 2008; Cavanaugh, 2001; Cavanaugh, Gillan, Kromrey, Hess, & Blomyer, 2004; U.S. Department of Education, 2009), showing that virtual education can reach underserved areas (Ferdig & Cavanaugh, 2011) and can close achievement gaps for students at risk for dropping out of school (Liu & Cavanaugh, 2012; Repetto, Cavanaugh, Wayer, & Liu, 2010). Barriers to entry, such as costs and prerequisite skills, are decreasing continually. A knowledge base of effective instructional practices has been established (Ferdig, Cavanaugh, DiPietro, Black, & Dawson, 2010).

Progress toward using online learning to increase educational access in developing nations like Nepal would be advanced if the United Nations provided a clearinghouse of programs and initiatives, and sponsored virtual and physical conferences for leaders and practitioners. There is little reason for online education to stay within jurisdictional boundaries; the United Nations is well positioned to lead in this arena. Such an international collaboration could help Nepal and other developing countries build a more educated workforce and national prosperity.

References

Allen, E., & Seaman, J. (2008). *Staying the course: Online education in the United States, 2008.* Needham, MA: Sloan-C.

Amnesty International. (2011). *Nepal: Briefing to the UN Committee on the Elimination of Discrimination Against Women.* London: Author.

Bokova, I., Clark, H., Lake, A., & Somovia, J. (2010, October). *Joint statement for World Teachers Day.* New York: United Nations.

Cavanaugh, C. (2001). The effectiveness of interactive distance education technologies in K–12 learning: A meta-analysis. *International Journal of Educational Telecommunications, 7*(1), 73–88.

Cavanaugh, C. (2009). *Getting students more learning time online: Distance education in support of expanded learning time.* Washington, DC: Center for American Progress. Retrieved from http://www.americanprogress.org/issues/2009/05/distance_learning.html

Cavanaugh, C., Gillan, K., Kromrey, J., Hess, M., & Blomeyer, R. (2004). *The effects of distance education on K–12 student outcomes: A meta-analysis.* Naperville, IL: North Central Regional Educational Laboratory.

Cavanaugh, C., Hargis, J., Munns, S., & Kamali, T. (2013). iCelebrate teaching and learning: Sharing the iPad experience. *Journal of Teaching and Learning With Technology, 1*(2). Retrieved from http://jotlt.indiana.edu/article/download/2163/3042

The Economist. (2011, January 27). Not just talk. Retrieved from http://www.economist.com/node/18008202

Evans, G. W., & Lepore, S. J. (1993). Non-auditory effects of noise on children: A critical review. *Children's Environments,* 10, 42–72.

Ferdig, R., & Cavanaugh, C. (Eds.). (2011). *Lessons learned from virtual schools: Experiences and recommendations from the field.* Vienna, VA: International Association for K–12 Online Learning.

Ferdig, R., Cavanaugh, C., DiPietro, M., Black, E. W., & Dawson, K. (2010). Virtual schooling standards and best practices for teacher education. *Journal of Technology and Teacher Education, 17*(4), 479–503.

Ferdig, R., Cavanaugh, C., & Freidhoff, J. (Eds.). (2012). *Lessons learned from blended programs: Experiences and recommendations from the field.* Vienna, VA: International Association for K–12 Online Learning.

Lee, C. S. Y., & Fleming, G. G. (2002). *General health effects of transportation noise.* Washington, DC: U.S. Department of Transportation.

Liu, F., & Cavanaugh, C. (2012). Success in online high school algebra: Factors influencing student academic performance. *Open Learning: The Journal of Open, Distance and e-Learning, 27*(2), 149–167.

Marcotte, D., & Hemelt, S. (2008). Unscheduled school closings and student performance. *Education Finance and Policy, 3*(3), 316–338.

Murphy, C. (2006). *Flu action plan: A business survival guide.* Singapore: Wiley & Sons.

Nepal Telecommunications Authority. (2010). *Management information system.* Kathmandu: Author.

Perry, A., & Wadhams, N. (2011, January 31). Kenya's banking revolution. *Time Asia.* Retrieved from http://www.time.com/time/magazine/article/0,9171,2043329,00.html

Powell, A. (2011). *A case study of e-learning initiatives in New Zealand's secondary schools* (Unpublished doctoral dissertation). Pepperdine University, Malibu, CA.

Powell, A., & Patrick, S. (2006). *An international perspective of K–12 online learning: A summary of the 2006 iNACOL international e-learning survey.* Vienna, VA: International Association for K–12 Online Learning.

Repetto, J., Cavanaugh, C., Wayer, N., & Liu, F. (2010). Virtual high schools: Improving outcomes for students with disabilities. *Quarterly Review of Distance Education, 11*(2), 91–104.

Sherpa, N. (2005, September). *Indigenous peoples of Nepal and traditional knowledge.* Paper presented at the International Workshop on Traditional Knowledge, Panama City.

Stansfeld, S. A., Berglund, B., Clark, C., et al. (2005). Aircraft and road traffic noise and children's cognition and health: A cross national study. *Lancet, 365,* 1942–1949.

United Nations Children's Fund (UNICEF). (2011, February). *The state of the world's children 2011: Adolescence: An Age of Opportunity.* New York, NY: Author. Retrieved from http://www.unicef.org/sowc2011/pdfs/SOWC-2011-Main-Report_EN_02092011.pdf

United Nations Educational, Scientific and Cultural Organization. (2010). *Education financial planning in Asia: Implementing medium-term expenditure frameworks—Nepal.* Bangkok: Author.

U.S. Department of Education. (2009). *Evaluation of evidence-based practices in online learning: A meta-analysis and review of online learning studies.* Washington, DC: Author.

Vosloo, S. (2012). *Mobile learning and policies: Key issues to consider.* Paris: United Nations Educational, Scientific and Cultural Organization.

West, M. (2012). *Turning on mobile learning: Global themes.* Paris: United Nations Educational, Scientific and Cultural Organization.

World Bank. (2013). *Migration and remittance flows: Recent trends and outlook, 2012–2016.* Washington, DC: Author.

14

ONLINE LEARNING IN AUSTRALIA

SCIL as a Case Study

Stephen Harris

Australia is often noted as a country that adopted distance learning many decades ago—a reputation almost entirely due to the well-known School of the Air (Australian Government, 2007). The School of the Air commenced in 1951 using shortwave radio and changing to satellite and wireless Internet technologies in 2003 (OPTUS, 2003).

Based on evidence gathered through the VISCED Project, Bacsich and Bristow (2012) summarized the status of virtual learning in Australia:

> As might be expected in a very large country with many isolated communities, there are a significant number of virtual schools in Australia. The largest numbers are in New South Wales and Queensland, with three in Victoria, two in Northern Territory and one each in South and Western Australia.

A VISCED project website lists 25 virtual school programs in Australia. The Schools of Isolated and Distance Education (SIDE) in Western Australia were characterized as "the largest, with thousands of enrollments" through schools on six campuses.

Despite this activity, it would be reasonable to say that online learning or e-learning is not yet on the mainstream education radar in Australia. Schools and jurisdictions talk about their online programs, but in most instances they are referring to components of courses that have online information delivered via learning management systems or, in some cases, components of courses undertaken online. Discussion about replacing paper-based texts in schools in most instances revolves around sourcing e-book versions of the same text, as opposed to creating a pedagogy that does not rely on textbooks at all.

There is more activity at the tertiary level. Universities are offering an increasing range of courses online. The Open University Australia (OUA) was established in 1993 as a consortium of several Australian universities and colleges, seven of which own it. The OUA is also a member of the Elite Athlete Friendly Universities (EAFU) national network (Australian Sports Commission, 2012). Many of its courses are delivered in entirely online formats, with no limits on how many government-funded students can enroll.

Different state governments have had online learning in mind as they have adjusted their school-relevant legislation during the last decade to allow for offering online learning programs at the school level. School communities in general have not taken up opportunities from this legislative change, relying more on the different state correspondence (i.e., independent study) schools to progressively shift their course offerings to include some blended or fully online options.

Education Services Australia (2013) has several initiatives that support digital or blended learning, including the National Digital Learning Resources Network and Scootle, a learning management system that allows teachers to create learning paths for students and engage in collaborative teaching and learning activities online.

The refined definition of *blended learning* for North American contexts as proposed by Staker and Horn (2012) further differentiates the concept of blended learning and e-learning from the Australian context:

> Blended learning is a formal education program in which a student learns at least in part through online delivery of content and instruction with some element of student control over time, place, path, and/or pace and at least in part at a supervised brick-and-mortar location away from home. (p. 3)

This refinement to the definition acknowledges the growth of the rotational model in many U.S. schools. This model, however, is quite removed from the Australian experience of blended learning. When linked to the refinement of the added wording of "a formal education," it is quite distinctly narrower than Australian understanding.

The Queensland University of Technology (2012) has captured the usage of the term *blended learning* in the Australian context, providing this definition:

> Blended learning is the designed integration of face to face, distance, and electronic approaches to enhance student learning. The particular blend of physical and virtual learning environments in a course or unit is chosen to provide optimal support for the desired learning activities and learning outcomes. (p. 1)

There is little evidence of rotational or formal blended learning models in Australian education to date.

Australian Legislation

An enormous gulf exists between states in Australia when it comes to legislation that relates to the possibility of undertaking online courses. The Sydney Centre for Innovation in Learning, a unit of Northern Beaches Christian School, is situated in New South Wales (NSW) and as such is subject to relevant legislation in that state. NSW enacted legislation in 2004 to enable online learning in elementary and secondary education. The registration and accreditation for such courses is through a governmental body, the NSW Board of Studies (BOS). The act makes provision for a school to deliver to its enrolled students all or a significant part of the courses in distance education mode. The BOS manual states,

> A school would not be considered to be delivering distance education to its students if the teacher with prime responsibility for delivering the course of study was regularly in the presence of students and supplemented the teaching with a range of audiovisual

Figure 14.1: Blended learning taxonomy

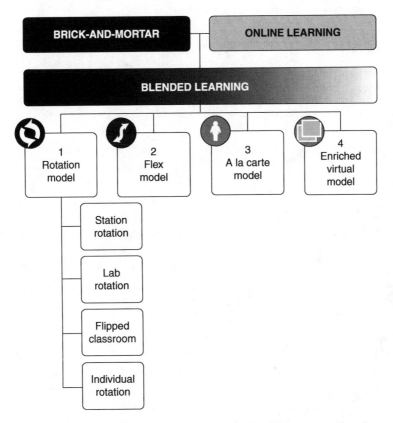

Note. Adapted from "Classifying K–12 blended learning," by Heather Staker and Michael B. Horn, p.2. Copyright © 2012 by Innosight Institute. Adapted with permission.

aids. . . . [A school may deliver] all or a significant part of courses from Kindergarten to Year 12 by means of distance education. When a registered non-government school delivers distance education to its students, the school must have in place policies and procedures that are appropriate to ensure the personal and social development of its students. (New South Wales Board of Studies, 2012a, p. 27)

If the legislation finished at this point, it would readily enable the widespread introduction of online learning as a flexible option. However, as stated in the manual, the NSW BOS also legislated that

these policies and procedures must include the provision of a minimum of fifteen (15) school days of "residential school" sessions for all students undertaking a full-time distance education program (pro-rata for students undertaking a part-time program). (p. 27)

By itself, this residential requirement could be incorporated into a program, even with the inconvenience for those living in remote areas of the state or indeed overseas to have to regularly travel to an on-site residential program. However, in separate policy areas, the registration and accreditation processes outline very stringent requirements for boarding or dormitory arrangements, effectively removing this as an option for schools that do not ordinarily have a residential program at the same time.

In effect, this policy detail has had two outcomes. Schools either have shelved online learning as an option, placing it into the "too hard" basket, or only offer online courses as a less than 50% component of a student's overall course selection, thereby keeping an online program at a contained level, with restricted possibilities for growth.

As it currently stands, legislation allowing for the registration and accreditation of online learning remains with Australia's different state governments. Undertaking online course delivery in all educational jurisdictions is possible within Australia, but the definitions of and requirements for *online learning* within those states vary quite widely.[1]

In South Australia, the definition of *online learning* falls within the government's very broad alternative schooling options: Students who are unable to attend a local school or access curriculum at their school may be able to undertake school externally. This is sometimes called "distance education." Recognized external education methods include telephone, videoconference, online lessons, specialized course booklets, DVDs, CDs and activity kits, face-to-face workshops, camps and excursions, and visits from teachers (Government of South Australia, 2011).

In Tasmania, students can enroll in a program conducted through the government-run Online Campus and CELO. The Tasmanian *e*School enrolls students who meet specific enrollment criteria, enabling the *e*School to be their base school. Students can enroll in the Tasmanian *e*School, which provides online courses either full-time or on a dual basis with another school.

In most situations in Australia, there are still only two main players in the online learning world: (a) the existing correspondence or distance education schools, which have only very incrementally adopted online pedagogies, and (b) the homeschool movement, often fueled by passionate supporters, which has availed itself of online programs where they exist as a means to strengthen educational options for learning.

As of 2012, there were only about 25 providers of K–12 online learning in NSW Australia. The number of providers appears limited when compared to a nation like the United States or Canada for a variety of reasons:

- The additional requirement for pro-rata residential schools
- Lack of understanding of online course frameworks
- Lack of familiarity with learning management systems
- Lack of broad (mass) media conversations about online learning
- Skepticism about the capacity to create an active learning community within online course environments
- Nonfamiliarity of face-to-face teachers with online course environments
- A perception that online course delivery equates with videoconference delivery

In the next section I present a case study of one virtual school that has overcome many of these constraints, Northern Beaches Christian School.

Case Study: Northern Beaches Christian School and the Sydney Centre for Innovation in Learning

The year 2004 was key in a number of ways for the development of the Northern Beaches Christian School (NBCS) online course program. New government legislation authorized the use of online learning courses as a potential mode for course delivery for the first time in NSW. At the same time, NBCS was on a growth curve in terms of student numbers, increasing by around 150 students and 10 staff every year for four consecutive years.

NBCS was keen to embrace the opportunities of online learning and recognized the need to learn all it could about the mechanics and possibilities of online learning. To do that, an action research cycle was proposed, focusing on the experiences of schools internationally that already had at least four to five years' experience of online learning delivery. As a member of the then Macquarie University School Partners program, NBCS applied for a 2005 travel fellowship to observe best-practice online course delivery for senior-secondary-level education in a range of European countries and in British Columbia, Canada (Harris, 2005).

In 2004 it was difficult to find schools in Australia to use as exemplars for the emergent online and blended learning world. Relatively few countries outside the United States and Canada were engaged in delivering online courses remotely. Our research identified a range of institutions in Finland, Sweden, Iceland, and Canada that had the potential to offer the best case studies as a point of reference for the intended NBCS programs. A number of other countries had explored the development of online courses or online course modules but had not situated those courses within a delivery framework.

One particularly useful point of reference and information was a 2004 paper by Ásrún Matthíasdóttir from the University of Reykjavík, Iceland. Much of the Macquarie University–sponsored study tour centered around schools or individuals identified in Matthíasdóttir's work.

A key purpose of the 2005 Macquarie University School Partners' Study Fellowship was to ascertain the most effective strategies used in best-practice European and Canadian schools as a framework to deliver secondary school courses via distance or blended learning pedagogies. Another purpose was to research and develop a viable e-learning framework ready for 2006 in order to deliver some Stage 6 (i.e., Years 11 and 12, equivalent to the 10th and 11th grades in the United States) secondary-school courses in a blended context. This framework would then be applied to course modules as suitable for the state government's BOS courses, such as Stage 6 Legal Studies.

The conclusion at the time of the tour was that no single model existed in terms of being the "best" way in which to incorporate the use of online content into pedagogical approaches, because the intentions of different models are so diverse. However, after analyzing the different impacts of observed exemplars, a model emerged that had the potential to be highly successful (Harris, 2006). It involved the teacher as the active developer of lesson-specific content, operating from a student-centered philosophy and using personalized and differentiated approaches to teaching. This teaching is supported by well-developed, comprehensive, web-based online content, which is delivered via a student-centered portal within a stable learning management system. Any online content used in this context should be in a format where it could easily be reformatted to operate as suitable for a blended delivery context or as independent modules for partial or complete distribution online.

Perhaps of most significance in the development of an online learning program at NBCS around the time of the 2005 Macquarie Schools Partners Travel Fellowship was the creation of the Sydney Centre for Innovation in Learning (SCIL). SCIL emerged as a concept during the tour. It was conceived as a practical means by which to create an environment where grassroots innovation was nurtured and resistance to change minimized.

The NBCS board supported the concept wholeheartedly, and it was decided that SCIL would operate as a research, innovation, and development unit within the wider structures of NBCS. It had no specific start-up budget. The intention was that any staff who wished to trial new ideas would be resourced from within existing budgets and that as natural vacancies in staff occurred, consideration would be given to creating new-paradigm roles better aligned with the emergent directions of the school.

By the time in 2006 when SCIL's online program commenced, a number of key factors had emerged in relation to the successful use of online curriculum. While technical issues such as selection of an appropriate portal or learning management system were important, clearly the key to long-term success in a program lay in the area of school culture and school vision. There had to be a clear resolve at the top end of school leadership to have a strongly articulated vision for the potential of online learning, matched with a resolve to enact it well—the relentless pursuit of excellence. School leadership also needed to be prepared to develop new nonteaching roles to facilitate online curriculum preparation, as well as tailor senior management roles to support implementation. Also critical for long-term success was the availability of passionate teachers with a clear understanding of the online pedagogic framework.

SCIL Online Tour

By late 2005 the decision was made to create two positions that would help advance the process of creating online courses: SCIL director of online school and SCIL online portal manager. Appointments were made to these positions, and an accelerated program of professional development was devised to support an immediate, but limited, commencement of online courses in 2006. This program included a second round of travel, the SCIL Online Tour, in February and March 2006, undertaken by the new appointees to nine exemplar institutions in the United Kingdom, Iceland, and Finland. These institutions are listed in Table 14.1.

The U.K. exemplar focused on the two institutions that had successfully created digital learning objects for cross-platform use within the United Kingdom, while in Iceland, four institutions were selected as positive exemplars of embedded online course programs. In Finland, three institutions were selected as exemplars of online learning delivery.

The accelerated professional development program worked very well. The nascent online learning team at SCIL gained a perspective that online learning not only was possible but also had immense potential to improve learning outcomes and create many new flexible learning pathways. The vision became broadly shared among people who had the capacity to grow it.

TABLE 14.1:
European exemplar institutions visited by SCIL administrators in 2006

Nation	*Exemplar Institutions Toured*	*Exemplar Use*
Iceland	Verzlunaskóli Islands, Reykjavik Fjölbrautaskóli Snæfellinga, Grundarfjörður Fjölbrautaskólinn við Armúla, Reykjavik Fjölbrautaskóli Suðurlands, Selfoss	Embedded online course programs, online learning delivery
Finland	Tampere Polytechnic, Tampere Sotunki School, Vantaa Kotka School for Adults, Kotka	Online learning delivery
United Kingdom	Thomas Telford School, Telford Shireland Language Academy, Birmingham	Creation of digital learning objects for cross-platform use

NBCS started offering fully online and blended education courses in the senior secondary school years in 2006. It was recognized as one of the first schools in Australia to undertake such a program. There was a high burden on NBCS to develop strategies so that its pedagogical approach was well suited to the online delivery framework used, and to demonstrate the online and blended learning program's success.

NBCS targeted further development of SCIL as an organizational means by which to support this program's growth. SCIL was strongly committed to the use of diverse information and communication technology tools to create and disseminate knowledge and improve student learning.

The strategic decision to embrace Moodle as the key platform for creating virtual classrooms to augment and extend the physical spaces at NBCS was made in late 2004. The use of Moodle replaced the initial use of HTML platforms. By 2006 NBCS provided every physical classroom and teacher with the capacity to supplement learning through a replicated online space housed within a Moodle framework. Three separate instances of Moodle were commissioned and developed. Primary Education Through E-Learning (PETE) was created as the tool for pervasive use within the primary section of the school (Northern Beaches Christian School, 2012c). LEARN was created as the secondary-student online platform (Northern Beaches Christian School, 2012b), supporting face-to-face teaching.

The interfaces for PETE and LEARN were kept highly visual, and Moodle as a platform offered significantly more flexibility and ease of access than other commercial platform solutions. Moodle is still used as the current platform. Since 2005, professional development programs for teachers have focused on capacity building so that every teacher within the school not only can use the adjunct virtual space but also is required to use components such as Moodle Markbook as the primary place for recording assessment information.

Sitting alongside PETE and LEARN, a third instance of Moodle was created for use by NBCS staff: HSC Learn Online (Northern Beaches Christian School, 2012a). Upon successful completion of senior secondary school, students in Australia attain the Higher School Certificate (HSC). This third Moodle instance was created to provide a cross-institutional platform for the online school program that supports HSC attainment.

Funding Models

Different financial models were considered at this time in order to create start-up capacity as an early provider of online course programs in NSW. Both the Macquarie University School Partners Travel Fellowship Tour in 2005 and the SCIL Online Tour in 2006 investigated as many different financial models for the creation and delivery of online learning as possible, so as to provide a strong basis for decision making connected to the financing of an online course program at NBCS.

Curriculum Development and Standards

Without separate start-up funding, the only viable model for online course development was to quickly develop the capacity of the average classroom teacher to create and upload online learning objects. To do that, three strategies were employed:

1. Accelerate on-the-shoulder teacher professional development.
2. Recurrently assess the developmental status of the virtual learning spaces of all existing courses.
3. Target those staff with capacity to develop online courses and provision them with sufficient time and resources.

When the number of digital objects in any one given course reached a certain number, or the sequence of uploaded activities formed the visible framework for a course, then time was allocated to transition those materials into a format suitable for online course delivery. In this way, the development of online courses was both gradual and attainable. In 2006, three courses were ready for use, and the program enrolled its first students.

With few Australia-based exemplars or standards for course delivery, NBCS continued to look overseas for guidelines and support. The most helpful framework for developing standards for online course creation was through those published by the International Association for K–12 Online Learning (iNACOL, 2011). The iNACOL standards framework has provided a practical template for quality for teachers and program leaders.

Program Partners

NBCS has been highly cognizant of the fact that Sydney-based schools could do a great deal more to provide quality education pathways for rural and other urban students who would otherwise not have access to a particular course or program. Course choices offered through the HSC Learn Online portal have been made with a rural clientele in mind—subjects that would be unlikely to run in a smaller school have been targeted for development and inclusion in the course choices. Since starting with three Preliminary Stage 6 courses in 2006, the number of online courses has grown rapidly. By 2012, over 350 students from more than 40 NSW schools had enrolled in one of more than 40 Stage 6 (i.e., Years 11 and 12) courses.

SCIL Stage 6 online distance education courses have been delivered to a variety of schools, systems, and regions. Enrolled students currently come from all sectors of the NSW education landscape—Department of Education and Communities (DEC) schools, independent schools, and Catholic schools. Students can enroll directly with the SCIL or through their own school.

Challenges

The development of any program has its inherent challenges, and the development of an online school in Australia is no different. While online learning is quite often talked about in general terms as a growing phenomenon within schooling, it is not yet on the radar of the average student or parent in Australia to the same degree as is evident in either North America or Europe. A growing number of students, when provided with the option of an online course, are keen to take one up for one or more reasons—for example, to experience such learning modes prior to university, to undertake studies in a subject otherwise not available, or because of the lower level of relational interactions with their teachers.

The learning environment at NBCS has been geared around developing strong, independent learning habits, and NBCS students have in many cases found the transition to the online environment an extension of a preferred mode of learning. This is not necessarily the case with the partner schools availing themselves of increasing their subject possibilities through the HSC Learn Online portal. One specific challenge has been to develop the capacity of the regional schools to understand the online learning environment and provide sufficient support for students undertaking online courses.

Another recurrent challenge has been financial. In a broader budgetary context, all programs within an institution need to move to self-funding status as quickly as possible. This creates an ongoing tension between having the capacity to provide adequate start-up time for teachers developing courses for online delivery and the time available for allocation. In this regard, being able to draw from the experience of other schools that had successfully initiated an online learning program was invaluable. A clear commonality existed among course development time, teacher costs, and course fees across countries and jurisdictions. Such commonality provided a baseline for NBCS thinking about budget frameworks around the online learning program.

As with funding models, a variety of models exist for course delivery. Those schools that had developed correspondence-style courses requiring little or no teacher moderation had the lowest cost. Some of these were able to better subsidize those courses, adding heavier teaching, preparation, or feedback requirements.

The school day and synchronization of courses have also impacted viability over a wider framework. The majority of NBCS/SCIL online courses have been developed for an asynchronous mode. Some courses such as language courses have included a regular synchronized videoconferencing component. A number of courses have included a compulsory fieldwork component or incorporated practical activities as ways to meet the mandated syllabus requirements. All courses offered through NBCS/SCIL have included the opportunity to attend a workshop day at the start of every school term.

Another challenge has been to determine and embed the most stable staffing formulas for the online courses. The school considered three models: a model where teachers work entirely as online teachers, a model where teachers are allocated face-to-face classes and online classes without any overlap of courses offered in two modes, and a model where teachers take both the face-to-face class and the online class in subjects where the courses are offered in the two modes. This latter model has been the most successful in our experience. In some instances, NBCS/SCIL has offered courses in a "supported online mode"; the course is essentially offered in online mode with the option of attending tutorials. All three course modes have been successful to varying degrees.

One early observation from external schools undertaking online course delivery has been the importance of creating a social or pastoral environment around the course delivery. No student should be left in a virtual world feeling isolated. NBCS/SCIL has sought to create time frames and expectations for responding to student questions, as well as developing social media frameworks to create ease of virtual conversations for course participants. The tendency for some teachers to withdraw to a less interactive mode is a recurrent problem, and the school monitors the frequency of online engagement of staff with students.

Learning Outcomes

The success of any program will be measured by its outcomes. The NBCS/SCIL online learning program has been developed with the intention of increasing learning opportunities for both NBCS and external students. The program provides a course structure that has a high success rate in terms of outcomes such as student course completion and course marks, which contribute to success in external tertiary admission processes. Course completion rates have remained very high (above 90%), which may be linked to the fact that most courses form part of a sequence of courses necessary for inclusion in tertiary admission processes. Students are less likely to undertake surplus (i.e., elective) courses in order to enable the noninclusion of some marks.

Of high interest (and challenge) is that where the same teacher has taught a course in the same year for both the face-to-face and online environments, in about 75% of cases over a number of years, the online student cohort has achieved a higher average mark for the course than the face-to-face contingent. This has sent an immediate challenge to teachers as it undermines an assumption that a teacher's physical presence is inherently the better mode of course delivery. Informal analysis would suggest that high motivation to undertake a specific subject, combined in some cases with a lack of relational tension in being in a context removed from the complexity of some face-to-face interactions, has generally allowed this higher outcome.

Almost every subject taught in an online mode through the final year of schooling (i.e., Year 12) has at some stage seen a student attaining a Band 6 result (90 or higher) in the HSC, which signifies the highest level of performance (New South Wales Board of Studies, 2012b). In three of the last six years, the highest individual course mark from the school has been attained with an online course delivery mode.

Conclusion

The NBCS/SCIL online course program is still very much in its infancy stages. The competing demands of budgets and course preparation times have not been resolved to the point of stability. Australia is gearing up for a national curriculum being implemented from 2014 onward in years up to Year 10. This will provide new opportunities for a national approach to online learning and fresh challenges for course preparation. The key challenge to Australian uptake of online learning modes remains the fact that it is yet to make the national agenda in education in a substantive or visible way. That will hopefully be the story of the next decade.

Note

1. Interestingly, as the authors pursued accurate information for this chapter, every state department had to take questions on notice (in writing) as they had no person available with sufficient understanding and experience to immediately answer direct inquiries about the online learning legislation in their state.

References

Australian Government. (2007). *The School of the Air and remote learning.* Parkes, Australia: Author. Retrieved from http://australia.gov.au/about-australia/australian-story/school-of-the-air

Australian Sports Commission. (2012). *University network.* Bruce, Australia: Author. Retrieved from http://www.ausport.gov.au/ais/athlete_career_and_education/university_network

Bacsich, P., & Bristow, S. F. (2012). *International research into K–12 online learning.* Retrieved from http://virtualschoolmooc.wikispaces.com/international

Education Services Australia. (2013). *Annual report 2012–2013.* Retrieved from http://www.esa.edu.au/sites/default/files/files/ESA-Annual-Report-2012-13-low-res.pdf

Government of South Australia. (2011). *External education.* Retrieved from http://www.sa.gov.au/subject/Education%2C+skills+and+learning/Schools/Alternative+schooling/External+education

Harris, S. (2005). *Online learning in senior secondary school education: Practice, pedagogy and possibilities.* Sydney: Sydney Centre for Innovation in Learning. Retrieved from http://scil.com.au/documents/nbcs-mq-report.pdf

Harris, S. (2006, June). *Common factors influencing success in the online environment.* Sydney: Sydney Centre for Innovation in Learning. Retrieved from http://scil.com.au/documents/scil_success_online.pdf

International Association for K–12 Online Learning. (2011). *iNACOL national standards for quality online courses.* Vienna, VA: Author. Retrieved from http://www.inacol.org/research/nationalstandards

New South Wales Board of Studies. (2012a). *Registered and accredited individual non-government schools (NSW) manual.* Sydney: Author. Retrieved from http://www.boardofstudies.nsw.edu.au/manuals/pdf_doc/reg-accred-individ-non-gov-manual-12.pdf

New South Wales Board of Studies. (2012b). *Understanding HSC results.* Sydney: Author. Retrieved from http://www.boardofstudies.nsw.edu.au/hsc-results

Northern Beaches Christian School. (2012a). *HSC learn online.* Sydney: Author. Retrieved from http://hsconline.nsw.edu.au

Northern Beaches Christian School. (2012b). *Learn.NBCS.* Sydney: Author. Retrieved from http://learn.nbcs.nsw.edu.au

Northern Beaches Christian School. (2012c). *PETE: The virtual learning environment for primary students at NBCS.* Sydney: Author. Retrieved from http://pete.nbcs.nsw.edu.au

OPTUS. (2003). *Rural education gets the picture.* Retrieved from http://www.optus.com.au/aboutoptus/About+Optus/Media+Centre/Media+Releases/2003/Rural+education+gets+the+picture

Queensland University of Technology. (2012). *Manual of policies and procedures. Chapter C, 6.3 blended learning.* Brisbane: Author. Retrieved from http://www.mopp.qut.edu.au/C/C_06_03.jsp#C_06_03.03.mdoc

Staker, H., & Horn, M. B. (2012, May). *Classifying K–12 blended learning.* San Madro, CA: Innosight Institute. Retrieved from http://www.innosightinstitute.org/innosight/wp-content/uploads/2012/05/Classifying-K-12-blended-learning2.pdf

15

USING VIRTUAL LEARNING ENVIRONMENTS TO PERSONALIZE LEARNING IN U.K. SCHOOLS

A Case Study

Helen Boulton and Lisa Hasler Waters

The United Kingdom's Open University was said to have revolutionized distance learning for adults. Today, it is still considered to be on the cutting edge of distance education, yet despite the advanced technologies employed for adult learners in the United Kingdom, some have described e-learning for younger students as slow moving (British Broadcasting Corporation, 2009; Hunt, Davies, & Pittard, 2006; Office for Standards in Education, Children's Services, and Skills [OFSTED], 2009). Beyond cultural aspects, schools must confront organizational challenges as they look to technology to support teaching and learning. Many schools are still unsure that benefits are associated with e-learning, and school leaders have placed little emphasis on learning through technology beyond the school walls (Hunt et al., 2006). Some contend that the lack of teacher proficiency with information and communications technology (ICT) has stymied its progress in primary and secondary schools (Tearle, 2004). Conversely, others have suggested that teachers have the skills but are reluctant to employ ICT because of deeper pedagogical implications of using systems not yet proven effective (Association for Information Technologies for Teacher Education, 2012). Additionally, there is the contention that the interoperability of learning platforms and management information systems has been problematic for schools. Others are encumbered by the lack of a combined curriculum and management network (Hunt et al., 2006).

Nonetheless, some schools are making good use of technology to enhance learning for their students, and some alternative schools are employing advanced interactive technologies to engage students who may not be able to attend traditional schools. This is especially true in schools where there is strong vision and leadership for ICT from senior management, as well as centralized resource allocation and whole-school strategies that focus on how ICT can enhance teaching and learning (Hunt et al., 2006). Some have found that when a school has reached e-maturity, e-learning can in fact promote higher school performance and "greater investment in learning by pupils" (Underwood et al., 2007, p. 4).

During the mid-2000s, there was an increase of e-learning in secondary schools, primarily due to government funding through credits for schools to acquire e-learning materials and the establishment of 10 regional broadband consortia to support the development of e-learning in schools (Boulton, 2008). The government provided £240 million to train teachers in the use of technologies in the classroom through New Opportunities Funding. Between 2000 and 2010, additional funding was provided under the Labor Government to increase the ratio of computers to pupils. Today, many younger students throughout the United Kingdom have access to computers and Internet technologies for learning. One recent study found average pupil/computer ratios were 6.1:1 for primary students and 3.7:1 for secondary students. Further, 54% of local authorities reported that all their schools with Internet access were connected at broadband speeds (Hunt et al., 2006).

To determine how effective schools were at using virtual learning environments (VLEs), OFSTED (2009) conducted a survey with 34 higher and adult education institutions, and primary and secondary schools. In schools where they found ineffective use of VLEs, they discovered that the systems were merely being used as a "dumping ground to store rarely used files" (p. 5). The authors concluded that schools were not using VLEs to the fullest extent possible, but they also found instances of good use of VLEs. In these instances, they encountered enthusiastic teachers who developed materials and encouraged students and staff to use the system, as well as school leaders who encouraged a whole-school approach to using VLEs.

Our objective in this chapter is to identify and describe how primary and secondary schools are currently using VLEs to personalize learning. A group of five schools, representing a broad spectrum of primary and secondary education in the United Kingdom, provides a useful snapshot of the current trends of personalization through VLEs. Included in this profile are two virtual schools (both of which are private) and three brick-and-mortar schools (two state schools and one private independent school).

Virtual Learning Environments

In 2005 the U.K. government published *Harnessing Technology: Transforming Learning and Children's Services*, which is still thought of today as the instrument that galvanized e-learning in U.K. schools (Department for Education and Skills, 2005). The VLEs seen in many U.K. classrooms today are, in part, manifestations of the recommendations contained within the 2005 document. VLEs have been recognized as a "new milestone in the development of e-learning in schools" (Boulton, 2008, p. 11). These online environments enable learners and school staff to access a range of learning materials through specially designed computer systems. However, some have suggested that teacher skills have not kept pace with rapidly advancing technologies, and advise that upskilling, particularly in new pedagogies to support use of ICT in learning and teaching, requires further development (Gillespie, Boulton, Hramiak, & Williamson, 2007).

Today, *VLEs* are still "an agreeably blank but versatile slate" (Crook & Cluley, 2009, p. 200). They have been defined as "any combination of distance and face-to-face interaction, where some kind of time and space virtuality is present" (Barajas & Owen, 2000,

p. 40). Typically, they involve some type of mediated space where individuals and groups can access information and resources to learning materials, such as notes and handouts, practice tests, PowerPoint presentations, video clips, and links to useful Internet sites (OFSTED, 2009).

Barajas and Owen (2000) created a summary of reasons why learners, teachers, and institutions might want to use VLEs. For example, learners might favor using VLEs to experience online learning, teachers might want to gain experience using a VLE, and institutions might favor VLEs so that they can give learners from different backgrounds a shared learning experience.

Personalized Learning

According to Gilbert (2006), personalized learning means focusing in a more structured way on each child's learning in order to enhance progress, achievement, and participation. Verpoorten, Glahn, Kravcik, Ternier, & Specht (2009) state that personalized learning "emphasizes the notion that learners consider given settings for learning as personally relevant" (p. 52). Verpoorten et al. also contend that personalized learning relies on three particular learning theories that are interrelated. The first is *constructivism*, which emphasizes that learning is a process whereby the student constructs his or her own knowledge, concepts, and competencies by interacting with the environment and others. The second, *reflective thinking*, emphasizes that learning is not merely about memorizing facts and acquiring knowledge but also about helping the learner engage in meta-levels of learning. The third theory, *self-regulated learning*, concerns how learners are able to control their learning. Verpoorten et al. (2009) saw motivation as a key concept of self-regulated learning and asserted that motivation occurs when the learner experiences perceived control of his or her learning, perceived value of the lesson or task at hand, and perceived self-efficacy or having the capacity to learn. But these aspects depend on the learner being fully aware of his learning processes. Verpoorten et al. (2009) also found that, at a minimum, personalized learning environments typically provide the learner with (a) materials for reading and learning, (b) websites to explore, and (c) assignments or tests to perform. However, the researchers contended that a truly learner-supportive VLE also provides the learner with tools to monitor his or her activities.

Some see personalized learning supported by technology as having great potential to transform learning (Gilbert, 2006). Indeed, in the mid-2000s, the government identified personalized learning as a key educational priority. In response, a review group was established to identify a clear vision of what personalized learning might look like for U.K. schools by the year 2020 and to provide recommendations that would be needed to effect systemic change. This group suggested several ways that technology might be able to contribute to personalized learning: (a) broadening the range of learning materials accessible to students, (b) enabling quick interactive assessments, (c) promoting development of a broad range of skills, (d) facilitating collaboration among peers within and outside with other schools, (e) blurring distinctions between informal and formal learning, (f) increasing motivation, and (g) increasing relevance through greater links between children's experiences and the technology-rich world outside (Gilbert, 2006). The group also contended that, in order for technology to effectively enable personalized learning through technology, there needed to be a planned whole-school approach and engagement with parents and students.

While little research is available on the effectiveness of personalized learning (Verpoorten et al., 2009), one comprehensive study conducted for the British Education Communications Technology Agency showed promise that technology could help facilitate personalized learning (Underwood et al., 2007). The study was conducted as a national-level investigation of the conditions under which e-learning was effective in schools. It included qualitative and quantitative data collected from 67 schools, which included responses from 3,700 teachers, students, and ICT staff. The researchers found the following:

- Primary-school-age students with greater opportunity to use ICT and who had positive attitudes toward computers reported having a more personalized learning experience.
- Teachers perceived that ICT was strongly associated with personalized learning.
- Computer use and e-maturity in schools where e-learning had been taking place for some time were associated with personalizing learning.
- Where homeschool links had been forged, there was greater support for the individual learner.
- Allowing content choice was one of the most frequent ways of personalizing learning.

However, in most of the schools studied they found absent two attributes considered critical in personalized learning. These attributes were *learner goal setting* and *student self-monitoring*. Further, they discovered a number of concerns held by participants that seemed to impede deep implementation of technology for personalization. Some participants had the perception that VLEs might cause a further divide between the haves and have-nots as they make their way into private homes. Others were concerned that because VLEs could be used anywhere and anytime, this might have led to "unnecessary attention to school work at home" (Underwood et al., 2007, p. 7). Moreover, some of those surveyed asserted that no direct link was shown between personalized learning and improved pupil performance, or that head teachers had a low level of familiarity with the concept of personalized learning in an online environment.

Profile of Schools Using VLEs to Personalize Learning

A group of five schools, representing a broad spectrum of primary and secondary education in the United Kingdom, provides a useful snapshot of the current trends of personalization through VLEs. Two virtual schools (both of which are private) and three brick-and-mortar schools (two state schools and one private independent school) are included in this profile of personalization of learning through VLEs.

Overview of Virtual Schools Profiled

Fully online schooling for younger children in the United Kingdom is still somewhat of a cottage industry. Only a handful of these schools are operating, most of which are privately owned.

The two virtual schools featured in this chapter are a small, privately held for-profit school and a larger, nonprofit school. Both schools charge tuition, and parents enroll their children by choice. The larger school also has provisions to serve local authorities, who can enroll their public school students to remediate or enrich their learning experiences. As the nature of their business is e-learning, the teachers and administrators in these schools are technology savvy and seem to welcome advanced use of Web 2.0 and other educational technology capabilities suited to serve younger students.

Briteschools is a small, fully online private school that serves students ages five to 18, Key Stages 2 to 5, as well as International General Certificate of Secondary Education (IGCSE) and A-Levels (standard for assessing suitability for entrance into university). Students are placed into classes according to their abilities. The school had 25 students enrolled in the 2011–2012 school year. At the time of this study, the majority of students were homeschooled children living in the United Kingdom and some were homeschooled children living overseas. Some students had special education needs (SEN), while others were expatriates living abroad who wished to continue their British education.

Courses were offered synchronously online, with teachers leading students through individual lessons or hosting group classes. Students worked at home on their own or with the help of parents. They could enroll in as many courses as they liked, and there was no mandated schedule of courses that students must take. The school hosted an annual event to enable students to meet each other and their teachers face-to-face. The success of the event has convinced it to host others.

There were six part-time teachers and one full-time teacher/administrator in 2011–2012. They were expected to be technology savvy, but ICT training was not mandatory. Teachers might also have attended ICT-related conferences to acquire new skills.

The school employed a customized system to manage teaching and learning. The system comprised a variety of online tools, such as Blackboard Collaborate, Keynote iLink, WizIQ, and other Web 2.0 tools. The school had plans to switch to Moodle to host its VLE in order to consolidate much of the functionality and to expand its services to other students.

InterHigh is a large, fully online private school. There were 600 students between the ages of 11 and 18, representing Key Stages 3 to 5 and IGCSE and A-Levels in 2011–2012. At the time of the study, 300 of the students were enrolled in InterHigh, a school that serves students who are enrolled by their parents and who are homeschooled or expatriates who wish to continue their British education. Some students may have disabilities or live in remote areas, or they may be professional athletes or actors who cannot attend traditional schooling. They may enroll in as many courses as they can handle. The other 300 students were enrolled in its Academy, an online program managed by Inter-High for local authorities providing supplementary education to students who may need extra assistance or may be advanced learners.

The school offered synchronous online courses scheduled during a typical school day, where a teacher leads a small cohort of students through the curriculum. In addition to hosting online classes, teachers also met online with students one-to-one to offer individual assistance. There were 60 full-time teaching staff, who were reportedly technology savvy. The school provided technology training for its teachers, and training was compulsory and ongoing. Additionally, the school hosted an annual event to enable students and their teachers to meet each other face-to-face.

There was a student-to-computer ratio of 1:1. The school's VLE was mature, built by the school to serve its specific requirement: to suit the needs of younger learners. The proprietary system was also licensed to others, such as local authorities. The school continued to evolve the VLE system, which included many of the same features found in other commercial VLEs, such as online communication and collaboration tools, library and internal resource storage, whiteboards, multimedia, and Web 2.0 applications.

These two fully virtual schools shared some common practices. For instance, they each had a student-to-computer ratio of 1:1, both schools relied heavily on technologies to provide and manage student education, and both had implemented robust online learning environments to accommodate their needs. Students in the two schools were placed in courses based on their age and abilities, and students engaged in their online courses synchronously.

Overview of Traditional Schools Profiled

Each of the three traditional schools profiled in this section follows the British national curriculum standards. All three schools reported that they had a range of technology-savvy staff members—some of whom were early adopters and others who were more reluctant to use technology in the classroom. While training in technology skills was not always mandatory, each school reported that it provided professional development training in technology through its ICT staff. All three schools also reported that their administrative staff and head teachers were very supportive of technology for teaching and learning and were keen to see effective use of VLEs across their schools.

Minster School is a state secondary school. Students generally come from a homogeneous background, comprising primarily a White and affluent population. The school is tied to the Church of England and has an academic emphasis in music. During the 2011–2012 school year it served 1,600 students ages 11 to 18 in Key Stages 3 to 5.

At the time of this study, the school had four information technology (IT) labs where there was a student-to-computer ratio of 1:1. There were SMART Boards and projectors in each classroom, and multimedia tools were also available. There were three full-time IT staff and two additional non-IT specialists on the teaching staff who worked part-time to support the ICT Department. In addition to developing and maintaining the school's ICT systems, the staff taught students and teachers on ICT. The ICT Department head worked with teachers to integrate technology into their classroom activities.

The school had recently switched from one VLE platform to Moodle, an open-source course management tool. Thus, the school was currently in what might be considered an early growth phase. The VLE hosted a wide range of applications, including online collaboration and communication tools and search engine capabilities, library functions, file storage, administrative tools, e-assessments and survey tools, course resources, multimedia, social networking tools, and so on. ICT staff were leading the way by using the system for teaching and learning. However, they reported that they had witnessed some progress among teachers using the VLE throughout the various departments. ICT staff have also realized an improvement in teacher attitudes toward using ICT in their classrooms, where many have set their own professional development targets for ICT skills.

Hampshire Primary State School (pseudonym) is a state primary school that serves students ages five to 11, Reception to Key Stage 2. It is located in an area of high depravation; the majority of residents reside in Local Authority Housing. During the 2011–2012 school year there were 256 students enrolled, almost half (44%) of whom were considered SEN students. Eleven percent of the students were statemented, meaning they were considered severely disadvantaged. Thirty percent of the students received free school lunches. A number of students were also considered as additional-language learners.

One ICT coordinator was on staff, receiving some part-time support from administrative staff. The ICT coordinator taught students technology skills and worked with staff to infuse technology into their curriculum. The school had one computer lab with 18 computers, so students typically shared computers when they worked in the lab.

There were two to three computers in the library, and some of the lower primary classrooms also had a few computers in their classrooms. Each classroom had a SMART Board and a laptop for the teacher's use. The school also had a trolley with 10 laptops, and the school acquired three iPads for use with SEN students. There was no mandatory ICT training, but some teachers took their own initiative to incorporate technology into their classroom activities. The ICT coordinator planned to offer in-house training on ICT in the next school year.

The school used WizKid, a VLE developed by the local county council to serve local schools. It was used mainly by teachers and staff for communication, administration, class preparation, scheduling purposes, and file storage. Some teachers also placed resources in the VLE for students to access at home, and a few might give students homework contained within the VLE. The system was still growing, however, and there were plans to shift from the current VLE platform to Google applications. This would enable the school to reach out to students beyond the limited and insular system that served as the VLE platform.

West Hill Park School is a private, independent prep school that serves students ages two to 13, Nursery to Year 8. During the 2011–2012 school year there were 280 students enrolled. The school primarily served White, upper-middle-class families. A number of students were also from military families.

Two ICT staff maintained the systems, and the head of ICT also provided instruction to teachers and students on ICT-related skills. Two computer labs served students, where there was a student-to-computer ratio of 1:1. Most of the classrooms had SMART Boards, projectors, and laptops for teachers, and a few classrooms held desktops for student use. The school acquired three iPads for trial use by teachers. In a few mandatory ICT training courses, ICT staff taught teachers about in-house data systems. Otherwise, teachers took their own initiative to attend ICT-related courses. ICT also worked with teachers to help them integrate technology into their classroom activities and worked to align ICT classes with content areas.

The school used a VLE system called EdModo. However, the system served only ICT staff and was considered to be in the testing phase. It facilitated communication between ICT staff and students and was a platform for storage of files and resources that students could access for ICT-related coursework. The head of ICT had plans to move the VLE to an open-source platform, such as Moodle, in order to serve the whole school. Otherwise, teachers typically worked with licensed technology products to manage students and prepare for class. There was also a schoolwide communication system for staff, teachers, and parents of students.

The case study schools used technologies beyond the VLEs in a variety of ways to enhance learning for their students. For instance, the state school used iPads to remediate and enrich learning for SEN students. West Hill Park was giving students hands-on computer building and programming opportunities using Raspberry Pi components, which were then installed into plastic cases that students built in their design technology courses.

Personalization: A Continuum

Our primary focus of this chapter is to explore and describe how schools in the United Kingdom were using their VLEs to personalize learning. Five schools, representing a diverse cross section of schools serving primary- to secondary-age students, were studied for the presence or absence of personalization characteristics (see Table 15.1). These characteristics are grouped into three themes: portaling, collaborating, and socializing. Where a characteristic was present in a school, the level of adoption of the characteristic was observed. The researchers could then summarize where each school was in general along the continuum of personalization from emerging to growing to maturing.

Based on the level of personalization characteristics found in each school, the two primary schools were located within the emerging phase; they were just beginning to structure their VLE and were still forming ideas on how it would be used. The ICT staff in these schools were testing options within the VLE and exploring other systems that could help expand their online services to teachers and students. In the middle of the continuum was the secondary school, which was in the growing phase on the continuum. It had a robust school website and was one year into the process of changing its existing VLE to a much improved version using Moodle. Its ICT Department was forging ahead with innovative ways to personalize learning while some of the other departments in the school were testing applications within the VLE and making progress and planning for broader use in the next school year. The two virtual schools were located within the maturing phase of the continuum by the very nature of their business models. They had fairly robust systems in place to personalize learning aspects for students within the VLEs.

Patterns of Activities Found Within the Continuum

Portaling

Portaling refers to the act of logging onto a VLE portal using a personal account and accessing tools, resources, and applications for learning. At a very minimum, each school in this study provided students with their own personal log-in to the school's VLE. This activity alone might have given students a sense of personalization. The depth of personalization in a school could be seen in what was made available to the student once he or she logged into the VLE, as illustrated along the emerging-growing-maturing continuum.

Emerging. At a very basic level, the log-in options exhibited by both the primary schools gave students access to internal e-mail accounts and course resources. Here, students could receive regular feedback from their ICT teachers for homework they may

TABLE 15.1:
Presence of VLE personalization characteristics in case study schools

Personalization Characteristics	Primary State	West Hill Park	Minster School	Brite-school	Inter-High
Portaling					
Whole-school approach to implementing VLE			✓	✓	✓
Curriculum customized and available online			✓	✓	
Choice of online courses that are student-selected				✓	✓
Ability-based placement into online cohorts				✓	✓
Learning targets set by students				✓	✓
Students work through curriculum at their own pace				✓	✓
Customized rewards; motivation provided online					✓
Online synchronous courses				✓	✓
Tracking system allows students to see their progress			✓	✓	✓
Online asynchronous courses			✓	✓	✓
Differentiation of materials based on abilities			✓	✓	✓
Assessments with immediate feedback			✓	✓	✓
Personal student log-in to VLE	✓	✓	✓	✓	✓
Communication tools for student, teacher	✓	✓	✓	✓	✓
Receive feedback from teachers for online work	✓	✓	✓	✓	✓
Remediate and enrich at student's own time/place	✓	✓	✓	✓	✓
Access resources available online beyond school walls	✓	✓	✓	✓	✓
Collaborating					
Web 2.0 tools for student collaboration, file share, blogs			✓	✓	✓
Differentiate online material and cohorts for group work			✓		✓
Collaboration across the curriculum			✓		
Socializing					
Socialization tools for communication and interaction			✓		✓
Common "room" for organizing and sharing community activities					✓

have posted within the system. They could also catch up on missed work, enrich their learning experiences by engaging in web resources aligned with content, and engage in remediation activities. While these activities might represent the basics of personalization, they gave the individual student opportunities to engage in school-related activities that might occur beyond the daily school schedule and might help to create a sense of personalization.

Growing. Portaling in Minster School included more advanced activities. The school, which had a robust website and was growing its VLE, presented students with opportunities not only to find out information relevant to school activities but also to communicate with other students and staff and access resources for subjects taught at the school. Students could also interact with content resources. For example, they could watch a video that they might have missed in English class or review a teacher's recorded presentation from a previous lesson and post a blog response. Some courses included asynchronous online course material. These types of courses were set up as highly structured and organized so that students could work their way through them independently and with little need for teacher intervention.

This more advanced level of log-in might have given the student a feeling of independence as he or she was able to access school-related resources in ways that extended beyond the classroom and could have offered a sense of responsibility by allowing the student to follow up with course materials as needed. Furthermore, students could take e-assessments that provided them with immediate feedback. Finally, the system incorporated SIMS Learning Gateway, an application that allowed students and parents the ability to track a student's progress and attendance and view academic reports.

Maturing. At the deepest level of portaling we find the two virtual schools. The very nature of their business model was to serve the unique needs of each individual student enrolled. In these schools, each student was placed in courses based primarily on abilities rather than age. In addition to the types of activities found within the emerging and growing phases, personalization also occurred between the routine connections the student had with teachers through synchronized online courses. In the case of BriteSchool, these courses were usually conducted in Blackboard Collaborate, where the teacher could engage students by calling upon them to answer questions using the audio or video communication tools or by eliciting their responses in writing using the online whiteboard. Briteschool also provided its students with curriculum customized specifically for their educational needs and made content and resources available to students through its VLE tools. InterHigh also provided similar applications, but the system it uses is proprietary.

In both schools the student could choose which courses to take. Once these were decided, the student log-in would enable access to content, resources, links, and classroom tools. Additionally, in these schools students were in charge of setting their own educational goals and working through the content at their own pace. At InterHigh, the student also had immediate access to progress reports because the system was embedded with a tracking system that followed and recorded student accomplishments and aligned them with educational targets. InterHigh also motivated the individual student through its credit card system, an application that rewarded the student for work done by issuing a credit that the student could then redeem for prizes.

Collaborating

Collaborating refers to the way in which a school unites students, teachers, staff, and parents through the VLE, and how the school sought to implement a whole-school approach to using the VLE for teaching and learning. The profiled schools were placed along the continuum in terms of how they collaborated. The two primary schools had plans to initiate collaboration among students, faculty, and parents, while the other three schools were actively engaging in a variety of collaborative projects that were mostly between students and their teachers.

Growing. Minster School provided students with opportunities to collaborate within the VLE. For instance, the ICT Department had created some of its coursework to include opportunities for students to work together in groups using VLE applications such as file storage and file sharing. Students also could post their completed presentations within the VLE and share them with the class during group presentations. The school also used blogs embedded within course sites, where the student posts responses to other students and receives feedback for his comments from his peers and teachers within the group forum. The ICT Department had recently trialed the group option in Moodle to differentiate course resources and materials for students that they placed into groups based on their abilities. This application allowed them to push materials that were appropriate for a given group of students who shared similar abilities. This approach facilitated more individualization in offering students materials that were more closely aligned with their own abilities.

Furthermore, Minster School also sought to incorporate collaboration between departments by adopting a whole-school approach to using the VLE. This cross-curricular method enabled students to work on projects that reached beyond one content-matter area, facilitating greater opportunities for them to experience how aspects of learning could be applied to other experiences.

Maturing. The two virtual schools practiced collaborative activities similar to Minster School but also made further use of online course applications to engage groups of students online in a hands-on way. For instance, during synchronous classes, a teacher might assign groups of students to engage in collaborative work and then place them in the break-out rooms, where they could work together online as a team. When the groups were done, they were invited back to the main whiteboard areas to present their group work.

Socializing

Socialization refers to the way in which the schools facilitate communications and interactions among students, teachers, staff, and parents. Only two of the profiled schools engaged in socialization as part of their use of the VLE to personalize learning.

Growing. The Minster School was beginning to develop an internal social networking tool that would allow each student to create his or her own profile, or e-portfolio. Here, the student could post work and share it with other students, teachers, and eventually parents. The student would also be able to communicate with other students using this tool in a way that aligns socializing in school with socializing off the campus.

Maturing. InterHigh's VLE featured an internal social networking system that enabled students to connect with their peers, share work, and communicate across the entire online school community. The sophisticated system also allowed a student to build his or her own website, and contained a chat feature where the student could set up groups and forums to engage with peers. A general discussion board feature enabled teachers and students to create discussions that the entire school community could join. The discussion board also featured a common room where students could participate in whole-school activities, such as rehearsing a presentation, listening to a guest speaker, viewing student works, and engaging in schoolwide competitions.

Concerns

Each of the schools had concerns regarding VLEs. The two primary schools shared that they were concerned with e-safety and ensuring that students access safe and appropriate websites. The schools were also sensitive to the amount of time that teachers needed to use technology and to the burden placed on them when extra training and time were required to implement technology. They proceeded with caution so as not to cause any concern among teachers. Funding maintenance and equipment acquisition was a challenge for the primary state school.

In Minster School, the ICT Department's main concerns were centered on providing a truly effective and efficient VLE. The department had set forth guidelines for ensuring quality by balancing the need to maintain consistency while engaging teachers and students in the creative and development process of the VLE. Another concern the school faced was overcoming the negative experiences teachers had in the previous year when ICT first introduced a VLE using another platform. That system was slow, and many teachers became frustrated. Installing the new Moodle system has been a delicate process whereby the ICT staff diligently modeled use of the system. ICT staff also provided in-house training for teachers, instructing them so that they would be well-prepared to navigate the new system and assured that the new system would achieve the school's intended goals.

Both virtual schools reported that their main concerns with the VLE were business-related. Briteschools was working on strategies to grow its business to keep up with expanding demands and increasing competition and was looking to new applications to support its VLE. InterHigh was planning to manage its growth to maintain a school size that enabled it the flexibility to be agile yet the capacity to accommodate new students.

Future Plans

All five schools expressed genuine optimism regarding the near-term potential they have to leverage VLEs to deliver personalized learning for their students. The primary schools had plans to evolve their current systems into more robust VLEs using Moodle or Google. They both endorsed the U.K. government's recent disapplication of ICT standards, which they regarded as a step in the right direction to move away from teaching students outdated computing skills. The head of ICT at West Hill Park found this "rethinking" of ICT rejuvenating and looked forward to focusing on opportunities that would allow his students to explore ICT in a more hands-on manner. Both schools also had plans to engage students in the maintenance of the ICT systems, creating what they termed *digital learner clubs*.

Interestingly, the main differences between the planned use of the VLEs could be seen in each school's characteristics. For example, because many of the students enrolled in the primary state school had special needs, the school actively involved students' parents. The school planned to build its VLE so that parents could interact more effectively with the school and with their children when they were doing homework. The private independent school, on the other hand—a boarding school where students do homework at school—was less reliant on parental involvement. Its plans did not necessarily include expanding access to parents. Rather, the school would focus its attention on building cross-curricular activities using the VLE and giving students more opportunities to work in the cloud and learning how to move with ease across platforms and systems.

Minster School continued to base its ICT efforts on a whole-school approach, as was evident in its method to ensure more cross-curricular implementation of the VLEs and its efforts to work with all departments to embed more multimedia elements for student learning. Minster School was also focusing its near-future efforts on creating socialization opportunities within the VLE. The school planned to implement e-portfolios so that students could showcase their works to other students and parents. Additionally, it planned to involve parents more by extending the VLEs to parents so that they could track their children's progress more efficiently and so that they could interact and communicate more readily with the school.

Briteschools was planning to leverage the tracking applications available in Moodle, while InterHigh was seeking to expand its services to students by implementing an upgraded library system and offering a wider variety of courses, including vocational education. This new system was also planned to provide deeper personalization for each student because it was to operate with an intuitive application that would track a student's status and then push the appropriate materials to the student to help progress continue.

Conclusion

In this study we have provided rich evidence suggesting that these five schools were making a substantial effort to personalize learning through VLEs for their students. The depth of personalization was determined by the level of e-maturity found in each school, which could be envisioned along a continuum. The schools engaged in three categories of personalization activities: portaling, collaborating, and socializing.

Portaling activities might have created a sense of personalization because, at a minimum, each student had his or her own log-in identification and password. Moving along the continuum, the more mature a school's VLE, the more that personalization activities were evident. For example, Minster School pushed differentiated learning materials to its students and enabled some to work through course content at their own pace. The two virtual schools were able to provide students with opportunities not only to monitor their progress but also to choose courses, and one of the schools enabled students to track their progress. Verpoorten et al. (2009) suggested that, at a minimum, personalized learning environments should provide the learner with materials for reading and learning, websites to explore, and assignments or tests to perform. They also asserted that a truly learner-supportive, personalized learning environment should provide students with tools to monitor their activities. Verpoorten et al. suggested that true personalization could be realized when students had control over their learning, could track their progress, and could choose courses that were meaningful for them—activities practiced by the more e-mature schools profiled in this study.

Two additional practices that Minster School and the two virtual schools engaged in were not necessarily reflected in Verpoorten et al.'s (2009) criteria, yet seemed to facilitate a sense of personalization for students: collaborating and socializing. The collaborating activities these schools engaged in offered students the chance to be parts of teams and may have created a sense of personalization by giving each individual student the experience of sharing one's own contributions with team members. Socialization activities extended the sense of personalization by giving students opportunities to communicate with their peers in ways that might have been similar to how they socialize during non-school-required activities.

The five schools represented in this chapter have shown activities resembling those associated with the criteria of personalization through technologies (Crook & Cluley, 2009; Gilbert, 2006; Grabe & Grabe, 2007; Underwood et al., 2007; Verpoorten et al., 2009). Moreover, the way in which each school implemented its VLE and sought to personalize learning was consistent with the school's vision, its targeted audience, its approach to pedagogy, as well as the scope of the school's initiative to implement ICT. These were among the characteristics found by Barajas and Owen (2000) as identifiable factors shaping the composition of VLEs in schools.

Most apparent was that each of the five schools included in this study had the determination to ensure that technology was used to benefit teaching and learning, and had a vision for how the VLE could be leveraged to support personalization. Minster School and InterHigh clearly had a well-defined approach to implementing personalization across the entire school, where head teachers, staff, and students were important members of the implementation process. This type of effort was found by Tearle (2004) as instrumental in ensuring effective integration of ICT. The two primary schools still faced some obstacles before full integration of VLEs could be realized across each school. These two schools were struggling with interoperability of learning platforms and management information systems, a problem still found in many schools across the United Kingdom (Hunt et al., 2006).

It would be reasonable to suppose that traditional schools in the United Kingdom, which are designed to serve groups of students, might place more emphasis on personalization of learning through student collaboration opportunities. On the other hand, virtual schools, which are in business to serve individual students, might place more emphasis on personalization of learning through more individualized opportunities. The very nature of the school would seem to direct its efforts of personalization through VLEs.

Much research is still to be done to fully understand how to effectively measure student outcomes that result from personalization through technologies. Additional research might also lead to effective strategies for implementing technology-supported personalization that fit within the goals for, and identity of, each school. These strategies may be especially important as the U.K. government moves toward a more hands-off approach to supporting ICT in schools. At the time of writing this chapter, the ICT national curriculum had been disapplied in the United Kingdom, which leaves schools in a state of flux. A new national curriculum is to be in place for September 2013 and is expected to have more focus on computer science and digital literacy as well as ICT. What is clear is that the role of the VLE in schools will be the choice of each individual school.

In this study we were not able to capture whether personalization in these schools led to improved student academic outcomes. Future research should consider how learners themselves are benefiting from personalized learning. A starting point might be to measure learners' perceptions of personalization against the three attributes suggested by Verpoorten et al. (2009) that lead to personalization: how learning is personally relevant to the learner, how the learner takes ownership of learning, and how the learner takes responsibility for learning.

Finally, these schools have shown that using VLEs to personalize learning for students is an evolving practice that takes continuous effort. Where a school lies along the continuum may not be as important as how its effort to use the VLE for personalization reflects its mission, vision, and capacity to support technology. It may not be advisable for a school to race along the continuum toward personalization. A slower, well-planned approach may lead to more purposeful and effective strategies that truly benefit teaching and learning.

References

Association for Information Technologies for Teacher Education. (2012). *Practitioners who are reluctant to use digital technologies in classrooms.* Oxford.

Barajas, M., & Owen, M. (2000). Implementing virtual learning environments: Looking for holistic approach. *Educational Technology & Society, 3*(3), 39–52.

Boulton, H. (2008). Managing e-learning: What are the real implications for schools? *Electronic Journal of e-Learning, 6*(1), 11–18.

British Broadcasting Corporation (BBC). (2009). *"Virtual learning a slow starter."* Retrieved from http://news.bbc.co.uk/1/hi/education/7824736.stm

Crook, C., & Cluley, R. (2009). The teaching voice on the learning platform: Seeking classroom climates within a virtual learning environment. *Learning, Media and Technology, 34*(3), 199–213.

Department for Education and Skills. (2005). *Harnessing technology: Transforming learning and children's services.* (2005). London: Author.

Gilbert, C. (2006). *Teaching and learning in 2020 review.* Nottingham: Department for Education and Skills (DfES).

Gillespie, H., Boulton, H., Hramiak, A. J., & Williamson, R. (2007). *Learning and teaching with virtual learning environments.* Exeter: Learning Matters Ltd.

Grabe, M., & Grabe, C. (2007). *Integrating technology for meaningful learning.* New York: Houghton Mifflin.

Hunt, M., Davies, S., & Pittard, V. (2006). *Becta review 2006: Evidence on the progress of ICT in education.* London: British Educational Communications and Technology Agency (BECTA).

Office for Standards in Education, Children's Services, and Skills (OFSTED). (2009). *Virtual learning environments: An evaluation of their development in a sample of educational settings.* London: Author.

Tearle, P. (2004). *The implementation of ICT in UK secondary schools*. Exeter: University of Exeter, Telematics Centre.

Underwood, J., Baguley, T., Banyard, P., Coyne, E., Farrington-Flint, L., & Selwood, I. (2007). *Impact 2007: Personalising learning with technology*. London: British Educational Communications and Technology Agency (BECTA). Retrieved from http://oro.open.ac.uk/34533

Verpoorten, D., Glahn, C., Kravcik, M., Ternier, S., & Specht, M. (Eds.). (2009). *Personalisation of learning in virtual learning environments* (Vol. 5794). Heidelberg: Springer.

16

A CASE STUDY OF KOREA'S CYBER HOME LEARNING SYSTEM

Hyeonjin Kim and Jeonghee Seo

The Cyber Home Learning System (CHLS) is the Korean government's national e-learning system for elementary and secondary education. *CHLS* is defined as

the Internet-based learning service that enables learners to undertake self-directed learning activities at any time, whether or not at school, via the Internet, through a one-to-one system of learning management, and that provides learning services that are customized for individual learners. (Jung et al., 2007, p. 44)

Why Was CHLS Developed?

While traditional distance education institutions (e.g., Air and Correspondence High Schools) in Korea have provided diplomas, CHLS was designed to support public education through both online and blended learning. For example, students can use CHLS at home via online learning to brush up and prepare for their schoolwork, and teachers can use it in the classroom via blended learning to support their teaching.

History

CHLS was established in 2004 by the Korea Education and Research Information Service (KERIS), a governmental organization housed in the Korean Ministry of Education, Science, and Technology (MEST), for the purpose of narrowing the education gaps between regions and between high- and low-income families, and to reduce private tuition expenses. In 2005, the first CHLS service was launched in all areas of Korea, covering 16 cities and provinces.

Table 16.1 summarizes the history of CHLS, focusing on the development of the e-learning content, the learning management system/learning and content management system (LMS/LCMS), the counseling system, and other aspects of the system. The service of CHLS has been expanded since 2005. In addition to providing services for learning core curricular and extracurricular subjects, CHLS also now provides career counseling for high school students.

TABLE 16.1:
The history of CHLS

2004	Initial development of CHLS nationwide
	Developed 16 CHLS modules for regular and extracurricular subjects for middle school students
2005	Launched the CHLS service for middle school students nationwide
	Developed 16 CHLS modules for elementary and high school regular and extracurricular subjects
	Developed parent tutoring service for high school students
2006	Expanded the CHLS service to elementary and high school students
	Incorporated video lecture content from EBS (Educational Broadcasting System)
2007	Developed the LMS for the Counseling and Telecounseling System
	Developed two levels (elementary and advanced) of CHLS modules for secondary school students
2008	Developed the next-generation LMS/LCMS
	Developed two levels (supplementary and advanced) of CHLS modules for elementary school students
2009–2011	Developed CHLS modules based on revised national curriculum

Note. Adapted with permission from Ministry of Education, Science, and Technology, & Korea Education and Research Information Service, *Adapting Education to the Information Age: The White Paper for ICT in Education of Korea* (Seoul: KERIS, 2012).

Stakeholders

CHLS was implemented by several different bodies, including MEST, KERIS, 16 Metropolitan Offices of Education (MOEs), and 16 MOE subsidiary agencies. MEST formulated the policy framework and monitored the effects of CHLS, while KERIS and the 16 MOEs developed and served the systems and content. KERIS supported and coordinated the MOEs through research, development, and consultation. Initially, KERIS developed the e-learning content as a prototype, and the MOEs developed their own content based on a standardized format.

The MOEs and the subsidiary agencies (i.e., Institutes for ICT in Education) administer the CHLS service for schools by developing content and implementing services. Each MOE implements CHLS based on its own regional needs. Accordingly, each MOE also has its own CHLS website. For example, the CHLS website for Seoul is www.kkulmat.com, while http://star.cbedunet.or.kr is Chungbuk's website. Figure 16.1 provides a screen shot of Seoul's CHLS website.

Stakeholders in the CHLS service cooperate so that they can implement the system successfully without overlapping or omitting services.

CHLS Design

CHLS was originally designed to support students' self-study at home. Its service has expanded to support teachers' classroom teaching and to provide career counseling. Figure 16.2 illustrates the concept and service structure of CHLS.

Figure 16.1: CHLS website of Seoul City (www.kkulmat.com)

Figure 16.2: The service structure of CHLS

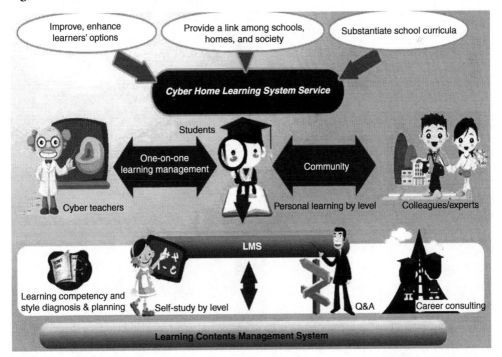

CHLS includes LMS/LCMS in order to manage and support students' e-learning and teachers' teaching both offline and online. For example, the LMS of CHLS provides services such as customized learning content and counseling from cyber teachers who are assigned to or voluntarily participate in CHLS. CHLS also provides a diagnostic service for measuring students' levels of performance and a videoconference service for counseling at a distance.

Cyber teachers are divided into cyber class teachers and cyber counseling teachers. Cyber class teachers are tasked with managing students' attendance and progress, providing assignments and supplementary materials, and providing feedback on students' work and questions. Cyber counseling teachers have the job of providing students with career counseling and answering students' questions about the subject matter. Parents and university student volunteers serve as tutors, supporting the cyber teachers by managing students' attendance and progress.

CHLS content is developed for elementary and secondary education in five regular curriculum subjects (e.g., Korean, mathematics, science, English, and social studies), as well as extracurricular subjects (e.g., essay writing, economics, and environmental studies). Because CHLS content aims to support adaptive learning based on students' levels of performance, it has been developed at three levels: supplementary, basic, and advanced. Supplementary content is developed for students with a low performance level, basic content for students at an intermediate level, and advanced content for students at a high performance level. The basic-level content includes Educational Broadcasting System (EBS) video lectures that can be used to support students' self-study and preparation for midterm and final examinations. Figure 16.3 presents screen shots of CHLS content in the two formats in which all of the content is developed—Flash-based (left) and video-based (right).

Core Service: e-Learning for Public Education

After completing six years of elementary school, Korean students complete six years of secondary education—three in middle school and three in high school. CHLS provides service to students beginning in the fourth year of elementary school and continuing

Figure 16.3: Screen shots of CHLS content

Figure 16.4: Learning process in CHLS

| Class-assigned learning | Start studying
Receive permission
Sign up for course
Select a course
Sign up for CHLS
Cyber class teacher
Cyber class teacher
Tutor |
| Self-study learning | Start studying
Select content(s)
Sign up for CHLS
Cyber class teacher |

through the first year of high school. Students wanting supplementary or advanced lessons after their regular school day ends may select CHLS content from the five subject areas based on their levels of performance.

Students can generally work with CHLS in two ways—class-assigned and self-study learning. The class-assigned CHLS service was designed for particular target students, such as students from low-income families, students who are handicapped, and gifted students. A cyber class teacher is assigned to each online CHLS class and manages his or her students' learning. Students wanting to be involved in class-assigned CHLS must register for particular courses. MOEs or teachers may facilitate the students' registration. While working within CHLS, class-assigned students receive support from a cyber class teacher, a cyber counseling teacher, and tutors (parents or university student volunteers). Teachers can volunteer to participate in CHLS as cyber class teachers or cyber counseling teachers.

However, the self-study CHLS service also allows students to sign up for CHLS voluntarily and to select the content they want to study. Students enrolled in self-study CHLS have their learning managed by LMS and cyber counseling teachers (i.e., without the assistance of a cyber class teacher). Figure 16.4 illustrates the learning process of class-assigned and self-study CHLS students.

Teachers make frequent use of CHLS content during their offline (face-to-face) classes as supplementary teaching materials. They also ask their students to use CHLS online lessons at home as a supplement to their offline class lessons. In other words, teachers use CHLS as blended learning to support their regular curricula.

Effects: Does CHLS Work—and if So, How?

To date, the effects of CHLS have been reported through policy reports and publications in scholarly journals.

Policy Effects

The effects of CHLS from a policy perspective can be viewed relative to the policy goals of the CHLS service—reducing private tuition expenses and the educational gap between high- and low-income families. Since CHLS was established in 2004, the service has been used by numerous students, half of whom have come from geographically rural areas or lower-income backgrounds. In 2011, over 4.1 million students used CHLS, an average of approximately 228,150 student log-ins per day (Ministry of Education, Science, and Technology, & Korea Education and Research Information Service, 2011). Just over 79% of students who used CHLS agreed that "CHLS [was] helpful for their learning," and 48.2% of students agreed that "CHLS [was] nice to be supplementary to classroom learning" (Ministry of Education, Science, and Technology, & Korea Education and Research Information Service, 2009a). Eighty-one percent of students answered affirmatively to the question of whether CHLS had led to changes in their study habits (Jung et al., 2007).

Specific effects of CHLS have included enhancing the quality of public education by making more educational resources available to all students. CHLS received high ratings with respect to accessibility (e.g., "easy access to the CHLS website" was rated at 71.1%), and 66.2% of users considered it to be a "convenient support system for learning" (Korea Education and Research Information Service, 2007). CHLS also plays a role in supporting public education when it is used as supplementary material and advanced course resources (Cho, 2007; Jung, Kim, Hong, Lim, Cha, & Ahn, 2007; Park, Joo, & Bong, 2007). Further, CHLS reduces the expenses of private education. Approximately 12.5% of parents whose children used CHLS responded that additional private education would not be necessary. In addition, 69.9% of parents perceived that they benefited from supplementary learning with CHLS. Finally, 15.5% of parents answered that they planned to stop or had already stopped providing private tutoring (Jung et al., 2007).

CHLS also addressed the educational divide for economically and geographically disadvantaged students. Since 2007, students from small schools in rural villages and from low-income families have received targeted services. Such efforts have enabled these students to have higher-quality supplementary learning services. Approximately 50% of the target students are currently using CHLS, and their teachers believe that CHLS contributes to the equality of education.

Effects on Learning

The literature indicated that CHLS contributed to student learning by enhancing self-directed learning skills, providing customized learning content, improving teacher-student interaction, and supporting the development of learning communities. CHLS supported student's self-directed learning skills by allowing students to choose content based on their academic level or other factors. Also, students can identify their own learning problems through evaluation and feedback, and address those problems by actively participating in CHLS (Shin & Lim, 2007). As students used CHLS more, their self-directed learning ability continued to develop, and they spent less time playing computer games or chatting online (Jung et al., 2007). Teachers and parents similarly considered

CHLS to be effective in developing self-motivated study habits (e.g., 38.8% of parents answered that their children had developed self-directed learning habits; Korea Education and Research Information Service, 2007).

CHLS also contributed to students' differentiated learning by providing different levels of content according to students' levels of performance (e.g., Kim & Hwang, 2007; Park, Ham, & Lee, 2009; Song, Oh, & Kim, 2009). For example, Kim and Hwang (2007) developed storytelling contents to improve high school students' reading skills based on their tailored learning needs. The results indicated that 80% to 90% of teachers and students were satisfied with the online content and 65% with offline classroom activities.

The literature also reported that CHLS improved interactions between teachers and students, and among students themselves. For example, Eom and An (2009) analyzed the interaction-supporting function of CHLS in 16 metropolitan cities and identified eight to 13 kinds of interaction functions, including messages, chat systems, bulletin boards, archives, and wikis. Parents also reported that CHLS use resulted in increased interactions with their children (Jung et al., 2007).

Success Factors

Numerous studies focusing on CHLS have been conducted in Korea since 2004. Seo and Koo (2010) reviewed 46 such research studies, focusing on the factors that influence the effects of CHLS. Approximately 60% of the studies used quantitative methodologies, and half of the studies were conducted by researchers from the field of subject-matter education rather than technology-related researchers. Target subject areas included Korean, English, and mathematics at the elementary and middle levels of education.

With respect to learner factors related to the effects of CHLS, Seo and Koo examined which student characteristics positively influenced students' learning. For example, self-directed learners participated more actively in CHLS and gave positive feedback regarding CHLS (Kim & Kim, 2007; Shin & Lim, 2007). Also, students with high motivation tended to have positive learning attitudes toward CHLS (Kim & Baek, 2008). The literature also reported that students who had self-confidence had more positive learning attitudes toward and higher satisfaction with CHLS (Yang & Baek, 2008).

Research on the CHLS teaching and learning models focused on developing a model to support teachers and students. For example, Song and Chung (2006) suggest six implementation models for cyber home learning: (a) supporting student-level-based classroom instruction, (b) supplementing teachers' school curriculum implementation, (c) addressing individual students' learning needs, (d) building the cyber learning community, (e) differentiating school instruction, and (f) assessing achievement in terms of the purpose of CHLS service. Similarly, Lee, Choi, and Cho (2007) proposed four CHLS implementation models: (a) combination of online with offline, (b) online-centered, (c) integrating afterschool activities, and (d) supporting online administration for extracurricular programs. These various teaching and learning models may contribute to school practices and teacher participation in each region by providing a framework to guide blended learning in primary and secondary schools.

The cyber teacher is one of the most important factors in CHLS. The literature indicates that cyber teachers' passion and commitment to CHLS, attractive management strategies, good blended teaching strategies, and technical literacy contributed to the success of CHLS (Cho, 2007; Korea Education and Research Information Service, 2007). Kim, Kim, Park, Ma, and Jung (2009) developed information literacy evaluation standards to identify the competence of cyber teachers. Further, Kang and Shin (2008) developed a scale regarding the tutor's role in elementary cyber home learning. Finally, Shin and Lim (2007) explored parents' contributions to their children's active participation in CHLS, noting that parents' interests and involvement were important because CHLS was a connected model of learning between the school and home.

Conclusion: How Should CHLS Evolve?

CHLS has contributed to Korean public education both offline and online. However, as society changes and evolves, the needs of teachers and students also change in terms of their preferences regarding interaction and learning. Accordingly, several lessons have been learned, and future directions for CHLS are addressed in this section.

First, although CHLS services have expanded since 2005 (e.g., career counseling through a conferencing system), the target students for CHLS need to be reassessed. A 2011 report by the Ministry of Education, Science, and Technology (MEST) and Korea Education and Research Information Service (KERIS) indicated that students in the elementary and secondary levels had different levels of satisfaction with CHLS services. Students in lower grades express a higher degree of satisfaction with CHLS services, which could be interpreted as meaning that CHLS content has been developed in such a way that it is more attractive for lower grade levels (e.g., Flash-based animation), rather than upper grade levels. Possibly as a result of this finding, in 2010 the Korean government decided not to develop high school content, instead focusing more on the quality of services provided for elementary and middle grades students.

Second, CHLS content and services need to be developed to create new learning environments by shifting from the developers' perspective to the users' perspective. Development based on this change in perspectives can facilitate participants' active engagement in their learning. For example, through Web 2.0 services (e.g., wikis, blogs, and RSS), students can share information easily, collaborate with their friends, and express their interests and creative ideas to others. User-created content and individually customized learning might become more popular in CHLS.

Third, CHLS should be enhanced to include a more interactive and dynamic learning environment. For example, teachers could provide more interactive and lively lessons with students through the video lecturing and consulting system. Students can chat with their cyber teachers and friends on the videoconferencing system. Added functionalities (e.g., group chatting, presentations, and writing on the online blackboard) have made CHLS a more interactive system than it was previously, although CHLS has experienced some technical problems when attempting to expand its video-based services nationwide.

Fourth, the advanced learning diagnosis and prescription service in CHLS needs to be enhanced through accurately analyzing and evaluating students' academic performance and learning patterns so that it can better provide services customized to individual learners. CHLS began operations in 2007, and the level of the service has been very limited until recently because of the quality of the diagnosis tools and prescription module. More advanced learning diagnosis and prescription services to provide students with more customized learning materials and environments will be developed after scrutinizing the need for and role of the service.

Fifth, effective blended learning models need to be developed for CHLS to further support public education. These new blended learning models need not be limited to the blending of online and offline learning; they should include blended models of classroom learning and home learning, as well as school activity and local community activity. These potential models could be effective frameworks for educational transformation.

Sixth, the meaning and value of CHLS services need to be shared from a learning perspective rather than a policy perspective. As mentioned previously, CHLS initially aimed to address such policy objectives as reducing private education expenses and educational gaps between regions and families. The degree to which these goals have been achieved is not clear because the original problems are complicated phenomena, affected by many factors outside of the realm of education. The fundamental success of CHLS should be evaluated based on whether it contributes to student learning—qualitatively and quantitatively. With respect to the quantitative aspect, students' educational opportunities enable them to gain an academic diploma as well as lifelong learning skills that should be transferable to various endeavors. These learning skills can help students to develop 21st-century skills, which are a recent focus of educational initiatives. Based on the experiences of the past several years of CHLS—and the existing supporting system—CHLS will be further developed to support the teaching and learning of these 21st-century skills using collaborative learning, problem-based learning, and project-based learning.

Finally, CHLS can contribute to the new generation of learning. *Smart Education*, which MEST announced in 2011 as an educational plan to support the 21st-century knowledge society, is defined as an "intelligent and adaptive teaching and learning system to enable new pedagogy, curriculum, assessments, teachers, etc. which are required for the twenty-first century knowledge society" or a "learning format which is integrating social learning and adaptive learning in the best communication environment" (Ministry of Education, Science, and Technology, & Korea Education and Research Information Service, 2011, p. 6). The Smart Education initiative emphasizes the importance of online instruction and evaluation. For boosting online learning, CHLS could serve as a primary platform for *SMART online learning* for students. In SMART online learning, various subjects and more sophisticated functions need to be developed to address students' needs. One of the biggest changes in the future will be to provide educational credits for online learning for students who cannot attend a physical school due to health (e.g., being ill), geographic (e.g., living in an isolated region), or environmental (e.g., earthquake, flood, epidemic disease) reasons. To support this service, more interactive and intelligent functions for online learning and online evaluation will need to be added to CHLS in the near future.

References

Cho, K. (2007). An analysis of learners' satisfaction and effectiveness awareness on Gyeongbuk Cyber Home Learning System. *Journal of Educational Information and Media, 13*(3), 159–188.

Eom, W., & An, B. (2009). Analysis of functions for interactions in learning management systems for Cyber Home Learning System. *Journal of Educational Information and Media, 15*(2), 47–66.

Jung, S., Song, J., Kim, Y., Hong, C., Kim, J., Lim, . . . Ahn, K. (2007). *Overview of the CHLS in Korea.* KERIS Issue Report RM 2008-8. Seoul: KERIS.

Kang, E., & Shin, J. (2008). Development of a scale for tutors' role for elementary Cyber Home Learning. *Journal of Educational Technology, 24*(2), 207–232.

Kim, B., & Baek, H. (2008). A study on the impact of the attitude of Cyber Home Study using structural equation model on effectiveness. *Journal of Digital Contents Society, 9*(3), 449–460.

Kim, C., Kim, J., Park, S., Ma, D., & Jung, E. (2009). A study on information literacy evaluation standards for Cyber Teachers. *Journal of the Korean Association of Information Education, 13*(3), 383–392.

Kim, J., & Hwang, S. (2007). Connecting on-class elementary school English learning with selected on-line differentiated contents. *Multimedia Assisted Language Learning, 10*(1), 130–154.

Kim, M., & Kim, J. (2007). Analysis of students' attitude and satisfaction level toward afterschool e-homeStudy. *Korea Contents Society, 7*(10), 44–58.

Korea Education and Research Information Service. (2007). *The effectiveness of the Cyber Home Learning System in 2007.* KERIS CPC 2007-6. Seoul: Author.

Lee, J., Choi, J., & Cho, K. (2007). A study on the linking model of Cyber Home Study with afterschool. *Journal of Educational Information and Media, 13*(3), 5–34.

Ministry of Education, Science, and Technology, & Korea Education and Research Information Service (2009a). *Adapting education to the information age: The white paper for ICT in education of Korea.* Seoul: KERIS.

Ministry of Education, Science, and Technology, & Korea Education and Research Information Service. (2009b). *Customized learning space, always open for you: Cyber Home Learning System.* KERIS promotional brochure. Seoul: KERIS.

Ministry of Education, Science, and Technology, & Korea Education and Research Information Service. (2011). *Adapting education to the information age: The white paper for ICT in education of Korea.* Seoul: KERIS.

Ministry of Education, Science, and Technology, & Korea Education and Research Information Service (2012). *Adapting education to the information age: The white paper for ICT in education of Korea.* Seoul: KERIS.

Park, C., Ham, U., & Lee, J. (2009). Research and development of Cyber-Home Learning System content in Korean subjects (1)—for 4th grade elementary school students. *Korean Language Education Research, 23*, 185–240.

Park, S., Joo, Y., & Bong, M. (2007). Investigation of the perceived effectiveness of and user satisfaction with the Cyber Home Learning System. *Journal of Educational Technology, 23*(3), 59–87.

Seo, J., & Koo, Y. (2010). Analysis of research on the Cyber Home Learning Service. *Journal of Korean Education, 37*(4), 207–238.

Shin, B., & Lim, K. (2007). A study on factors that affect the participation of students in Cyber Home Study. *Journal of Child Education, 16*(4), 119–129.

Song, J., Oh, H., & Kim, H. (2009). Research and development of Cyber-Home Learning System content in Korean subjects (2)—for the 1st grade of middle school students. *Korean Language Education Research, 23*, 241–287.

Song, S. H., & Chung, H. M. (2006). An exploratory research on implementation models of instruction for Cyber Home Study System in Korea. *Journal of Educational Information and Media, 12*(3), 259–298.

Yang, S., & Baek, H. (2008). A study on the effects of learning motivation factors of the Cyber Home Study contents using structural equation model on learning satisfaction and activation. *Journal of Digital Policy and Management, 6*(2), 145–155.

PART FOUR
Summary Thoughts

17

ONLINE, BLENDED, AND DISTANCE LEARNING IN SCHOOLS

Summing Up

Michael K. Barbour and Tom Clark

I n conceiving this edited volume, we sought to answer two questions: What can North American and international educators learn from each other about online and blended learning? and What are some key policy and practice issues in the field that might be addressed through advice from experts and program leaders? We asked experts and experienced administrators to contribute chapters that would help us answer these questions, wherever possible referencing the existing research literature. Some were asked to provide chapters sharing insights on key aspects of practice and policy, while others were asked to develop illustrative case studies.

In this chapter, we begin by summarizing lessons shared by the authors of our North American and international case study chapters in response to the first question. We then consider what our authors say about policy and practice issues. Finally, we consider where things are heading by proposing some possible future trends.

Lessons Shared by Educators and Programs

Revenaugh (Chapter 10) presented a case study of Nexus Academy blended charter schools in two U.S. states that provided data-driven personalized learning for every student in a small high school setting. Math and English were taught face-to-face, with a focus on data-driven intervention, remediation, acceleration, and enrichment; science, social studies, electives, and enrichment courses were taught online. Students attended in morning or afternoon shifts in an open, collegelike environment. An on-site success coach provided academic support and guidance. Lessons learned included the need to provide in-depth training for on-site teachers to help them move away from whole-class instructional techniques and adopt the use of data-driven intervention strategies focused on small groups. Revenaugh foresaw blended charters like Nexus becoming an alternative for families and students who might otherwise choose charter, private, or home schools. She noted that historically Black colleges and universities were partnering to develop Nexus-style early-college high schools.

Ebert and Powell (Chapter 11) presented a case study of a district-led online and blended learning program in Clark County, Nevada. The district began a virtual high school in the late 1990s. The early adoption of course development guidelines allowed content development teams to develop high-quality and engaging courses. A strong emphasis on ongoing professional development helped build instructional quality. Updates to technology infrastructure made it easier to capture data and offer courses in both district buildings and students' homes. The authors cited policy changes in the state and district that have supported program growth, such as revisions to school law that removed the need for students in online courses to meet attendance requirements. The district continued to educate state- and district-level stakeholders about the benefits and opportunities that online and blended learning provide students. These practices and policy changes helped the district move online and blended learning into the main-stream. These forms of learning became an integral part of the district improvement plan, which called for use of choice and innovation to drive school reform and included an initiative to incorporate blended learning in traditional district schools.

Smallwood, Reaburn, and Baker (Chapter 12) offered a study of the evolution of the Virtual High School (VHS; Ontario), a private online school that began in the mid-1990s as a spinoff from a program within a school district. Early challenges included developing a learning management system (which later formed the basis of a commercial LMS, Desire2Learn) and obtaining accreditation needed to offer high school courses for credit. The school has since grown into the largest private, nondenominational online high school in Canada. The authors identified several keys to the school's success: There was a strong team atmosphere among mostly colocated staff. All learning was individualized and asynchronous, with active communication during coursework, including teacher responses to student inquiries within 24 hours. To develop challenging online courses, VHS used a collaborative team approach with a strong focus on formative assessment with constructive feedback. As the school was tuition-based, the authors saw parents and students as having high expectations of the program. They saw a student-centric approach that combined personalized education, challenging curriculum, responsive teaching staff, and a robust learning environment as essential for building a successful school of this kind.

Based on the case of Nepal, a least-developed country that faced many challenges to educational access, Cavanaugh (Chapter 13) addressed the potential for online learning to meet the needs of all students. Cavanaugh profiled Open Learning Exchange (OLE) Nepal, a Nepali organization that sponsors an initiative in public primary schools where students engaged in project-based learning related to local ecosystems, indigenous cultures and arts, and the nation by contributing to an open online repository. The repository also served as a portal to open education resources, experts, and mentors. While OLE Nepal was a good first step, the author noted, it served a limited number of schools and students, and many children in Nepal lacked good access to school-based learning. She believed that as mobile technology became more cost-effective and widespread, it had the potential to leapfrog Nepal into an online education system. To make online learning a reality in Nepal and other developing nations, Cavanaugh recommended strengthening data systems, providing tutoring and other support needed to promote engagement in mobile learning, building a stable learning environment for high-need students, and developing a full digital curriculum that supports flexible lifelong learning. Cavanaugh (foreword; Chapter 13) asserted that sustained access to quality educational resources and experiences required a permanent systemic commitment on the part of collaborating governments and agencies. Cavanaugh cited an initiative of UNESCO (a UN agency), to promote mobile learning as a strategy for reaching its Education for All program goal, and advocated that the United Nations take additional steps to develop systemic commitment.

Harris (Chapter 14) described the evolving role of the Sydney Centre for Innovation in Learning (SCIL), a unit of Northern Beaches Christian School (NBCS), in the provision of K–12 online learning in New South Wales (NSW), Australia. The author noted that while all Australian states now permit K–12 online learning, legislative restrictions limit its use. The NSW state legislature first authorized online learning in 2004 but required a face-to-face residential education component. This led NCBS, a large private residential school, to begin planning work in 2006 with the development of a blended learning model. The relative lack of Australia-based exemplars led SCIL to look overseas for guidance and support, including the iNACOL standards for course development and programs in the United Kingdom, Iceland, and Finland as the best models. The SCIL model of blended learning involved the teacher as the active developer of lesson-specific content, a student-centered philosophy, and use of personalized and differentiated approaches to teaching. Teachers often teach the same course online and face-to-face. The high level of teacher involvement in course development allowed content to be easily reformatted for online or face-to-face delivery. The author said that completion rates had remained above 90%. Today students across NSW can enroll in SCIL through their regional school on a supplemental basis. This new role led to new challenges in terms of helping regional schools understand online learning, develop needed technical capacities, and provide sufficient support for their enrolled students. The author noted that online learning has yet to make the national agenda in education in a substantive or visible way, but hoped that a new national curriculum being launched in 2014 would provide new opportunities.

Boulton and Hasler Waters (Chapter 15) described the use of virtual learning environment (VLEs) to personalize education in the United Kingdom. These authors saw personalization via VLEs as the next generation of technology integration in education. They found differences among the five schools profiled in how they used VLEs to personalize learning. While the traditional schools used VLEs mostly for authentic student collaboration, the virtual schools used VLEs primarily to provide individualized learning opportunities. The two virtual schools and a traditional secondary school had the most experience with VLEs and appeared to offer higher levels of personalization, allowing students to have more control over their learning, track their progress, and choose courses meaningful to them. The two traditional primary schools profiled were still struggling with technical issues that prevented full integration of VLEs. The authors noted the lack of national leadership in online and blended learning. The existing ICT national curriculum had been removed from the statutes, and a new national curriculum due in fall 2013 was to focus more on digital literacy, meaning that the role played by VLEs in the United Knigdom would remain the choice of each individual school.

Kim and Seo (Chapter 16) presented the case of the Cyber Home Learning System (CHLS), South Korea's national e-learning system for elementary and secondary students and teachers. This system was originally developed to address a policy goal—reducing the educational gap between families that could afford private after-school tutoring and families that could not—by supporting students' self-study at home. CHLS has since expanded to support teachers' classroom teaching and guidance counseling for students. Students used CHLS online at home for voluntary self-study of content of interest, while teachers used it in the classroom to provide class-assigned study for targeted groups such as remedial and gifted students. CHLS content supported study in core courses and electives through early high school, and was adaptable to low-, intermediate-, and high-performing students. The authors noted that the original policy goal was not a good fit for the program's evolving mission. They believed grade levels served should be reassessed, so that CHLS covered key content in all high school grades. They saw the system as designed for didactic learning and advocated shifting to a more interactive and dynamic learning environment. They also saw the CHLS learning diagnosis and prescription services as ineffective in differentiating learning. The authors asserted that CHLS lacked connections to effective blended learning models and advocated development of models for classroom and home learning that might become effective frameworks for educational transformation. With these enhancements, the authors believed that CHLS had the potential to become the platform for a new generation of learning, Smart Education—a national educational plan to support the 21st-century knowledge society.

Addressing Key Policy and Practice Issues

We asked our policy and practice chapter authors to provide insights on key policy and practice issues. In profiling North American and international programs, our case study authors often addressed these issues as well. What our authors said about policy and practice issues is summarized in this section. Issues related to practice are presented first—organized according to four key program components: teaching, content, technology, and management—followed by general policy issues.

The first key component related to practice is teaching, specifically how to address the growing need for K–12 educators trained in high-quality online and blended teaching. Kennedy and Archambault (Chapter 2) described multiple pathways to meeting this need, including coursework, field experiences, and professional development. They emphasized the importance of aligning training and credential requirements with standards frameworks. To better prepare educators for online and blended teaching, they believed that teacher education programs needed to model both effective technology integration and high-quality online and blended teaching. They considered a mentored online field experience to be a key part of teacher preparation.

Yang and Rice (Chapter 9) presented a case study of Boise State University's Online Teaching Endorsement program, designed to meet the state of Idaho's corresponding online teaching endorsement. The program and endorsement were both built around competency-based, flexible, and adaptable evaluation frameworks. The authors encouraged other states to consider this model, as only four U.S. states had such an endorsement in 2012. Like Kennedy and Archambault, they emphasized the importance of online field experiences. Both chapters cited the need for government and higher education to support high-quality online and blended teaching.

Oliver and Weeks (Chapter 8) described how evaluation feedback led North Carolina's state virtual school to improve professional development by emphasizing three pillars—synchronous contact, meaningful feedback, and instructional announcements—and by developing online professional learning communities. The roles of teachers varied considerably across case studies. Smallwood, Reaburn, and Baker (Chapter 12) described the "high-touch" online instructional model of an elite Canadian private school, while Harris (Chapter 14) documented an Australian private school where teachers developed and teach both online and face-to-face versions of their courses. The case studies and our experiences in the field suggest that preservice teacher education and professional development in digital technology use, online learning, and blended learning are growing in prominence around the world. However, much remains to be done to ensure global access to effective training.

The second key component is course content. Keeler (Chapter 3) introduced instructional design principles for online and blended learning, noting that online courses could be extremely time intensive and costly to produce and that high-quality online course content typically came from a course team or third-party developer. She said that developers must consider how to ensure functional and consistent educational experiences for all enrolled students, including those requiring accommodations, and should use multiple forms of media to support learning. Keeler also argued for incorporation of new design methods, such as those incorporating immersive and gaming technologies, but noted the additional affordability and usability issues they raised.

While high-quality, team-based instructional design that includes learner accommodations may be optimal, online learning programs often begin on a budget with a few teacher-developed courses. With the recent growth in district-led programs, teacher-designed courses are likely to remain common. Contributor chapters suggested ways to ensure course quality. Harris (Chapter 14) described how Australian teachers who became online course developers had better academic outcomes online than face-to-face. Oliver and Weeks (Chapter 8) described development of cascading style sheet (CSS) course templates by the North Carolina Virtual Public School (NCVPS) to address accessibility. The blended Nexus Academy described by Revenaugh (Chapter 10) used well-established, high-quality online content and learner accommodation processes. However, these effective practices in well-funded programs also raised general questions for small and district-led programs on a budget. When teachers act as course developers, how does that impact course quality? Can use of shared design templates, content resources, and multimedia tools help ensure quality? Can "high-touch" blended learning help address course design limitations and accommodation needs? Similar questions about content quality arise when teachers develop massive open online courses (MOOCs) and incorporate them into classes.

Technology is the third key component. Darrow (Chapter 4) reviewed technology infrastructure and tools. He described a wide range of Web 2.0 tools for communication, productivity, and creativity that could be integrated into online or blended learning, as well as open education resources and learning objects that naturally support a social constructivist approach. Darrow saw mobile learning technologies as bringing new challenges and opportunities. He advised designers and teachers to select tools with specific functionalities that can improve student learning experiences and outcomes within a course. This raised the question of how school policymakers can support them in doing so.

The fourth key program component is management. One key management issue that must be addressed during program planning is whether to build or buy technology, content, teaching, and management functions. For example, Darrow said that district-led programs must make technology decisions early on, such as whether to use a commercial or open-source LMS. The latter choice requires building up district technology staffing capacity. Boulton and Hasler Waters (Chapter 15) noted that a charter school's authorizer might outsource all program functions to an educational management organization.

Another key management need is to ensure program effectiveness and continuous school improvement. Oliver and Weeks (Chapter 8) addressed this issue through a case study of a partnership between the NCVPS and North Carolina State University that demonstrated how program evaluation could inform practices, procedures, and policies in online and blended learning programs. During the program's start-up period, evaluation findings were used to revise course design, teaching, and policy. Over time, findings led to development of new training for participating schools, and improved procedures—such as a streamlined registration process, a standardized instructional design model, and a technical needs assessment process—at the course level. Evaluation also helped the school think strategically about its future. However, not many new programs have the resources available to NCVPS.

Beyond these key issues related to program practice, a number of policy issues also need to be addressed. Academic quality based on student performance is one of the most important. As online learning has become widespread, jurisdictions have increasingly focused on academic quality. Many U.S. states are monitoring the academic performance of online schools, and some are instituting student growth models that can help determine their impact on individual student learning. As Darrow (Chapter 4) noted, developers should consider early on how the various information systems in their online or blended learning program will generate needed performance data. Ferdig, Cavanaugh, and Freidhoff (Chapter 5) asked what the research about online learning really means. Since most studies have found no significant difference in learning outcomes for online and face-to-face learning, they encouraged researchers to focus instead on the conditions under which online learning works best. For example, the authors noted that students who were self-directed and motivated had the best results, and that more research was needed on how online learning can work best for other students.

Ferdig et al. also acknowledged that some online learning programs had poor academic results, while Raish and Carr-Chellman (Chapter 6) expressed concerns based on recent large-scale studies that many large full-time online charter schools were not academically effective. Their research suggested that cyber charters might not be a good fit for many students and parents. Therefore, they asserted that more research on effectiveness was needed before use of cyber charters was expanded. However, Raish and Carr-Chellman also noted examples of small cyber charters that met a local need or educational goal and had a positive relationship with local school districts. Blended charter schools, such as those described by Revenaugh (Chapter 10), serve students residing in a specific region. They might be part of the answer to quality concerns raised about large-scale statewide cyber charters.

Another important policy issue is the role that government should play in enabling or restricting K–12 online and blended learning. All U.S. states and Canadian provinces have at least some K–12 online learning opportunities. However, many jurisdictions worldwide have policies that restrict the development and growth of K–12 online learning. In most nations that completed an international survey, technology integration in the classroom and blended learning via virtual learning environments was more acceptable than online learning (Barbour et al., 2011). National policies often support digital learning and digital literacy. Developed and developing nations around the world now provide centralized LMSs and content repositories for use in local schools. South Korea (Chapter 16) and Nepal (Chapter 13) are good examples. School laws restricting online learning may in some cases encourage development of blended learning models. NSW, Australia (Chapter 14), is an example. Overall, it appears that blended learning may be a better fit for the current policy environment in most nations.

How to promote educational equity is also an important policy issue. This issue was addressed by Rose, Smith, Johnson, and Glick (Chapter 7), with a focus on the United States. These authors asserted that if underserved and special populations of students were provided sufficient access to computers and the Internet, well-designed and well-taught online courses and programs could increase access to equitable education. They cautioned programs to be vigilant for unintentional biases that could discourage some learners, and not to use pretests or screening to discourage participation. Instead, they encouraged local schools to identify and provide the supports that students need to succeed, and to create updated policies that enable rather than restrict new learning opportunities. This chapter supports the idea that online learning with face-to-face remediation and supports (i.e., blended learning) might work better for at-risk students.

Cavanaugh (Chapter 13) addressed international education equity issues in her Nepal case study. She noted that about 88% of the world's 1.2 billion adolescents live in developing nations that often lack the educational and societal infrastructure needed for school-based learning. She saw a sustained systemic commitment by collaborating governments and nongovernmental organizaton as necessary to ensure access to quality online resources and mobile learning experiences in these nations, and the United Nations as a key force for change. This chapter raises an important equity question: What are the prospects for a shared international vision supporting online and blended education systems in the developing world?

Some Trends in Online, Blended, and Distance Learning in Schools

Online, blended, and distance learning is a rapidly growing phenomenon at the K–12 level. Evidence presented by our chapter authors and other sources suggests that, in the future, online, blended, and distance learning in schools will be global and evidence-based, mobile and open, blended and facilitated, and personalized and adaptive.

Figure 17.1: Eight key trends for the future of online, blended, and distance education

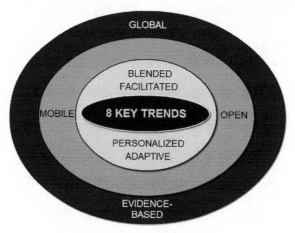

Figure 17.1 shows the relationship of these eight trends that will impact the future development of online, blended, and distance education in schools. Global and evidence-based underlie the other trends. Open and mobile are worldwide trends that apply to teaching and learning. Decisions about facilitated and blended instruction and personalized and adaptive learning must be made at the program level.

Global and Evidence-Based

Learners around the world will participate in education enabled by digital technologies. "Digital technology is now an utterly integral but wholly unremarkable component of educational conditions and arrangements around the world" (Selwyn, 2012, p. 5). While a digital divide clearly exists, young learners around the world "are ultimately more ready than the schools or educators [for] learning in an online and blended learning environment . . . [and will drive] public demand [that] may actually serve as a catalyst for systemic change" (Barbour et al., 2011, p. 30).

Program administrators, evaluators, and researchers must actively work to build trust-based relationships that can inform program improvement and advance knowledge in the field. A good example is the partnership between a state virtual school and a university described by Oliver and Weeks (Chapter 8). One challenge here is data sharing across programs. Cavanaugh (2012) piloted the idea of a a massive open online research community (MOORC), where researchers can join in open-source research and publication efforts that may help disseminate evidence-based practice more widely.

Mobile and Open

In 2013, "The number of connected mobile devices, the vast majority of which are mobile phones, will surpass the world's population for the first time in history" (UNESCO, 2013, p. 40). Darrow (Chapter 4) found that mobile learning technologies were already being used to support teaching and learning in schools, bringing new opportunities for ubiquitous learning. As Cavanaugh (Chapter 13) asserted, mobile learning might be the mechanism that allows developing nations to leapfrog into personalized learning.

As Darrow noted (Chapter 4), open-source LMSs (e.g., Moodle), education resources (e.g., the Khan Academy), learning objects, and online repositories provided new tools for developers of online and blended learning programs. The growth in single-district online and blended programs in the United States reflects the local technical-capacity building needed to use open resources effectively. As Revenaugh (Chapter 10) noted, as some blended schools moved away from cohort-based classroom models, they embraced an open school environment like a college lounge.

Blended and Facilitated

Outside the United States, distance education and online learning are generally seen as options when face-to-face education is unavailable. Full-time online learning as an option for all K–12 students appears to be a uniquely American invention. The need for parental supervision places a natural limit on its growth in the United States and elsewhere. Blended learning can bypass this restriction. In the United States, single-district programs, many of them both online and blended, are the fastest-growing type, and full-time blended schools are an increasingly important category (Watson, Murin, Vashaw, Gemin, & Rapp, 2012). In a survey of 54 nations (Barbour et al., 2011), blended learning was much more commonly reported than online learning. Christensen, Horn, and Staker (2013) see blended learning as sustaining (supporting the existing classroom model) or disruptive (untied to the classroom model), predicting that elementary schools will mostly use sustaining blended models while secondary schools experiment with disruptive models. Added experience with online learning may give U.S. providers an advantage in developing innovative, "disruptive" blended learning programs such as the Nexus Academy profiled by Revenaugh (Chapter 10). Outside the United States, sustaining models may be widely adopted across K–12. For example, Korea's CHLS profiled by Kim and Seo (Chapter 16) might support "flipped classroom" learning, where instead of doing homework, students study a new topic at home, then apply what they learned at school. Developing nations that lack traditional educational infrastructure may use blended and mobile learning to leapfrog development of their education systems.

The need for teachers does not disappear in online and blended learning; rather, teachers take on important new roles as facilitators, guiding and shaping student learning. These roles require a shift in the focus of teacher education programs and professional development, creating new pathways to proficiency in K–12 online and blended teaching with the support of standards associations, accreditation agencies, and governments (Kennedy & Achambault, Chapter 2; Yang & Rice, Chapter 9). The challenge is for K–12 teachers to move away from direct instruction—and go beyond the use of technology to enrich instruction—by combining on-site guided learning with online learning that includes some student control over time, place, path, or pace.

Personalized and Adaptive

In personalized learning, "Teaching and learning are focused on the needs and abilities of individual learners" (Izmestiev, 2012, p. 3). According to U.S. Department of Education

(2010), personalization refers to instruction that is "paced to learning needs, tailored to learning preferences, and tailored to the specific interests of different learners" (p. 12). Darrow (Chapter 4) noted the trend toward increasing personalization through technology. Revanaugh (Chapter 10) described data-driven personalized learning in a blended school, where student mastery data is used to dynamically group students for on-site learning activities. Harris (Chapter 14) described how an Australian virtual school personalizes learning through individualization. Boulton and Hasler Waters (Chapter 15) documented similar activities in U.K. virtual schools but found conventional schools in their study more likely to personalize learning through authentic collaborative activities.

Technology-based adaptive learning systems, which use learner interactions to adjust remediation and content, can be seen as another form of personalization—but they deserve separate mention. Watson et al. (2012) believe that any definition of *blended learning* should include "a way in which students' online work generates data that are used by the instructional system—teacher, technology, or both—to personalize and improve instruction for each student" (p. 17). Many higher-education institutions are integrating adaptive learning systems into entry courses (Education Growth Advisors, 2013), and blended schools like Nexus Academy are doing so as well.

Taken together, these eight trends—global and evidence-based, open and mobile, facilitative and blended, and personalized and adaptive—appear likely to impact future development of K-12 online, blended, and distance education in schools. They also may serve to inform those involved in setting future research agendas for this rapidly evolving field.

References

Barbour, M. K., Brown, R., Waters, L. H., Hoey, R., Hunt, J. L., Kennedy, K., . . . Trimm, T. (2011). *Online and blended learning: A survey of policy and practice around the world*. Vienna, VA: International Association for K–12 Online Learning.

Cavanaugh, C. (2012). *MOORC: Massively open online research community*. Paper presented at the New Trends on Global Education Conference, Kyrenia, North Cyprus.

Christensen, C. M., Horn, M. B., & Staker , H. (2013). *Is K–12 blended learning disruptive?* San Mateo, CA: Innosight Institute. Retrieved from http://www.christenseninstitute.org/publications/hybrids

Education Growth Advisors. (2013). *Learning to adapt: Understanding the adaptive learning supplier landscape*. Stamford, CT: Author. Retrieved from http://edgrowthadvisors.com/research-paper-1

Izmestiev, D. (2012). *Personalized learning: A new ICT-enabled education approach*. Moscow: UNESCO Institute for Information Technologies in Education. Retrieved from http://iite.unesco.org/pics/publications/en/files/3214716.pdf

Selwyn, N. (2012). *Education in a digital world*. London: Routledge.

UNESCO. (2013). *UNESCO policy guidelines for mobile learning*. Paris: Author. Retrieved from http://unesdoc.unesco.org/images/0021/002196/219641E.pdf

U.S. Department of Education. (2010). *National educational technology plan*. Washington, DC: Author. Retrieved from http://www.ed.gov/technology/netp-2010

Watson, J., Murin, A., Vashaw, L., Gemin, B., & Rapp, C. (2012). *Keeping pace with K–12 online and blended learning*. Evergreen, CO: Evergreen Education Group. Retrieved from http://kpk12.com/reports

Editors

Michael K. Barbour is director of doctoral studies for the Isabelle Farrington College of Education and an assistant professor of educational leadership at Sacred Heart University in Fairfield, Connecticut. He completed his PhD in instructional technology from the University of Georgia. Dr. Barbour is originally from the Canadian province of Newfoundland and Labrador, and his interest in K–12 distance education began after accepting his first high school teaching position in a regional high school in a rural community of approximately 3,500 people. Having been educated in an urban area, Michael was troubled by the inequity of opportunity provided to his rural students and began a program to offer Advanced Placement (i.e., university-level) social studies courses over the Internet to students at his own school and other schools in the district. For more than a decade now, Michael has worked with numerous K–12 online learning programs in Canada, the United States, New Zealand, and around the world as an online teacher, course developer, administrator, evaluator, and researcher. His current research interests focus on the effective design and delivery of online learning to K–12 students in virtual school environments, particularly those in rural areas.

Tom Clark is president of TA Consulting. In this role, he has undertaken many successful evaluations for state and federal agencies, universities, school districts, museums, and for-profit and nonprofit organizations. He led the evaluation of a five-year, $9.1 million project for online professional development and K–12 online learning funded through the U.S. Department of Education. TA Consulting served as contractor for team-based evaluations in the 2000s of state virtual school programs in Illinois, Georgia, Mississippi, and Missouri, and the Chicago Public Schools Virtual High School. Dr. Clark has many related publications. He coedited *Virtual Schools: Planning for Success* (Teachers College Press, 2005) with Dr. Zane Berge; coauthored one of the first American books in the field, *Distance Education: The Foundations of Effective Practice* (Jossey-Bass, 1991), with Dr. Richard Verduin; and authored an early overview of K–12 online learning in the United States, *Virtual Schools: Status and Trends* (2001). Recognized as an author in distance and online learning in *Who's Who in America*, he was an advisor for U.S. Department of Education's Evaluating Online Learning (2008).

Series Editor

Michael Grahame Moore is Distinguished Professor Emeritus of Education at The Pennsylvania State University. He is known in academic circles for pioneering the scholarly study of distance education, nowadays commonly referred to as e-learning and online learning. Retiring from teaching in 2013, Moore now consults internationally and focuses on his editorial work, especially The American Journal of Distance Education and the Stylus Publishing series Online Learning and Distance Education.

Contributors

Leanna Archambault is an associate professor at Arizona State University. Her research areas include teacher preparation for online and blended classrooms, the nature of technological pedagogical content knowledge, and the use of innovative technologies to improve learning outcomes. Most recently, she has collaborated on the Hartwell Sustainability Education Project to create, teach, and study a newly developed blended course, Sustainability Science for Teachers. Together with her coauthor, Dr. Kathryn Kennedy, she cochairs the Virtual Schooling SIG for the Society for Information Technology and Teaching Education (SITE). In 2012 they won International Association for K–12 Online Learning (iNACOL) Online Learning Innovator Award for Outstanding Research.

Stephen Baker founded Virtual High School in 1997 while teaching high school in Ontario, Canada. The original concept for the online school involved personalizing the education experience in order to accommodate the particular needs of each student. If anything, Virtual High School has moved even closer to this goal, thanks to the flexibility and leveraging power of online education.

Helen Boulton is reader in technology-enhanced learning and teaching at Nottingham Trent University in the United Kingdom and a National Teaching Fellow. Her research is focused on emerging pedagogy for new technologies in learning, and teaching the use of new technologies to support the development of reflective practice and building communities of practice. Helen has coauthored several books focusing on learning and teaching. She is vice chair of the National Association of Information Technology in Teacher Education and reviews for a variety of journals and conferences. Her work is published nationally and internationally.

Ali Carr-Chellman is the head of learning and performance systems at Penn State University and a professor of learning, design, and technology. She received her bachelor's and master's degrees from Syracuse University and her doctorate in instructional systems design at Indiana University, Bloomington. She has taught elementary school, jet fighter pilots, graduate students, and many in between. Ali has many publications and presentations on the topics of systemic change, e-learning, diffusion of innovations, qualitative research, and gender and gaming. Her current research focuses on how boys can be reengaged in their educational experiences through video gaming.

Cathy Cavanaugh is director of teaching and learning in worldwide education at Microsoft Corporation, working with education leaders and organizations around the world. Her research and publications focus on technology-empowered teaching and learning in virtual schools, online and blended learning, teacher development, mobile learning, and integration of devices into schools, and she has received international awards recognizing the impact of her work. Cathy held faculty and leadership appointments in U.S. universities and a college in the Middle East and was a Fulbright Senior Scholar advancing e-learning in Nepal. She also directed professional development centers and was a classroom teacher.

Rob Darrow advises colleges and school districts about implementing online and blended learning. He is also an adjunct professor in the educational doctoral program at California State University, Fresno. Rob is the former director of member services with iNACOL, was the principal of an online charter online school, and has taught every grade level from kindergarten through eighth; he also served as a school and district librarian during his 33 years in California public schools. His research interests include blended and online learning, professional development, costs of online learning, creating a social presence in online courses, and school libraries.

Jhone M. Ebert has served the Clark County (NV) School District, the fifth-largest school district in the nation, for over 20 years. With the call to ensure that every level of the organization nurtures a culture of innovation, she oversees the Innovative Teaching and Learning Unit, which is responsible for supporting 357 schools with assessment, accountability, curriculum, instruction, and technology. An advocate for capitalizing on technology and innovation to increase access for all students, Jhone is also a sought-after speaker and author, was named one of 20 to watch by the National School Boards Association's Technology Leadership Network in 2013, and was inducted into the CCSD Excellence in Education Hall of Fame in 2012.

Richard E. Ferdig is the Summit Professor of Learning Technologies and professor of instructional technology at Kent State University. He works within the Research Center for Educational Technology and also the School of Lifespan Development and Educational Sciences. He earned his PhD in educational psychology from Michigan State University. Richard's research, teaching, and service focus on combining cutting-edge technologies with current pedagogic theory to create innovative learning environments. His research interests include online education, educational games and simulations, the role of faith in technology, and what he labels a deeper psychology of technology.

Joseph R. Freidhoff is the director of the Michigan Virtual Learning Research Institute, a division of the Michigan Virtual University that focuses on policy, knowledge, and network development in the field of K–12 online learning. He earned his PhD in educational psychology and educational technology from Michigan State University and his BA in English Education from Grand Valley State University.

David Glick is currently the director of Cyber Village Academy, a hybrid charter school in St. Paul, Minnesota. He received his bachelor's degree from Carleton College and holds master's degrees from the University of Minnesota and Hamline University. He is particularly interested in how online programs can reach disenfranchised populations and how online programs can avoid replicating the biases found in our traditional school systems. Current interests also include measurement and evaluation systems applicable to small charter schools.

Stephen Harris is founding director of the Sydney Centre for Innovation in Learning (SCIL; www.scil.com.au). He is also principal of Northern Beaches Christian School (NBCS) in Sydney, Australia. Stephen is a part-time doctoral student at the University of Technology in Sydney, with a focus on the SCIL as a case study of educational transformation. He has been in school education for 36 years since graduating from the University of Sydney, teaching all primary and secondary grades. He spearheaded the creation of an online learning unit at NBCS in 2005 and was also Australian Principal of the Year (New South Wales) in 2012.

Karen Johnson is the director for South Central Regional Area Telecommunications System (SOCRATES) Online. The regional collaborative provides elective, career-oriented online courses to area high school students. She has also been the online learning specialist for the Minnesota Department of Education. Her work includes development of an undergraduate online learning program and a hybrid graduate program for rural educators. She serves on the Minnesota Online Learning Advisory Council.

Christy G. Keeler has research interests including educational technology, instructional design, and social studies education. In addition to chapters in edited books and textbooks, her work appears in a variety of peer-reviewed journals, including *American Journal of Distance Education, Journal of Computing in Teacher Education, Social Studies Research and Practice*, and *Journal of Geography*. In 2009 she received the esteemed Mildred A. Wedemeyer Award for Outstanding Scholarship in Distance Education with coauthor Dr. Mark Horney. Many recognize her from her online presence, where she offers content- and pedagogy-specific resources, such as her acclaimed site on virtual museums at christykeeler.com.

Kathryn Kennedy is a senior researcher at MVU's Michigan Virtual Learning Research Institute. She formerly served as the director of research for iNACOL and professor of instructional technology at Georgia Southern University. She had practical experience as a preservice and in-service teacher, technology specialist, school librarian, technology integration trainer, and instructional designer in traditional, blended, and online learning environments, and is a researcher in the same areas. She earned her PhD in curriculum and instruction with a concentration in educational technology from the University of Florida.

Hyeonjin Kim is associate professor of educational technology in the Department of Education at the Korea National University of Education. Prior to her current position, she was senior researcher at the Korea Education and Research Information Service (KERIS) and researcher at the POSCO Research Institute. She received her PhD in instructional technology from the University of Georgia and her master's in educational technology from Ewha Women's University in Korea. Her research interests include professional and teacher education and design of technology-enhanced learning environments.

Kevin Oliver is an associate professor of digital learning and teaching in the Department of Curriculum and Instruction at North Carolina State University. He received his doctorate in instructional technology from the University of Georgia and his master's in educational media and instructional design from the University of North Carolina at Chapel Hill. His research focuses on emerging issues in virtual schooling and distance education, and his teaching on digital leadership in the schools.

Allison Powell is the vice president for state and district services/new learning models of iNACOL, which provides expertise and leadership in K–12 blended, online, and competency-based learning. Before joining iNACOL, Allison taught in both face-to-face and online K–8 environments. She helped build the Clark County School District's Virtual High School and an online professional development program for the Nevada school district. She has served as a board member for several organizations and universities. Allison completed her doctorate from Pepperdine University in educational technology.

Victoria Raish is a doctoral student in the Learning, Design, and Technology program in the College of Education at Penn State University. She received her bachelor's degree from Mercyhurst University and master's degree from the University of Southern California. She has focused her research efforts on how students learn and experience school in the online environment, specifically within virtual science classrooms. Currently, her research involves creating digital badges for students to earn in an asynchronous digital environment.

Jennifer Reaburn has been working and learning at Virtual High School since 2010. She received a bachelor's degree in anthropology from Wilfred Laurier University and her TESL Ontario certification from Conestoga College. She came to online education after years of teaching in ESL and literacy classrooms. She cares deeply about scaffolding online learners to succeed in a supportive environment. This goal fuels her interest in continually investigating and improving online content delivery and assessment practices.

Mickey Revenaugh is cofounder of Connections Academy and executive vice president of Connections Education, which provides online/blended learning services to schools, districts, and consumers, and recently launched the new network of Nexus Academy blended charter schools. Mickey has served twice as chairman of the board of iNACOL and is currently vice chairman. Previously, she helped launch the E-rate program to wire American schools to the Internet and served as education technology editor at Scholastic. Mickey has an MBA from New York University, did her undergraduate work at Yale University, and lives in Brooklyn, New York.

Kerry Rice is a 2012–2013 Senior Fulbright Scholar and professor in the Department of Educational Technology at Boise State University. She is author of *Making the Move to K–12 Online Teaching: Research-Based Strategies and Practices* (Pearson, 2012), and she led the development of the Idaho K–12 Online Teaching Standards and the Idaho K–12 Online Teaching Endorsement. Her research focuses on best practices in K–12 online education, with articles appearing in *Journal of Research on Technology in Education (JRTE)*, *Journal of Educational Technology & Society (JETS)*, and *British Journal of Educational Technology (BJET)*.

Raymond M. Rose, an online learning evangelist, has been in the forefront of equity and online learning since helping create the country's first virtual high school. He holds a bachelor's degree in education from the University of Bridgeport and a master's in counseling from Rhode Island College. He has been a junior high science teacher, high school guidance counselor, and administrator. In addition, he has extensive experience in civil rights issues, as a member of the Massachusetts Department of Education and staff member and associate director for an equity assistance center. He also served on the faculty of a teacher preparation program.

Jeonghee Seo is principal researcher at the Korea Education and Research Information Service. She received her PhD and MA in science education from Seoul National University in Korea. Her research interests include biology education, teacher education, and information and communication technology in education.

John Smallwood, a veteran teacher in southwestern Ontario, has taught for more than 40 years in different contexts—from secondary schools, to Western University, to Virtual High School (VHS). His varied work, combined with new approaches that have come about through e-learning, allow him to make the claim that new technologies have revolutionized learning by liberating students from methodologies that no longer serve teachers or students well. As a senior member of the VHS team, he sees unlimited opportunities for innovative approaches to learning while increasing student interest and maintaining high standards.

Alese Smith is online instructional designer at the Center for Learning Enhancement, Assessment, and Redesign (CLEAR) at the University of North Texas and serves as chief learning officer at Rose & Smith Associates. Her work focuses on guiding learning institutions through the process of moving into the online learning environment, and designing online professional development courses that teach sound online pedagogical approaches. She has previously been involved with online faculty development and curriculum development for the Concord Consortium and VHS Collaborative.

Lisa Hasler Waters received her PhD in educational technology from the University of Hawaii. She is currently a technology integrator at Flint Hills School—an Apple Distinguished K–12 independent school in Northern Virginia. Previously, she was a research associate for the Institute for Alternative Futures. She has over 10 years of experience as a research and instructional design consultant specializing in K–12 online and blended learning. She has taught K–8 and has conducted professional development in technology integration. Her research agenda focuses on educational futures, K–12 online/blended learning, and parental involvement in online learning.

Tracy Weeks is currently chief academic and digital learning officer at the North Carolina Department of Public Instruction. She is an experienced educator who previously served as executive director and chief academic officer of the North Carolina Virtual Public School (NCVPS), an adjunct university instructor, a district technology director, and a high school technology specialist and math teacher. She received her PhD in curriculum and instruction with a concentration in instructional technology from North Carolina State University.

Dazhi Yang is an associate professor in the Department of Educational Technology at Boise State University. Yang is an associate professor in the Department of Educational Technology at Boise State University. From 2012 to 2013, she developed and implemented the university's K–12 Online Teaching Endorsement program. She earned both her MA and PhD in educational technology (now learning design and technology) from Purdue University. Her current research focuses on engineering education, in terms of online and distance education, assessment and evaluation, and preventing student misconceptions of science and engineering.

The Power of Potential

At Microsoft, we believe limitless potential lives within every student, every educator, every school. Together we can unlock this potential by providing technology that not only fits the needs of different learning environments, but also expands the power of education.
To learn more, visit Microsoft.com/Education.